PROPERTY OF U.P.E.I.

THE CHALLENGE OF WAR:

BRITAIN'S SCIENTIFIC AND ENGINEERING CONTRIBUTIONS TO WORLD WAR TWO

THE CHALLENGE OF WAR:

BRITAIN'S SCIENTIFIC AND ENGINEERING
CONTRIBUTIONS TO WORLD WAR TWO

by

GUY HARTCUP

TAPLINGER PUBLISHING COMPANY
NEW YORK

First Published in the United States in 1970 by
TAPLINGER PUBLISHING CO., INC.
29 East Tenth Street
New York, New York 10003

For

A. P. ROWE

who gave the idea
and whose criticism
and encouragement enabled
the book to be completed

Standard Book Number 8008 1431 2

Library of Congress Catalog Number 70-106910

Printed in Great Britain

CONTENTS

LIST OF ILLUSTRATIONS

9

FOREWORD

By LORD BOWDEN

MA, PhD, MSC Tech, MIEE

Principal, The University of Manchester Institute of Science and Technology

It is extraordinary for anyone whose whole life was disrupted and changed and transformed by the last war to realise that more time has passed since 1939 than the interval between the outbreak of the French Revolution and Napoleon's defeat at Waterloo. Half the population of this country cannot even remember VE-day and to them the events which are so dramatically described in this book are matters of history, almost as remote as the Crusades.

It is very good for us to be reminded in 1970 of the extraordinary events which made it possible for us to be here today and to reflect on the possibility that, if things had turned out differently, if a few ingenious men had failed us, most of us would have died twenty years ago, and the whole of Europe might have been a desert at this moment.

Men have never worked together more enthusiastically and to better purpose than they did during the Second World War. There never can have been a time when the ingenuity of so many able men was concentrated so narrowly on one particular purpose. The courage of brave men has always inspired us, but the war showed dramatically how courage, which was not reinforced by technical innovations, was completely frustrated and impotent.

Without some of the devices which this book describes, our soldiers and sailors would have been as helpless as the troops of the Mahdi at Omdurman who were mown down by the Maxim guns of the British Army.

A bomber equipped with radar could do as much as half-a-dozen without. A Coastal Command aircraft could search the seas for enemy submarines indefinitely and fail to find them unless it had an ASV set. All the courage of Fighter Command and the skill of the Few would have been wasted, had it not been for the timely installation of the primitive radar system which saved us in 1940.

11

But even technical ingenuity was not enough. If there is one lesson to be learned from this book, it is that at a time when all seemed lost, we survived because of extraordinary effective collaboration between the fighting men and the civilians who helped them. The RAF was more successful in developing and using new scientific techniques than any other armed service on either side.

The Nazi Party rose to power by sowing dissention among its adversaries and it had within it the seeds of its own decay. If the German Army and its Air Force had recruited the help of the German scientists who still remained after the great exodus of the thirties, it is almost certain that they could have developed simple apparatus to jam the radar chain and open the whole of the South of England to the Luftwaffe. Had the German Army confided in the German Navy, our microwave ASV sets would never have been able to defeat the submarines in the Bay and we might never have been able to invade Europe and liberate it. Anyone who reads Mr. Hartcup's book must marvel that we survived—and won.

Mr. Hartcup has assembled information from an enormous field. No one could have known half the facts at the time : if only because of the Official Secrets Act. Members of Fighter Command understood radar, but few of them can have known that the struggle in New Guinea would be decided as much by dysentery as by bullets. Our medical services kept men alive to fight another day. The Japanese were so weakened that they could not resist.

It was said of Nelson that 'no man ever trusted less to the inspiration of the moment—or made better use of it'. A hundred and forty years after the battle of Trafalgar, the Normandy landings were a triumph of planning, of skill and improvisation. When we worry about the difficulties of building new roads or of clearing our slums, we should remind ourselves that thirty years ago we built a harbour on a hostile shore and landed thousands of troops and millions of tons of equipment in spite of all that the enemy could do to stop us.

It is a pity that Mr. Hartcup has not told us more about the remarkable feats of the Russian Army. How were they able to manœuvre their armour so effectively in the greatest tank battle that was ever fought, and annihilate the German armies which were besieging Stalingrad? How did they make their equipment so astonishingly rugged that it could withstand the demands of their armies in one of the worst climates in the world? However proudly we may remember our own achievements and those of the Americans, we must never forget that most of the German Army was defeated in Russia.

This is a fascinating story and despite the complexity of some of the devices with which it is concerned, it is a story which can be understood by anyone who is prepared to read it. It will remind all middle-aged men of some of the most strenuous and exciting and frustrating and anxious years of their lives. It is part of the history of our time and it should not be forgotten.

PART ONE

INTRODUCTORY

Chapter I

The Basis of Selection

The Second World War forms a watershed in the progress and organisation of science. Six important developments or devices arose or grew to stature because of the war. They were atomic energy, radar, rocket propulsion, jet propulsion, automation and operational research. Most of them have revolutionised post-war life in some respect. We accept all these things for better or worse, but how much attention is given to the origin of scientific or engineering ideas which helped to win the war? Already an attempt has been made to analyse the origins of the principal inventions of the nineteenth and the first half of the twentieth centuries,[1] but nothing comparable has been written about the passage of an idea from the mind of the originator to its arrival as a piece of equipment or a device in the hands of the service user.

A. P. Rowe, superintendent of one of the most successful wartime research groups, the Telecommunications Research Establishment (TRE) has written : 'Is necessity usually the mother of invention and of scientific progress, or does success more often come directly from basic work having no known application? Whence and in what proportions stemmed the important ideas in pure and applied science of the war and post-war years? Some of the obvious sources are university teaching departments, university research institutes, government research establishments, headquarters of government departments, industry and the general public. How often were they the product of rare and individual minds, and how often the result of mass attacks by groups of workers having little claim to genius? In the latter case, were the groups usually homogeneous, or were they groups of workers from different disciplines and specialities? Were the successful workers subject to rigid programmes of specific objectives or free from such restrictions? After the conception of an idea, how long before there was a resulting practical application? What factors accelerated or retarded the transition from idea to

17

practical application? The possibilities are many : contemporary climate of opinion, secrecy, personal friendships and animosities, propinquity, engineering difficulties affecting mass production and deliberate suppression in peace and war.'[2]

For the purpose of this book a list of forty-one items was compiled for analysis. In order to avoid bias by the author, a number of leaders from the three services and defence scientists were asked to name the scientific contributions which they considered to have had the most important influence on the outcome of the war. They included the late Lord Hankey, secretary of the Committee of Imperial Defence, both before the First World War and in the inter-war years and, in the early part of the Second World War, a minister without portfolio with a special responsibility for the orga-nisation of scientific effort; Admiral Sir Charles Daniel, Flag Officer, Combined Operations, later Vice-Admiral of the British Pacific Fleet; the late Admiral Sir William Tennant, who commanded the Mulberry harbour organisation during the Normandy landings; Admiral Sir Caspar John, a post-war First Sea Lord and Chief of Naval Staff; Field Marshal Lord Slim, Commander of the Four-teenth Army in Burma; General Sir Frederick Wrisberg, associated with the scientific aspects of air defence in pre-war years and a war-time Director-General of Weapons and Instrument Production in the Ministry of Supply; Marshal of the Royal Air Force Sir John Slessor, Commander-in-Chief of RAF Coastal Command during a critical period of the U-boat war; Air Marshal Sir Robert Saundby, Deputy Commander-in-Chief of RAF Bomber Command from 1942 to the end of the war; the late Air Chief Marshal Sir Philip Joubert, who served on the Air Staff before the war and later commanded RAF Coastal Command; Air Vice-Marshal D. C. T. Bennett, origi-nator and commander of the Pathfinder Force in RAF Bomber Command; the late Sir John Cockcroft, nuclear physicist and, during the war, responsible for army radar development; Professor P. M. S. Blackett, physicist and member of the famous Tizard Committee and later one of the originators of military operational research, and Professor R. V. Jones, physicist and wartime Director of Scientific Intelligence in the Air Ministry.

The urgency of the time inevitably threw up a number of ideas that were failures. Some of them were encouraged to the detriment of better ideas. For the purpose of this study, some failures have also been selected for analysis.

Undoubtedly the scientific development in the Second World War which has had the widest repercussions was the atomic bomb. But although a great scientific organisation was built up for its development, the effect on the course of the war was, until the very end, negligible (radar was far more important and involved the leading physicists in this country). It was, therefore, decided not to include the development of the atomic weapon.

Chapter 2

The Organisation of Scientists for War

(i) The First World War and Inter-War Years

In the military field, scientific ideas rarely emerge from the minds of individual inventors working in isolation, but from scientists working in service laboratories. But before rearmament began and, indeed, in certain cases before the war itself began, these scientists did not, with notable exceptions, have the qualities needed. We shall see that the big advances were made after the influx of scientists recruited from the universities and industry.

It was the Germans who first applied science to operations in the First World War. Fritz Haber, the distinguished German chemist who had been working on the utilisation of nitrogen from the air, was called upon to supervise the production of gas when, in 1915, the Germans were trying to end the deadlock on the Western Front. The British, on the other hand, were slow to appreciate the value of scientists, and it was not until pressure of events—in particular, the extension of the war in the air and under the sea—had become acute that new government establishments began to grow up.

The Royal Aircraft Factory, later known as the Royal Aircraft Establishment (RAE) at Farnborough, founded before the war, expanded and held a brilliant group of scientists working on problems of flight. At Orfordness, in 1916, an experimental station was founded for the investigation of gunnery, bombing and navigation, and at Martlesham Heath new types of aircraft were tested. These two establishments were the brain child of Bertram Hopkinson, Professor of Engineering at Cambridge, whose death in an air accident was considered by Tizard to be 'a real national calamity'.[1]

In July 1915, the Admiralty Board of Invention and Research was formed with Lord Fisher as chairman, and included such distinguished scientists as Sir Ernest (later Lord) Rutherford, Sir Charles Parsons, inventor of the turbine, and Professor W. H. Bragg. A

section of the panel concerned itself with the detection of submarines, first, by acoustic methods and later, using electrical, electromagnetic, and magnetic methods. The most significant was the
system in which echoes were obtained using quartz as a receiver and
which became known as 'asdic'. But asdic was not ready for operational use before the war ended, and this was because, in spite of
their talents, the work of these scientists was largely ignored. They
were refused a submarine for their experiments; they were refused
any data relating to the destruction of U-boats that had already
occurred. It was on failing to arrive at one of these panel meetings
that Rutherford excused himself with his celebrated apology, 'I have
been engaged in experiments which suggest that the atom can be
artificially disintegrated. If it is true, it is of far greater importance
than a war.'[2]

At the end of the First World War the principal scientific devices
had been tested in action, such as aircraft, tanks, automatic guns,
submarines, radio communications, and poison gas. Yet little was
done to draw conclusions about the use of these weapons either by
staff officers or by technical experts among the general public.

In the immediate post-war years the keyword was retrenchment
based on the assumption of 'no war for the next ten years'. The
scientist employed by the government did not rank high in the
hierarchy of the services. Nevertheless, in the post-war years direc-
tors of scientific research were appointed, first at the Admiralty, and
then at the Air Ministry, with small staffs under their control.

In 1920 the Admiralty founded the Admiralty Research Laboratory, its task being to carry out 'scientific research of a fundamental
and pioneer character which might bear naval interests and for the
prosecution of which no outside agency existed.'[3] It was under the
direct control of the newly-appointed Director of Scientific Research,
Sir Frank Smith, a distinguished pure scientist, but also inventor of
the magnetic mine. In spite of financial stringency, it was able to
make a useful contribution in the fields of fire control, electro-
magnetics, range-finding, and acoustics, among other items. Three
other Admiralty establishments began to do limited but useful scientific work in the inter-war years—the Signal School at Portsmouth
(later Admiralty Signal Establishment), the Mining School at HMS
Vernon and HMS *Osprey*, the Underwater Establishment at Portland. At the first-named, long-range radio transmission was
developed and a section concerned itself solely with the development

of valves. The Mining School worked on the protection of harbours from submarine attack. At *Osprey*, the development of asdic, begun during the war, was continued, principally from 1927 to 1939.

For the RAF there was the Royal Aircraft Establishment. But in these years policy fluctuated as to whether the establishment should pursue lines of basic research or whether it should be an aeronautical laboratory for the Air Ministry. The prevailing view seemed to be that basic research was the responsibility of the National Physical Laboratory and the RAE was to concern itself with development. More alive and go-ahead was the small Air Ministry laboratory set up under Wimperis, largely through Tizard's influence, at the Imperial College of Science, South Kensington. Here in a secret room in the basement experiments were made with engine fuel, research into the nature of bomb explosions took place, and a highly skilled workshop staff made, or modified, special types of equipment, especially navigational instruments.

The Army unfortunately tended to get a smaller share of the available resources than the other services. The War Office scientific establishments centred round Woolwich—ordnance research and signals—while chemical warfare was studied at Porton. At Farnborough, the Mechanical Warfare Experimental Establishment, consisting of a handful of officers and men, became the most important experimental establishment for the testing of all mechanical vehicles, including tanks, in Europe, if not the world. The Secretary of State for War had turned down a proposal to create a similar establishment in Egypt, but in 1931 a 'camouflaged' branch was opened in Cairo and vehicles from Farnborough were tested in the desert. It is ironical that this branch was subsequently disbanded. Had it continued, betters designs for tanks and vehicles operating in the Western Desert during the war might well have been achieved— a notable example of lack of foresight.

(ii) *Organisation of the British Scientific Effort in the Second World War*

Although rearmament was long delayed, Britain was the only country involved in the war which had organised cadres of scientists to be ready to assist the services. The first step taken was the compilation during 1937 and 1938 of a schedule of reserved occupations to provide against the mistake made in the First World War of enlisting into the forces skilled men essential for war production. Secondly, a central register of volunteers for war service with technical, professional and higher administrative qualifications was drawn up with the aid of the Royal Society, the universities and the principal technical and professional institutions. This was indirectly inspired by the action of two scientists at the time of the Munich crisis in 1938. Professor G. T. R. Hill, an early glider enthusiast, and Dr. C. F. (later Sir Charles) Goodeve, whom we shall encounter later in connection with mine warfare, aware of the possibility of war, realised that if it came scientists would be deeply involved. An organisation was required, they believed, whereby scientists could learn about an appropriate branch of one of the services so that when called upon they could at once take an active part in the war effort. They therefore wrote to the three service departments. The only one interested (the War Office did not reply) was the Air Ministry from which Hill's brother, Air Commodore R. M. (later Air Marshal Sir Roderic) Hill, an officer deeply interested in science and then Director of Technical Development,* replied.[4] There must have been brotherly collusion behind the scenes. They also wrote to the Royal Society where they met with a favourable response. By July 1939 the scientific section of the central register contained the names of 5,000 scientists.

At the outbreak of war Sir Maurice Hankey was summoned by the Prime Minister to become Minister without Portfolio in the War Cabinet, one of his tasks being, as he later said, 'to put science on the war map, and as a by-product of that exciting field of activity I had to assume important responsibilities in connection with higher technical and scientific manpower.'[5] With the startling new developments in radar, there was by 1940 an urgent requirement for skilled personnel; without them the services were threatened with a critical situation. Hankey, then Chancellor of the Duchy of Lancaster in Winston Churchill's government, became responsible for filling the immediate deficit and ensuring the future supply of trained personnel. In the first case the Central Register was invaluable, as were the universities and industry, and the gap in the critical first year was filled. In the second category, special courses were established by education authorities and a system of state bursaries

* He was Commander-in-Chief, Fighter Command, during the 'V' weapons period and after the war became Rector of the Imperial College of Science and Technology.

was devised to attract qualified persons who became known as 'Hankey Bursars'. Eventually, over 50,000 men and women were selected for basic scientific instruction and passed to the services, research and industry.

The war compelled a great expansion of government laboratories. One of the most significant was the evolution of the Air Ministry's Bawdsey Research Station on the Suffolk coast at which radar was first developed, and it became a Mecca for scientists of all three services. Bawdsey was conveniently close to the Cavendish Laboratory, Cambridge, then containing the cream of British physicists picked by Rutherford. As early as the Munich crisis, due to the foresight of Watson-Watt and Rowe, there was a to and fro between the Cavendish and Bawdsey Manor, and the latter with its cricket pitch, beautiful grounds, and the sea at hand became almost an adjunct to the famous laboratory.

The brilliance of many of the temporary staff and the university-like atmosphere was probably responsible for the introduction of the 'Sunday Soviet', one of the unique features of Bawdsey, or the Telecommunications Research Establishment (TRE) as it came to be known. This was a free for all discussion held by Rowe in his office on Sunday mornings and attended by senior service officers and civil servants, scientists, and aircrew often straight from operations. The latter were able to tell the scientists how the latest equipment worked and what faults needed rectifying, while senior officers could say what requirements were needed. Much time and effort was saved and the Soviets became a shop window in which TRE sold its goods to the 'customers'. It became a dictum that anything could be said in Rowe's office on a Sunday, and there was nothing like it in the other service scientific establishments. The second significant point about TRE was that it inherited the spirit of improvisation (sealing wax and glass tubes) which was characteristic of the Cavendish (having to make do on limited funds).

In wartime it is essential to discover how to shorten the period between the birth of an idea and its full-scale use in operations. TRE's answer to this problem was to set up an engineering unit which was able to produce a small number of equipments for immediate operational use while industry was preparing for mass manufacture. The motto of TRE was 'Second Best Tomorrow', and even the Americans, surprised at the results, were quick to copy the idea. Conversely, the inability of the Germans to fit radar into aircraft quickly and their too highly finished equipments were due to lack of an imaginative approach. The unit was also able to help the aircraft designer with the problem of fitting equipment into an already overloaded machine.

Finally, TRE realised that its task did not end with originating devices but extended to discovering how they behaved under operational conditions. A post-design service under J. A. Ratcliffe, a physicist from the Cavendish, was established in which parties of scientists were sent to operational squadrons using new radar equipment to find out how it worked. Without their reports, which should not be confused with operational research described later, much of the work of the laboratory scientists would have been in vain.

But the Ministry of Aircraft Production, which was responsible for TRE, did not have a monopoly of the best scientists. The Admiralty had allowed for a wartime expansion of forty scientists and technicians but, in fact, by the end of the war the total number engaged was more like 40,000. Much of the credit for recruiting suitable scientific staff for the Admiralty's scentific establishments must go to F. (later Sir Frederick) Brundrett, who ensured that scientists went to jobs that were most suitable for them. The Admiralty's special contribution to the scientific effort was, we shall see, the setting up of a unique inter-service organisation for valves, in particular transmitting-valve production, in which the Royal Navy had always had a special interest. In addition to the Admiralty Signal Establishment, an important contribution was made by the Anti-Submarine Experimental Establishment—as *Osprey* became known. The only organisation which was principally composed, like TRE, of temporary staff was Goodeve's Department of Miscellaneous Weapons Development. Its approach, as will appear, was quite different. There were more engineers than physicists and there was a proclivity towards the creation of gadgets. Moreover, no interchange of ideas took place between scientist and service user as was cultivated in the 'Sunday Soviet'. Consequently a number of devices were evolved for which no requirement existed.

One other war activity in which civilian scientists were engaged was operational research, or the subjection of military operations to quantitative analysis. Perhaps that prolific originator of new technological ideas, F. W. Lanchester, was the first to apply operational research to modern warfare with his treatise on aerial combat written before the First World War. Certainly A. V. Hill (later a member of the Tizard Committee) conducted with a small group of scientists the first operational research in the field in connection with anti-aircraft gunnery. But the first operational research section arose in the RAF and originated through the need to assess the operation of the first radar chain, though before this an Air Ministry scientist and RAF officers had already developed the technique of interception that won the Battle of Britain. Operational research spread to all commands of the RAF and to the other services, as well as to the US Navy and Air Force.

Of all countries engaged in the war, the closest collaboration between scientist and serving officer was undoubtedly achieved in the British armed forces. This was not only fruitful for the user but also for the scientist, for as a radio engineer, R. H. Barfield, has written : 'There is no doubt that without such mediating influence of this kind, research workers tend to get into a state of isolation when they find their work is not being followed up.'[6]

(iii) The United States Scientific Effort

The American military scientific organisation was quite different from that of the British. In 1915, largely through the initiative of Thomas Edison, then nearly seventy, President Woodrow Wilson approved a 'Department of Invention and Development' to devise counter-measures against the submarine. Edison was put in charge and much of his work anticipated operational research in the Second World War. The Assistant Secretary of the Navy at that time was Franklin D. Roosevelt.

In the crucial summer of 1940 Dr. Vannevar Bush, then chairman of the National Advisory Committee for Aeronautics (an independent federal agency responsible to the President) and also inventor of one of the first high-speed computers, asked several other distinguished scientists to discuss an idea for an emergency war research organisation. Bush sold the idea to President Roosevelt who, a month later, and perhaps remembering Edison, set up the Office of Scientific Research and Development (OSRD) which could make its own assessment of what the services needed. Bush was made director. The OSRD reported directly to the President and received funds from Congress by direct appropriation. It administered these funds by negotiating contracts (usually cost plus overhead) with private or governmental laboratories (time was too short to set up its own laboratories) or by the direct intervention of Bush.[7] Today, as a result, American universities are strong and government establishments relatively weak.

The policy of OSRD was supervised by the National Defence Research Committee (NDRC), whose chairman was the celebrated scientist, James B. Conant. The Committee for Medical Research was responsible for activities in the medical field; for example, the manufacture of penicillin. The administration of NRDC's work was carried out by nineteen divisions, each responsible for a particular subject such as rockets, radar, fire control, transportation, etc. The Radar Division is of particular significance in our story. Naval and Army laboratories had done some research into long-range radar, but Karl T. Compton, who became responsible for radar, appreciated the importance of short-wave radar and set up a Microwave Committee. But since no satisfactory source of power for such wavelengths was then known, the committee was groping in the dark until the arrival, in August 1940, of the Tizard Mission from Great Britain with the cavity magnetron which proved to be the solution to the problem. The cavity magnetron was the most important and far-reaching of the devices revealed to the Americans by the Tizard Mission, which will be described later. The Americans lost no time in setting up a civilian laboratory to concentrate on short-wave radar and made a contract with the Massachusetts Institute of Technology to establish a laboratory. Its cover name was the Radiation Laboratory—so-called because many scientists at that time considered nuclear physics a harmless activity. It at once began research on airborne and gunlaying radar equipment and long-range navigational aid for aircraft.

The drawback to the NDRC was that, being so compartmented, the exchange of ideas was restricted and there was a lack of contact with the services. The sheer weight of resources did produce results but it was a wasteful method. Rowe, for instance, remembers Dr. Lee Du Bridge, director of the Radiation Laboratory, asking him what percentage of TRE devices was eventually accepted by the user service, and telling him that in his case it was 25 per cent. 'I hardly knew how to reply,' says Rowe, 'because the close association we had between user and scientists rendered stillborn the many foolish or impracticable ideas we had proposed.'[8]

However, one laboratory, the Radio Research Laboratory set up in July 1942 to deal with radio countermeasures independently of the

Radiation Laboratory (as it was thought it would harm the more positive work of the latter), resembled the British system in that far closer liaison was maintained with the services.[9]

(iv) The Tizard Mission

At this stage it is appropriate to describe the Tizard Mission previously mentioned. Due to it the Americans were in possession, sixteen months before they entered the war, of the most important British scientific devices including, in addition to the cavity magnetron, radar for detecting surface vessels, asdic, the proximity fuse, rockets, aircraft identification techniques, the Kerrison anti-aircraft gun predictor, the RDX explosive, and other devices. Cockcroft said that: 'Our disclosures increased the power available to US technicians by a factor of 1,000.'[10]

A. V. Hill, who went to Washington as scientific adviser to the British air attaché, impressed on Tizard (who had sent him there) the great research facilities and manufacturing power in the United States. He made the daring suggestion of providing the Americans with information on British scientific devices. But if this was done, what happened if information imparted to the Americans leaked out to the Germans? Hill believed that there was more to be gained than lost in such an arrangement, but this idea of offering information to the Americans on a non-reciprocal basis had not gained much ground by the time the British Army had to be evacuated from Dunkirk. Even Churchill, who had just become Prime Minister, did not think that a British offer of military secrets would count for much. By this time, however, Britain, fighting in isolation, had engaged the sympathies of the Americans, especially the scientists. Moreover, the Americans, as Hill has written, 'suddenly realised that for a hundred years the Royal Navy, and not some law of Nature, had made this traditional isolation possible.[11] They were eager to help. Hill wrote to Tizard from Washington, 'We could get much more help in the United States and Canada if we were not so damnably sticky and unimaginative.'[12]

On 25 July the British government at last approved the despatch of the mission which was to be led by Tizard himself. The possibility of security leaks was overlooked on the grounds that it was more important to be a year ahead of the enemy than for the enemy to know what the Allies were doing six months back. Tizard was accompanied by Cockcroft, E. G. Bowen, the founder of airborne radar, and several service officers who had had recent operational experience. The first stop was Ottawa and Tizard's arrival stimulated the Canadians who had felt that insufficient use was being made of their country's scientific resources. After cautious overtures on both sides, the vital information was imparted to the Americans. It was now possible for the United States not only to use British devices for her own purpose but to become the arsenal for the hard-pressed British, undisturbed by air attack and without the handicap of priorities which British industry, working against the clock, had to face.

(v) Comparison with the Scientific Effort of the Enemy

By 1939, because of the Nazis' hostility to science, Germany's great scientific potential was dispersed and most German scientists with international reputations, such as James Frank, Max Born, Richard Courant, Albert Einstein, Fritz Haber, R. E. Peierls and G. Hevesy, had all left the country for the United States, Britain or Sweden. Only two leading physicists worked wholeheartedly in the war effort. There was no equivalent of Blackett or Cockcroft or Tizard. Assuming that the war would be a short one, the Nazis did not organise scientists for war or initiate long-range projects until 1942. (Basic research on radar had been stopped by Hitler in 1940.) It has been suggested the the lack of co-ordination was because experimental establishments had had to develop clandestinely, and that when rearmament came into the open it was too late to amalgamate the separate groups into a coherent organisation. Useful scientists had by then been drafted into the forces and many killed.

Certainly, there was little collaboration between scientist and service user. For example, trials of a radio-controlled torpedo at the Kaiser Wilhelm Institute in Berlin failed because the scientists were unable to borrow a torpedo from the Navy for their experiments. On another occasion when radar equipment was being tested, only one engineer from the firm that manufactured it was allowed to be present. Scientists were not asked to advise on the U-boat war until the end of 1943, though, later, some of them were belatedly sent to sea to discover the nature of Allied radar and radio emanations. There were no searching discussions like the 'Sunday Soviets'. In May 1943, a meeting of 200 leading scientists was given two elementary lectures on U-boats, a simple talk on radar, then everyone dispersed. If Germany had developed operational research she would not have spent such a disproportionate time on developing useless weapons.[13] A German scientist summed up the situation : 'Germany lost the war because of incomplete mobilisation and utilisation of scientific resources.'

The leading scientists of Italy, such as Fermi, Pontecorvo and Gullicini, had likewise fled, but earlier than the German exodus because of the longer establishment of the Fascist régime. As in Germany, there was no collaboration between scientists and the armed forces, nor was there any exchange of information with the technically superior Germany. One exception was that the Germans gave the Italians their second-best radar (Italy had no radar on the outbreak of war) in exchange for Italian torpedoes which were superior to those of the Germans.

The Japanese services were rigidly conservative in outlook. There was no collaboration between the Army and Navy, the former being the dominant service. It was said by a Japanese scientist that a general would rather lose the war than shake hands with an admiral. The Army and the Navy each had its own radar equipment. An army radar was unable to distinguish between an enemy and a friendly naval aircraft and the same confusion applied to naval radar when trying to locate enemy aircraft. Not until the autumn of 1944 did the Japanese Army and Navy set up a joint technical control committee with civilian representation, but then it was too late. Deep distrust of scientists by the services existed, especially if the former had been trained, as many of them had, in the United States, Great Britain or Germany. Only in the technique of combined operations was Japan ahead of the Western powers. They could not begin to compete with the Western radar, asdic or signals equipment[14] because of the low standard of technology and the hierarchical structure of their services.

PART TWO

THE WAR AT SEA

Page 33: German magnetic mine with parachute attached recovered near Shoeburyness, 23 November 1939.

Page 34: (above) Degaussing cables on HMS *Repulse*; (below) 'Hedgehog' in position on the forecastle of a corvette.

Chapter 3

Countermeasures Against Non-Contact Mines and Torpedoes

In the Second World War the most effective weapons at sea were the mine (especially the non-contact variety), the submarine and long-range aircraft able to carry depth-charges or mines. Previously, Britain had foolishly permitted the building of submarines by Germany, and not nearly enough attention had been paid to the potentialities of aircraft against submarines, or of aircraft and submarines operating in a *guerre de course* against merchant shipping. Even more disastrous, as events were to prove, was the fact that little had been done to improve methods of destroying U-boats or of detecting them while travelling on the surface.

(i) Magnetic Mines—Degaussing

From 17 September 1939, the Germans began laying non-contact mines off the east and south-east British coasts. These mines were usually dropped from aircraft and sank to the seabed on reaching the water.

The story of how the first non-contact mines were found in the early hours of 23 November, near Shoeburyness, has often been told. Although due credit has given to Lt.-Cdr. J. G. D. Ouvry, of the Enemy Mining Section of the Mining Department of HMS *Vernon*, for dismantling the external fittings of the mine, it was Dr. A. B. Wood, chief scientist of the Mine Design Department who, in fact, in a beach hut at Southsea, supervised the detailed dissection of the mine. This was done by two naval scientists, W. F. B. Shaw and H. W. K. Kelly. Wood at once realised that the mine operated on the change of the vertical magnetic field and required about 50 milligauss to fire it. The following morning Wood despatched his report to the Admiralty, entrusting it to a colleague—an RNVR officer who in civilian life was a physicist—C. F. Goodeve. Wood concluded : 'It is now clear that the German mine is of the pivoted magnet type operating on changes of the vertical magnetic field . . . in the direction of the North Pole downwards—a feature common to all steel ships in northern latitudes. Assuming all the German mines possess this characteristic (although it certainly does not apply to British magnetic mines), then a simple method of making ships immune at once presents itself, ie, to magnetise the ships so as to have no North Pole downwards, or if any polarity is shown it should be south downwards, a method obviously simpler than that of demagnetising.'[1] This was a stop-gap measure before demagnetising methods were introduced.

Magnetic mines had been used by the British in the First World War, and their use should not have caused the Admiralty any surprise in the autumn of 1939. Yet the outbreak of war found the Navy unprepared to meet the threat of non-contact mines. Why was this so? We must go back to the First World War to find the answer.

In 1917, F. E. (later Sir Frank) Smith, later the first Director of Scientific Research at the Admiralty, developed the first magnetic mine, (the M Sinker) and the following year a number were laid off the Dutch coast to prevent U-boats entering the North Sea. It was activated on the change of direction of the earth's vertical magnetic field. Magnetic mines sank a small number of U-boats.

In the inter-war years the magnetic mine, along with the acoustic mine (also devised in 1917 by Admiralty scientists and manufactured in large numbers but never laid), was suppressed largely through fear of the consequences. There was the fear that Britain, necessarily relying on sea communications, would be more vulnerable to sea mining than other nations and would suffer accordingly if magnetic and acoustic mines were devised which were unsweepable. (At this time it seemed that there was no antidote to the magnetic mine.) There was also a long-standing tendency among senior naval officers to believe that mining was an activity only resorted to by second-class naval powers. However, when rearmament began in the mid-thirties, the decision was made to reintroduce the magnetic mine. After some disputes between the Admiralty and the Air Ministry, a new mine, operating on the rate of change in the magnetic field, was designed. It was to be laid by aircraft, and work on the mine was largely carried out at *Vernon*. Air Commodore (later Air Chief

Marshal Sir Arthur) Harris, then in charge of the Operations and Intelligence Branch at the Air Ministry, pointed out that it was only by developing and experimenting with these weapons that the right antidote to them could be found.[2]

Nevertheless, in spite of extreme financial stringency and lack of staff, valuable research work in the field of magnetism had been carried out in the post-war years by the scientists of the Mine Design Department of *Vernon* and the Admiralty Research Laboratory at Teddington. By 1928, knowledge of magnetic fields and methods of measurement was fairly extensive. But this work seems to have been principally designed to protect warships rather than merchant shipping. Naval scientists, despite the example of the M Sinker mine, failed to see the value of mines laid on the sea bottom and, according to Sir Charles Wright, did not appreciate, 'the importance of the effect of gas bubbles* on a ship's structure.'[3]

In 1936, after receiving reports that the Germans were making a magnetically-fired torpedo, the Admiralty set up the Anti-Non-Contact Committee to investigate the problem of devising countermeasures to torpedoes operated by magnetic pistols, and magnetic mines. The problem which the committee had to solve was this: 'Given a complicated steel structure (ie, a ship) moving in a magnetic field and also possessing permanent magnetism, how can it most effectively be prevented from activating a magnetically-sensitive unit, or alternatively, to activate it at such a range that the resulting explosion is not dangerous to that structure?[4] The committee decided that the latter alternative, ie, magnetisation, was the most effective method. This was to be achieved by a current-carrying cable which horizontally girdled the steel hull. The *Curaçao* and, later, the *Iron Duke*, were chosen for experiments for magnetisation. At trials held at Weymouth in the spring of 1938 the coil set off the magnetic pistol of an approaching torpedo at a fairly safe range.

However, Wood, who had recently been appointed chief scientist of the Mine Design Department at *Vernon*, disagreed with the decision of the committee. Wood, it should be noted, was a scientist of considerable experience, one of a number of outstanding young men

---

* In an underwater explosion, the bubbles form an oscillating system, the movement of which is relatively slow at the stage of full expansion and very fast at the stage of maximum contraction. The second or third shocks reaching a ship's hull, although intrinsically weaker, are nevertheless in a position to do considerable damage.

who had studied atomic physics under Rutherford at Manchester University before the First World War. He had written papers with Rutherford and it was due to the latter that, in 1915, he joined the Admiralty Board of Invention and Research, after the war becoming an established Admiralty scientist. He became fascinated with the science of acoustics and long before the Second World War was one of the leading authorities on this subject. Before joining *Vernon*, Wood had been working on acoustical problems at the Admiralty Research Laboratory and had then gone on to the Signal School at Portsmouth. Writing many years later about the committee's decision he said : 'it was playing into the hands of the enemy, as it was much easier to make a very *insensitive* magnetic pistol than a very *sensitive* one. Why not try to demagnetise the ship instead?'[5] And this was what had to be done after the discovery of the first German magnetic mine in November 1939. Wood's opinion should have been taken more seriously.

At least the Anti-Non-Contact Committee set in motion a number of experiments to discover the best method of turning a ship into a very strong electro-magnet using current-carrying coils. A model of the *Curaçao*, magnetically to scale, was made at the Admiralty Research Laboratory and this served as a guide to determine the ampère turns and the most suitable arrangements of coils for the full-scale ship. The experiments succeeded in their object of countering British standard types of magnetic pistols. This work was largely supervised by Stephen Butterworth, another Manchester University physicist, who had joined the Signal School at Portsmouth in 1918 and later went to the Admiralty Research Laboratory where he was to remain until after the Second World War. 'He had a great facility', wrote Wood, when Butterworth retired, 'for writing down the mathematical equation appropriate to a problem and solving it "while you wait". To some extent this had a demoralising effect on those of us who worked near him as we found it much easier and quicker to obtain Butterworth's solution of a problem than to solve it ourselves.'[6] The experiments at Teddington were greatly expanded after November 1939, when Butterworth organised a model ship-yard for investigating the magnetic properties of all classes of ships and the best means of demagnetising them.

The alternative to making a ship invulnerable to the magnetic mine was, of course, to sweep the mines. Minesweeping was also the responsibility of the Mine Design Department, and several sweeps were evolved for non-contact mines. For the latter there was the 'A' sweep consisting of a loop of cable towed astern of two ships, carrying sufficient current to explode magnetic mines as it passed over them. The return current was carried by earths at each ship. The other sweep was called the Single 'L' (longitudinal) and was a straight cable with an earth return towed by one ship. But when using the 'A' sweep it was difficult to avoid sweeping buoys and fouling the moorings of ships. The small currents used in the 'L' sweep considerably restricted its range. Magnets towed along the seabed were also used but where the seabed was rough there was a danger of losing them. Then, in January 1939, plans were made to build into the bows of a ship a giant electro-magnet weighing 300 tons which produced a strong magnetic field sufficiently far ahead so that the ensuing explosion of the mines would not sink the ship.

Thus at the outbreak of war the Royal Navy had no real answer to the magnetic mine, and the almost unsweepable British magnetic mine could not be used until countermeasures were ready, in case it fell into the enemy's hands. We will, in due course, discover that on several occasions during the war devices were not developed for fear that they would be of more use to the enemy. No one knew what sort of mine the Germans would use. The Admiralty believed that as a mine operating on the vertical change in the magnetic field had been used in the First World War it would be unlikely to be used again. Furthermore, naval scientific research had been starved of money in the inter-war locust years and this had caused a rigidity of mind in the scientists. The scientific and technical staff at *Vernon* (only twenty-four at the outbreak of war) was far too small to cope with an adequate programme of countermeasures. The established scientists themselves were unable to influence naval policy and it was a tragedy that more use was not made of men like Wood and Butterworth when at the height of their powers. There was little idea of how to run an effective research and development organisation, yet when shipping losses began to mount because of non-contact mines, the scientists were strongly criticised by naval officers.

The work of the scientists at *Vernon* assumed the highest importance after Wood's and his assistants' analysis of the first magnetic mine. It was now possible to put into practice schemes which had formerly been rejected (ie, demagnetisation) and to shelve other more elaborate ones then being worked on. Within a few days of the submission of Wood's report, the decision was taken to demagnetise all naval and merchant shipping—a vast undertaking involving 500 of the former and 6,000 of the latter. This work was supervised by the Mine Design Department of *Vernon*, but before long a special organisation responsible for devising countermeasures against non-contact mines was set up at the Admiralty under Vice-Admiral Sir Richard Lane-Poole.

Fortunately, civilian scientists brought in from the universities, technical colleges, Greenwich Observatory and the National Physical Laboratory, by F. (later Sir Frederick) Brundrett, on the staff of the Director of Scientific Research at the Admiralty, introduced a wave of fresh air into the Admiralty laboratories, stuffy with inter-departmental jealousies and frustrations imposed by lack of money. They had a healthy critical attitude and saw no reason to be cowed by senior officers. Within a few months the personnel of the Mine Design Department had been increased to five or six hundred. At the same time it should not be forgotten that the small staff which had laboured in the inter-war years against such odds provided an essential nucleus of experience.

As we have seen, experiments with coils had already taken place before the war. Now they were used to demagnetise ships on the line of Wood's original proposal to the Anti-Non-Contact Committee. Demagnetisation became known as 'degaussing' (after J. K. F. Gauss, specialist in magnetic fields); the latter expression was acceptable to unscientific mariners because of its similarity to the expression 'delousing'. The relative crudeness of the setting of the first magnetic mine made it easy to counter. The first ship to be degaussed was the mine-sweeping trawler *Sawfly*, and afterwards came the turn of the light cruiser *Manchester*. Quantities of electrical cable were purchased and degaussing of ships began at all major British ports. The cable was simply hung round the ship and a current passed through it, thereby producing an equal magnetic field in opposition to that of the ship. Later, more sophisticated forms of coiling were introduced. The work of Butterworth and his team at the Admiralty Research Laboratory now assumed great importance and many scale models were produced to discover the magnetic fields of various types of vessel. Degaussing techniques were also improved by introducing main, fore and quarterdeck coils; this elaborate system was used only for the larger and more valuable ships in the Royal Navy and Merchant Navy, but all large warships and merchant vessels were coiled.

Electric cable was expensive and when, very soon, it was in short supply it became necessary to think of other methods of degaussing. The French had produced large coils which were temporarily passed round a ship and through which enormous currents were momentarily passed. They degaussed the ship successfully but the equipment was very costly and its effect did not last for more than one to six months, depending on the steel of which the vessel was made. This system was known as 'flashing'.[7]

An easier and cheaper method of flashing which avoided the use of giant coils and high-power installations at docks was suggested by Goodeve. It was known as 'wiping'. Goodeve, it has been seen, was a scientist in uniform. He was a Canadian who had come to England twelve years before the war began and was a Reader in Physical Chemistry at University College, London. He had always retained a deep interest in the Navy and had joined the Canadian Naval Volunteer Reserve, transferring to the RNVR when he came to England. He had been able to study all aspects of naval warfare and had recently been specialising in countermeasures to the magnetic torpedo. This had brought him in touch with Wood, and when he was called up at the time of the Munich crisis, Goodeve had speculated with Wood as to what would be the chain of events when war broke out.

All that had to be done in the process of wiping was for a line of sailors standing on deck to raise horizontally a long electric cable attached to ropes and carrying a current of several thousand ampères, up the sides of the ship. The heavy current in the cable made it cling to the steel plates. As with flashing, sufficient residual magnetism was retained to compensate the natural magnetism. There was an additional advantage to the wiping process in that different parts of the ship could be treated separately and subjected only to the right strength of magnetic field. Even more important was the speed with which ships could be degaussed. Small ships could be done in a few hours and bigger ships in half a day. As with flashing, ships had to be re-wiped at three-monthly intervals but as the process was so easy this did not constitute a major problem. Wiping was used extensively for small ships, particularly for those without electric power on board.

Large ships were treated to a variant of wiping known as 'deperming'. Steel ships have a certain amount of magnetism hammered into them, during construction, of a permanent or semi-permanent nature. This became a great nuisance to the accurate degaussing of ships and it was removed or compensated for by the wiping process. Deperming was used on ships in southern latitudes where there were different magnetic variations. This method was an adjunct rather than an entity in itself.

Degaussing in its various forms, coiling and wiping, was essential throughout the war. A total of £20 million was spent on degaussing cable but it was a safety belt which 'saved countless ships from destruction and became the sailors' greatest friend.'[8] The greatest triumph for the wiping process was during the evacuation from Dunkirk when 400 ships were wiped and only two ships were lost as a result of magnetic mines out of a total of 218 sunk in the operation. It created an atmosphere of confidence among sailors and a legend was created of the invulnerability of ships to mines. There could even be too much confidence as on one occasion when, after a ship had anchored and the captain had signalled : 'Finished with engines', the engineer switched off the current in the coils thus reintroducing the magnetism in the ship's hull. He said afterwards : 'It was just as if I had switched the mine on'—which indeed he had.[9]

Yet as Sir Edward Bullard, like Goodeve associated with this work, has pointed out, the principle of degaussing and 'kindred techniques of making ships impervious to magnetic mines was based on elementary and classical physics. This was characteristic of wartime science.' It was, wrote Bullard, not 'the production of startling new ideas (but) the application of rather humdrum and well-known principles to new problems. Success often depended more on having the foresight and confidence to lay plans on a large enough scale at an early stage than on anything profoundly "scientific" in the ordinary sense.'[10] As Goodeve wrote of degaussing, 'although in technical achievement it is not in the same class as the radar or anti-U-boat battles, it was the first technical battle in which we won a decisive victory over the enemy; but more important still, it was one which brought science fully into the war in the very early days.'[11]

(ii) Magnetic Mines—Sweeping

Degaussing gave immediate protection to ships. However, it was more effective to destroy the mines for then they could do no further harm. Some thought, it has been seen, was given before the war to sweeping non-contact mines, and experiments were made with a towed magnetic sweep in July 1939. After the analysis of the magnetic mine, the various methods of sweeping then in existence were reviewed, and it was apparent that a more effective type of sweep had to be devised. There were a number of difficult problems to overcome. Obviously the idea of towing a magnet (known as the 'Bosun's Nightmare') just above the sea bottom was impracticable. The alternative was to have a floating coil or cable. Hence the idea of a raft carrying coils of wire through which current would be passed from a generator in the towing craft to create a strong magnetic field. But high seas would upset the raft and the towing ship might be destroyed if it struck a mine. The easiest method was to tow a cable which floated. But buoyant cables did not then exist and would have to be designed. It was Wood who pointed out that a floating cable carrying a current gave no vertical magnetism on the seabed immediately below and thus would not explode a mine in a position close enough to destroy the cable.

In the first place Professor B. P. Haigh, Professor of Applied Mechanics at Greenwich Naval College, put forward the idea of a longitudinal sweep with two ships, each towing a length (one short and one long) of buoyant cable, each with an electrode at the end. The current would pass down one cable and back through the other and create a magnetic field in the water, thereby exploding the mine. There were three disadvantages to this scheme. The distances between the electrodes would be such that a continuous current of 3,000 ampères was required continuously; secondly, the channel swept would be very narrow; and, thirdly, the sweep did not float. Out of Haigh's idea came the Double Longitudinal, or Double-L sweep, proposed by the Mine Design Department. This also involved the use of two towing vessels, but enabled a much wider channel to be swept. An enormous amount of current was still required. Calculations by Dr. J. L. Tuck, a physicist then working at the Admiralty who later went on to work on the atomic bomb at Los Alamos, and Dr. E. A. Guggenheim, a mathematician of University College, London, later Professor of Chemistry at Reading University, enabled the power required to be greatly reduced. Instead of a continuous flow of current, short pulses would be passed through the cables as the ships moved forward on a parallel course. These pulses had to be synchronised exactly. Goodeve was placed in charge of the project.

Could this scheme work? An experiment must be made on quiet water but it had to be salt water. Close to *Vernon* was the Canoe Lake, Southsea—a favourite place in peacetime for sailing model boats. Buildings overlooked the lake so that the experiment could not be concealed. A friend of Goodeve's had a flat overlooking the lake and this was taken over as an office. A cover plan was then devised by Goodeve in which experiments for the detection of ships were to be made. A number of model ships were towed by sailors backwards and forwards across the cables in the lake. The procedure for sweeping was reversed, the electric cables being laid on the lake bed instead of floating. A crowd curiously watched them. Meanwhile, under cover, a magnetic mine was placed in a rowing boat. When the current was switched on, a recording instrument on the mine showed that it would have been exploded. The sweep worked.[12]

After the success of this experiment two tugs at London docks were equipped to tow the first Double-L sweep. Ford V8 engines drove 55-kilowatt generators, which provided the current for the cables. Later, fleet minesweepers were equipped for towing the sweeps. In the first sea test conducted by Goodeve on Boxing Day 1939, one of the tugs ran aground on a mudbank with its cable wound round the propeller. The sweep, however, had worked and immediately the Admiralty issued orders for the production of cable and the training of crews. But much work had still to be done. The first sea tests were made with the cables lashed to logs; buoyant cables had to be found. Rumour had it that a firm in the USA manufactured buoyant cable but Lease-Lend had not yet begun. Through Goodeve, two British cable-making firms were given the job. The first buoyant cables were enclosed in a sorbo sheath, and it was afterwards discovered that they were, in fact, the first cables of this kind ever to be made. In February 1940 the Double-L sweep destroyed its first magnetic mine in the Thames Estuary.

Other but less satisfactory methods of sweeping magnetic mines were by means of aircraft fitted with a giant coil and a petrol-driven motor generator, and by an electro-magnet fitted to the bows of a ship. Like degaussing, the Double-L sweep had a great moral effect as well as physically sweeping channels through which ships could sail with impunity. French craft being evacuated down the Seine from Rouen at the time of the fall of France refused to sail until they were preceded by minesweepers. The Royal Navy duly obliged by sweeping a channel, even though the Double-L sweep did not, in fact, conduct an adequate amount of electricity in fresh water.[13] Later, when the Allies returned to the Continent, the Double-L sweep was invaluable in clearing mines from harbour entrances and estuaries.

(iii) Acoustic Mines

The Germans continued to lay magnetic mines but they were made bi-polar, operating on either North or South Pole. They were now more sensitive and therefore easier to sweep, requiring only about ± 20 milligauss to fire them. Even more sophisticated magnetic mines were made which automatically adjusted themselves to north or south latitudes, their sensitivity to actuation being increased to four or five milligauss.

In the early autumn of 1940, the Germans began to lay what were suspected as being acoustic mines, and one of their first victims was the cruiser *Galatea*. A special meeting was held at the Admiralty to discuss the possible nature of these mines, but the idea that they might be acoustically activated was greeted with a certain amount of scepticism. Yet, as we have seen, an acoustic mine had been designed in the First World War by Wood, tested and manufactured, but never used.[14]

Between the wars the acoustic mine was neglected to an even greater degree than the magnetic mine, although much valuable data were collected on the propagation of sound underwater. Why was this? Again the reasons must be the lack of scientific staff due to financial stringency, and the fear that effective countermeasures could not be found. Technically, Wood has stated there was also some prejudice against the mine because of its variability.

The fact that the Germans were laying acoustic mines was confirmed early in November 1940, when acoustic mines were discovered near Cardiff and at Birchington in Kent, and Fowey, in Cornwall. The Admiralty responded to the new threat by setting up a special countermeasures section under Bullard at the Mine Design Department which was to work in conjunction with a naval section from *Vernon* under Lt.-Cdr. R. J. Cooper, RN. They worked in laboratories and offices installed on Clarence Pier, Portsmouth. Bullard had come from Cambridge where he was a lecturer in geophysics and, unlike Goodeve, he had joined the Admiralty as a civilian scientist at the outbreak of war. That summer he had been investigating the Continental Shelf. But Bullard also understood the workings of the naval mind. It was a mind, he states, which was suspicious of scientists before the war—an attitude which gradually changed after the solution of the magnetic-mine problem. This was possible because the naval staff at the top was small; it still resembled Nelson's Band of Brothers.

Wood's and others' knowledge of acoustic mines made it possible to devise an acoustic sweep within a few weeks. This was a hammerbox consisting of an electrically-driven road drill which struck a rapid succession of blows on a steel plate forming part of the casing. In the sea, this noise made acoustic mines explode up to a distance of one mile away. The hammerboxes were known as 'Kango hammers' after the road drill of this type. They were immediately successful and were the core of acoustic minesweeping throughout the war, although several other devices were used with which we are not concerned here.

In January 1941 a critical moment in the mining war was reached. The Mine Design Department on Clarence Pier was destroyed through enemy bombing and a decision had to be made whether to disperse it or not. It was now realised, initially by Capt. E. V. Collingwood, a fine mathematician and a member of the well-known naval family of Collingwood, that the enemy was going to introduce a number of different types of non-contact or 'influence' mines. Largely at the insistence of Cdr. (later Capt.) Oliver-Bellasis, it was decided to organise special sections in the Minesweeping Department of *Vernon* and in Bullard's sweeping section in the Mine Design Department to investigate future countermeasures in anticipation of further developments in German mine warfare. A joint establishment of the civilian Sweeping Division, another Minesweeping Department of *Vernon*, was set up that April on the Firth of Forth, with its headquarters in one of the boarding-houses of Fettes College. A. T. Pickles, a physicist who eventually became senior scientist after joining the Admiralty from Bristol University, has written that it was: 'an unusual form of organisation which arises from the special requirements set by work on countermeasures. Here the essential requirement is for speed of reaction once the enemy weapon, prepared in secrecy, is disclosed : for this a very flexible organisation is necessary, since operational as well as scientific considerations are involved. At one extreme, tactical countermeasures (eg, re-routeing, zig-zag, slow speed) may serve to tide over the immediate danger; at the other extreme, the development of a countermeasure may require a great deal of abstruse scientific work which has to be carried out as a series of purely academic investigations, preferably before the threat materialises. In terms of personnel, the requirement is for a team of naval officers, engineers and scientists to work together in the closest relations.'[15]

The new establishment was set up none too soon, for by June of that year the Germans were laying mines with combined magnetic and acoustic firing devices. They contained anti-sweeping devices and sometimes booby traps. Appropriate sweeps were devised by the Sweeping Division and their skill was more than matched by the courage of the crews of the minesweeping flotillas.

(iv) Pressure Mines

Pickles set up a civilian section parallel to the special section in *Vernon* which dealt with future sweeps, to explore possible methods of actuating influence mines, in particular, high- and low-frequency acoustic mines and hydrodynamic actuation. 'I think it may be arguable,' Pickles continues, 'whether our preparatory work led to better countermeasures being devised, but its existence meant that meeting new weapons was no longer a matter of crises involving the personal attention of very senior officers who could now turn to problems of the offensive.'[16]

A group of the Sweeping Division devoted itself to working at countermeasures against pressure-, or oyster-mines, as they were called. These mines were operated by suction under a moving ship and the Germans had set great store by them because they were virtually unsweepable. They were not used until June 1944, after the Allies had landed in Europe. For the Germans, the situation was then desperate. By that time the Sweeping Division scientists had obtained a complete understanding of pressure mines and related phenomena. Much had also been learned from developing British influence mines, especially information about wave periods, wave height and suction pressures on the seabed, and the British

mines, unlike the German, were designed to cope with these different probabilities. This bears out the lesson already defined that
the development of a new weapon invariably suggests possible
countermeasures to it.

Like the analysis of the first magnetic mines, an accident gave the
game away, for on 19 June 1944, thirteen days after the landings,
the German Air Force dropped two of their pressure mines by
error into the Normandy beachhead. Each weighed about a ton but
they were at once shipped over to *Vernon* and dismantled during
the night of 21 June. On the following morning the sensitivity of
the units was measured, and that afternoon a meeting was held at
the Admiralty to decide on countermeasures. Pickles, then senior
scientist of the Minesweeping Division, was present, and he proposed tactics which had been worked out over the past three years.
It had been found that if ships travelled below a certain speed the
suction effect would not be enough to set off the mines. Maximum
speeds for different types of ship had been calculated and set out
in a table on the assumption that the mines would require a pressure decrease equivalent to six inches of water to detonate them.
The mines dropped in Normandy operated on a pressure charge
equal to one inch of water. All that had to be done, therefore, was
to divide these speeds by two and a half, which is roughly equal
to the square root of six, for the pressure variations at depth are
proportional to the square of the speed of the ship. That evening
the Admiralty issued orders for shipping to proceed at slow speed
in shallow water off the beachhead.

In the event, the most effective sweeper of influence mines proved
to be the sea itself, and many influence mines were exploded by the
Atlantic swell coming up the Channel. The Germans continued to
lay acoustic and magnetic mines with influence mines, but they
had no effect on the conduct of operations.

What is significant to the development of an idea for an invention from this brief account of countermeasures to sea mines?
Scientists who are concerned with developing a new weapon have
to ask themselves the question : how can the weapon be improved?
Scientists concerned with countermeasures, however, must ask
themselves : how can the weapon be countered or, at least, how can
its effects be minimised? This depends on very extensive scientific
knowledge of the phenomena involved. Mining and countermining,
like anti-submarine weapons, were sadly neglected in the inter-war

years. As Capt. Stephen Roskill has pointed out: 'The big gun was still the arbiter in naval warfare.'[17]. Yet, in the event, more ships were sunk through mines than by any other weapon.[18] Magnetic mines took the Admiralty by surprise at the outset of war, but thanks to the knowledge acquired by the small group of Admiralty scientists, and the fresh blood injected by civilian scientists who came in during the war, the threat was overcome.

After 1941, because of its organisation designed to anticipate enemy mining developments, the Royal Navy kept abreast of the enemy in the field of underwater weapons, although towards the end of the war appreciation of the possible lines that enemy weapon developments might take revealed that the German designers were not exploiting technical opportunities to the full. And when they did succeed in capturing one of the newest British minesweepers in the latter stages of the Mediterranean campaign—a ship capable of sweeping both acoustic and magnetic mines—it was too late for them to reap the benefit.

(v) Acoustic Torpedoes

The Germans had been working some time before the war on a torpedo which would home on to the noise made by a ship's propellers. It operated on a gyro device. Launched from the submarine, the torpedo, acting like a human ear, turning from side to side, finally homed on the target. A special safety system ensured that the torpedo only exploded at a safe distance from the submarine.

The Wren (*Zaunkönig*), or 'Gnat', as it was called by the Allies, was planned to be used against Allied escort vessels in the Battle of the Atlantic, and was first used in September 1943. Its use had been anticipated by the scientists of the group from the Sweeping Division responsible for anti-torpedo work under M. N. Hill (son of Professor A. V. Hill). On the basis of theoretical calculations, made by Dr. R. Roscoe and other scientists, a complete scheme of defence and a prototype decoy were ready to counter the new weapon. Countermeasures consisted of noise-makers, usually hammerboxes similar in design to the acoustic mine sweeps, which were towed behind the ship so that the torpedo homed towards them instead of on the ship's propellers. This device was known as 'Foxer'. The scientists also worked out a system of slow speed

for ships when an attack by acoustic torpedoes was anticipated.

Foxer had a number of disadvantages. As it could not be towed
at speeds over 15 knots, escorts were vulnerable to the homing
torpedoes when they were following up a radar contact or radio
signal at high speed. Foxer also interfered with the operation of
asdic, and when destroyers were turning at high speed the device
was liable to get entangled in the propellers.

The Admiralty now instructed the Acoustics Group of the
Admiralty Research Laboratory to develop an expendable decoy or
noise-maker. F. Rock Carling was in charge of this group and was
responsible for a device called 'Publican' which would not have the
disadvantages of Foxer. Carling was an engineer with a deep
interest in acoustics from his student days, and had worked on
the development of loudspeakers before the war.

Publican was a small hammerbox contained in a rocket and was
fired from a projector on the deck of a destroyer. A small parachute was opened by the explosive gases of the projectile and this
kept the hammerbox in suspension below the water for about three
minutes. Publican was introduced towards the end of 1943 and was
immediately effective. By that time, however, the U-boat had
already been mastered by Allied radar devices and the combined
action of aircraft and surface vessels.

Page 51: (*left*) Sir Charles Goodeve; (*right*) Professor P. M. S. (later Lord) Blackett.

Page 52: A 'Sunday Soviet' at Malvern College including Lord Cherwell, members of TRE and RAF officers.

Chapter 4

Anti-Submarine Warfare

Little seems to have been written about the lack of anxiety, during the pre-war years, concerning the submarine as a threat to the survival of Britain. The menace of the enemy bomber to our cities and industries dominated efforts in the direction of scientific novelty. Yet, in the event, Germany and her people withstood immeasurably more bombing effort than we did before a vital effect on the outcome of the war was achieved. In those pre-war days, none foresaw that, with the fall of France and the threat of invasion, what was to matter most was not the bombing of cities but attacks on fighter aerodromes from which the Germans so foolishly turned away at a critical time.

Lack of anxiety about the outcome of a submarine war is indeed puzzling. Certainly it would have needed the vision of a poet rather than that of a man of war to have foreseen that the coastline available to the enemy for submarine bases would be far-flung from Norway to Bordeaux. Yet history records that, with a far smaller coastline available to Germany, the submarine nearly brought about our defeat in 1917. In the pre-war years, improvements were made in known anti-submarine devices and techniques but there was no call, analogous to that for defence against bombing aircraft, for a revolution in the science of anti-submarine warfare. Even when the revolution came, it was in a way an accident, a side-product of efforts towards defence against night bombing.

By the end of 1941 the U-boat campaign had become so serious that Churchill told the First Lord and the First Sea Lord that less than two submarines were being sunk per month, while they were increasing by nearly twenty. A special anti-U-boat committee, presided over by the Prime Minister himself, was set up to remedy the Navy's deficiencies. It is possible that the Admiralty believed that asdic and the system of convoys developed in the First World War were adequate countermeasures against the submarine, and certainly by 1939 British asdic equipment was well ahead of any other country.

The basic principle of asdic was to obtain echoes of high-frequency sound from a submarine. A short train of waves of supersonic sound is transmitted in a beam, similar to a searchlight beam, from the detecting ship. Any obstruction in this beam, such as the hull of a submarine, will reflect some of the sound and after the appropriate interval this arrives back at the detecting ship and can be picked up by a suitable receiver. Asdic could indicate the bearing and range of a submarine and in its more sophisticated forms it provided additional information, but it was subject to severe limitations. It lost contact with a submarine at ranges over two hundred yards and it was easily confused by background noise, such as waves breaking against the hull of a ship, air bubbles created when a ship is moving at high speed, the temperature of the sea, to say nothing of the explosion of depth charges and the noise of ships' propellers. Asdic could not detect a surfaced submarine, and the fact that submarines had to spend much of their time on the surface, either to recharge batteries or to move at speed, gave the other means of detection—radar—its great opportunity.

The performance of the U-boat used in the Second World War in terms of speed and endurance, surfaced and submerged, differed little from its predecessor of the 1914-18 war. Belatedly, the Germans built boats with improved underwater performance using hydrogen peroxide as a means of propulsion but, as with so many of their weapons, sufficient of them were not ready in time. On the other hand, the U-boats built in the early years of the war could dive deeper, were more manoeuvrable, and their hulls were made of thicker and stronger steel.

DETECTION

(i) Airborne Radar

In the autumn of 1936 E. G. Bowen, an original member of the Bawdsey team, instigated the formation of a team for research on airborne radar. 'Taffy' Bowen was a Welshman—a tower of strength in any team and an excellent cricketer. In the whole vast canvas of radar it is difficult to name specific fathers, but certainly Bowen was the father of airborne radar, both in Britain and later in the United States. That it fell to one possessing Bowen's demonic energy to initiate radar in aircraft was fortunate indeed.

The airborne radar equipment for night defence was known as AI (Air Interception) and will be described in Chapter 5. The earliest experimental sets used a wavelength of 6·8 metres, later reduced to 1·5 metres, the smallest then available. With these wavelengths, narrow beams were unattainable and the curse of this early form of AI was the return of echoes from the ground, thereby limiting the useful range of the set to the height of the aircraft above the ground. Curse it certainly was for AI, but for the birth of ASV (Air to Surface Vessel) a blessing. During experiments with 6·8-metre AI early in 1937, Dame Fortune took Bowen over the sea, and ships were observed at short range. It is no disparagement of those concerned to say that the practicability of ship detection was then obvious and involved no more than a modification of the AI set. Thus ASV was born, though none could know that, speaking of vastly different forms of ASV yet to come, Admiral Doenitz would one day say in a speech at Weimar: 'The enemy has deprived the U-boat of its essential feature—namely the element of surprise—by means of radar. With these methods . . . he has conquered the U-boat menace. The scientists who have created radar have been called the saviours of their country.'

During the summer of 1937 strong signals* at a range of five miles were obtained from the *Rodney* and the *Sheffield*, using a wavelength of 1½ metres. The next major step, taken in 1938, was the determination of the direction of a ship with respect to the observing aircraft and the use of the overlapping beam technique provided for homing on to a ship target. Aerials were mechanically switched and the resulting signals were applied to a single cathode-ray tube giving range and left-right indications of a form which was characteristic of all subsequent versions of ASV operating on metre wavelengths.

The winter of 1939/40 was, for the use of ASV, a period of training and by the summer of 1940, Mk. II ASV sets with a range of about four miles on surfaced submarines were available for operations. During this period they did little to assist RAF Coastal Command in a problem which, judging only and optimistically by the extent of shipping losses, was not acute. At that time the

* A description of how radar works will be found on pages 94-5.

enemy possessed few submarines and there was no indication of the appalling losses which were to result from the loss of the Bay of Biscay ports. ASV proved, however, to be extremely useful when aircraft had to find a convoy for the purpose of escorting it.

With the fall of France, ASV received an added impetus and a higher priority. The threat associated with an enemy-held Bay of Biscay was at last obvious to all, but success in the shape of sunken submarines was, however, long in coming. Until the war neared its end, submarines were forced to surface, either by day or by night, in order to charge their batteries. If surfacing by day proved dangerous, there was nothing to prevent a submarine from surfacing by night. During most of 1941 all that ASV could usefully do was to force submarines to surface only at night; this was useful in many ways but unless submarines could largely be prevented from attacking our convoys, the sea war could only end in one way—victory for Germany. It was not until 20 November 1941 that ASV was the direct cause of the sinking of a submarine, the best method of all of saving our ships.

In June 1942 there began a period of oscillating ascendancy which was to continue throughout the war. For a time, the submarine would be largely robbed of its power of destruction, followed by a period of successful enemy measures to deprive ASV aircraft of their victims. And so the battle of techniques and of wits went on. Until June 1942, the submarine was in the ascendency for reasons that were all too clear. ASV had succeeded in causing submarines to remain submerged for most of the daylight hours but at night a surfaced submarine could regard itself as tolerably safe. To home on to a submarine at night was one thing, to attack it in darkness was quite another. There seems to be no record of this problem being envisaged or investigated before the war. In June 1942, a device was fitted to Wellington aircraft, fitted with $1\frac{1}{2}$-metre ASV, which temporarily turned the tide of battle against the submarine. A Leigh Light, named after its proposer, was fitted to the aircraft and when switched on after ASV had brought the attacking aircraft to within a mile or so of a submarine, produced something like daylight conditions for an attack.

At best, the life of a submarine crew in war is a nerve-racking business. Owing to the submarine's own noise, aircraft could not be heard approaching and it is not surprising that to be subject at night to daylight conditions of attack had a devastating effect on the morale of submarine crews. During June and July 1942, in spite of heavy losses, U-boats making the passage of the Bay of Biscay, essential to their deadly work, continued to surface at night, but in August of that year they were driven to the desperate measure of charging their batteries in daylight. Sightings of submarines by day rose sharply and the sinkings of mercantile vessels declined for the first time.

The position in the late summer of 1942 was that only under cloudless skies by day were submarines able to detect the approach of hostile aircraft and dive to comparative safety. Meanwhile Germany, having given up hope of a speedy end to the war, had turned to the submarine as a main means of victory and with increased submarine construction. Shipping losses were still heavy, but declining, and much less than the 600,000 tons of June 1942.

To make their large new submarine fleet fully effective, the Germans were faced with the task of countering the ability of ASV aircraft to locate and home on to submarines. All that was necessary was for every U-boat to be fitted with a radio listening device which would receive energy from the wide beam inseparable from 1½-m ASV and which would provide a visual or aural signal indicating that a radar-fitted aircraft was in the vicinity. The U-boat would then dive and find safety, for radar was useless against a submerged submarine. No doubt these provisions took the Germans time which was precious to us, but by the early winter of 1942/43 submarine sightings were few and after a seasonal lull the shipping losses again rose to alarming figures; 400,000 tons in the month of March 1943.

The next step in the fateful play of measure and countermeasure was the most dramatic and decisive of all. It was the use of the magnetron (see Chapter 5) operating on a wavelength of ten centimetres.

Useful though 1½-metre ASV had been, it had many disadvantages. Today, most people are aware that radar signals are recorded on a kind of moving map, with the aircraft or ship position as centre. As a rotating radar beam continuously sweeps the area below or around an aircraft or ship, the relative positions of objects are clearly recorded. By comparison with this arrangement, the indications given by the 1½-metre ASV were difficult to interpret. Other disadvantages were that its range was limited to three or four miles; the wavelength used had become known to the enemy and, not least, a continuous signal from our 1½-metre ASV told the U-boat commander with fair certainty that he was being approached by an enemy aircraft.

With 10-centimetre ASV, all of these disadvantages disappeared. The range was eventually many times that of the 1½-metre ASV equipment and a new wavelength—and a very strange one to the Germans—meant at least a breathing space against listening. The presentation of plan position rendered interpretation of signals possible without crew fatigue and strain. Moreover, with 10-centimetre ASV, indications would be received by any listening device whenever the continuously rotating beam swept through the U-boat's position, whether or not the aircraft was approaching the U-boat. A possibility open to a U-boat commander would be to dive whenever there was the slightest danger, but his vessel would then be of little offensive value and his crew would soon become nervous wrecks.

Bowen went out with the Tizard Mission and stayed to give the results of his experience to the Americans. On 27 January 1941, he wrote a draft specification for 10-centimetre ASV, and this seems to have been the first documentary record of the project. The progress made at the Radiation Laboratory was rapid and the first flight test was made off New England on 27 March 1941. The object of the flight was to test the performance of the equipment for the detection of ships and submarines. 'The equipment performed admirably, and for what was probably the first time an airborne microwave radar was tried out for aircraft-to-surface vessel (ASV) purposes. Tests on a 10,000-ton ship gave strong signals, and the "sea return", ie, interfering echoes from the surface of the water, was much less than had been feared.'[1]

On the United States' entry into the war, large-scale production of centimetre ASV went ahead without major discomfitures.

Meanwhile, the British research effort on ASV was centred at TRE, then near Swanage. As will be explained in Chapter 6, the centimetre applications team was headed by Mr. (later Professor) P. I. Dee, and a prominent member of his staff Dr. A. C. B. (later Sir Bernard) Lovell, after the war to become well known in connection with the radio telescope at Jodrell Bank, was responsible for research on 10-centimetre ASV and on the similar H_2S equipment. During 1940, there was much discussion at TRE on the possibilities of a plan position presentation of radar echoes and of a centimetre form of ASV. It was not, however, until June 1941 that the project became a part of the official programme. The use of centimetre waves for submarine location had, however, an earlier origin in one of the most significant demonstrations ever given at TRE, described on page 64, and which led to the introduction of centimetre radar into the Navy—the first service to use 10-centimetre radar operationally.

Not until 1 March 1943 was the first operational flight with British 10-centimetre ASV made, though the research programme had begun nearly two years before (June 1941). Before considering the causes of delay, it is useful to examine whether the heartaches and the frustrations of the scientists with top-level service chiefs and their staffs were worth while in what most mattered, ie, sunken submarines and acceptable shipping losses.

On 17 March a submarine was detected at a range of nine miles but a faulty Leigh Light prevented an attack being made. From then on, the magnificent story can be briefly told. In April 1943 U-boats were once again forced to surface in daylight, during which for a time they tried the desperate counter to radar of fighting it out in packs of three or four. Success was so clear that the pessimists in Coastal Command and elsewhere were transferred to other posts. In May 1943 there was a slaughter of U-boats. Shipping losses fell from 400,000 tons in March 1943 to a comparatively trifling 40,000 tons in August of that year. As we shall see, the trial of wits, of measure and countermeasure, was not over but never again was the U-boat a menace and a threat to our existence. It was at this time that Hitler himself admitted that the setback (surely a masterly understatement) was due to a single technical invention of the enemy. 'It is not surprising that some important judges have seen in the change in the U-boat struggle, brought about primarily by the use of not more than fifty sets of H_2S radar equipment, the most significant single event which happened in the whole war of 1939-45. In the development of H_2S and this sea war application, much is owed to Dee, Lovell and their team at TRE.'[2]

If this is true, as surely it is, it may well be wondered why the Dee-Lovell team should have suffered so much discouragement and frustration. Essentially, as we shall see in Chapter 6, the main reasons were the nightmare which centimetre radar installations in aircraft presented to the aircraft designer, intent on aircraft performance; the entirely new techniques in the maintenance and use of which service personnel had to be trained, and in the reluctance to present the enemy with a magnetron, an event certain to happen sooner or later in operations.

There were, however, delaying factors which were peculiar to the use of centimetre radar against U-boats. One was the priority given to the bomber offensive and which received the special support of Lord Cherwell. In a deadly game of wits, such as that played with the U-boats, all that can be done is to keep ahead of the enemy; to buy time. This involved giving high priority to all means for frustrating the war against our merchant shipping. This was never given in full measure to 10-centimetre sea search equipment and, curiously enough, it seems likely that it would not have been given at all had not the H_2S set, a bombing aid, been substantially identical with centimetre ASV—so much so that the equipment was called $H_2S/$ASV. Until Air Marshal Sir John Slessor took over Coastal Command in mid-1943, the Command gave little encouragement to the $H_2S/$ASV equipment and failed to see that it was not a second-best ASV set but, as was proved in action, a highly efficient set for sea search, and that a combined set accelerated production. Perhaps the attitude of the Command accentuated the difficulties that the TRE team were to encounter at the RAF base from which the Wellington ASV aircraft were to operate. Lovell recalls a senior officer at that base saying in March 1943, 'We're giving up the old stuff too soon. There is nothing wrong with it. It is all a matter of joss, just joss.'

When at last a change of heart occurred in Coastal Command it is not altogether surprising that Bomber Command looked with a jealous eye and spoke with resisting voice against every $H_2S/$ASV set earmarked for Coastal Command.

The late summer of 1943 saw the end of dangerous losses to our merchant shipping but not of the trial of wits, involving measure and countermeasure. Although the 10-centimetre ASV presentation (the plan position indicator) was such that listening from a U-boat was less rewarding than it had been with the homing technique used with $1\frac{1}{2}$ metres, it was nevertheless a worthwhile countermeasure. The German device for listening to 10-centimetre ASV, known as 'Naxos', was introduced in August 1943. Rowe remembers that on 31 August, Lord Hankey and C. P. Snow were visiting TRE to investigate the need for senior research staff to be taken from elsewhere. In the middle of the discussions, a messenger came panting into the room to announce that the Germans were now listening to

10-centimetre ASV. Snow was never quite convinced that this was not a piece of stage management, which it was not.

As before, the answer to listening was a change of wavelength. During 1942, basic research on 3-centimetre equipment had been done at TRE under H. W. Skinner and, later in that year, this group fitted an American Boeing aircraft with 3-centimetre H₂S. This equipment became potentially available for the anti-U-boat war, and in October 1943 we find a coatless Commander-in-Chief ensconced in Lovell's office concocting a letter of protest to the Air Ministry concerning the delays in making 3-centimetre equipment available for ASV. Had such a scene been possible in Germany, the war might well have had a different ending. Some 3-centimetre sets became available but, for the conventional submarine, the war was over and at this stage the very small shipping losses were having no effect on the outcome of the war.

The Schnorkel, introduced in August 1944 enabled the U-boat to charge its batteries below the sea surface and so escape radar detection. Operationally, however, it was too late. With the advance of the Allied forces in Europe, Germany lost the coastline from which her U-boats had operated, and the deadly battle between radar-fitted aircraft and the U-boat was over. British compromise, epitomised by the TRE motto, 'Second best Tomorrow' had triumphed over German thoroughness, the results of which could be summed up in two words, 'Too Late'.

(ii) Surface Radar

In March 1935, the Tizard Committee discovered that the only instrumental aid for providing warning of hostile aircraft was the telescope. However, there was an alternative system of detection. Since 1925, the Admiralty Research Laboratory had been exploring the possibilities of locating ships and aircraft by the radiation from hot surfaces such as funnels and exhausts. But with the widespread adoption of radar there was no large-scale requirement for the infra-red equipment.

However, the possibility of using radio waves for the detection of ships had not escaped the attention of one of the scientists attached to the Signal School at Portsmouth. In 1928 L. S. B. Alder took out a patent which was countersigned by the captain of the Signal School for a scheme of radio-location. It is as C. E. Horton, one of his colleagues and later chief scientist, Admiralty Signal Establishment, said after the war : 'a most beautiful patent which can be read with intellectual satisfaction to this day. It gives convincingly and lucidly the fundamental principles on which the various types of radar have been developed. Nevertheless, nothing much was done about that patent and it lapsed. It fell on very unfertile soil. This Establishment failed to see the significance of radar, and as late as 1937 it was a matter of great difficulty to get workshop and drawing office effort to put on to it. The reason was always the same—other and more obvious demands took priority. The user had had no previous experience of radar on which to base his sense of value.'[3]

Nothing more was heard of radio location until A. B. Wood, then attached to the Admiralty Research Laboratory, made a number of visits to Orfordness and then to Bawdsey during 1935-36 to see to what extent radar could be applied to naval problems. 'Previous to visiting the research station at Orfordness', wrote Wood, 'I would have prophesied that the radio location of aircraft by echo was unlikely to succeed. But, of course, the asdic detection of submarines also seemed unlikely to succeed when it was first proposed in 1915-16.'[4] Wood soon appreciated how important radar could be in the detection and location of aircraft, ships and especially, submarines. He realised that the detection of submarines would require much shorter wavelengths than were being used for the detection of high-flying aircraft. On account of Wood's close interest in radar, he was, in December 1936, transferred to the Signal School. He and three other scientists carried on radar research at Eastney Barracks, Portsmouth, at the same time keeping in close touch with developments at Bawdsey. However, in October 1937, Wood was transferred to the Mining School where he was to achieve distinction with his analysis of the first German magnetic mine.

By 1937, the naval scientists at Eastney were obtaining echoes from the pylons on Portsdown Hill with their transmitter and by the end of the following year the battleship *Rodney* and the cruiser *Sheffield* had been fitted with an aircraft early warning system operating on a seven-metre wavelength. This type of set warned the British fleet of the presence of Italian warships before the Battle of Cape Matapan in March 1941. Although the Admiralty failed to grasp radar the first time, Churchill's criticism in the summer of 1939 when he asked why it was not 'hot on the trail' of radar is perhaps a little severe. Indeed, the year before the Director of Scientific Research, Dr. C. S. (later Sir Charles) Wright, had already appreciated 'the need', as he later wrote, 'for small aerials at maximum height in small ships and the need for narrow beams to detect small objects on the sea surface in spite of background returns from the sea waves. Indeed, for horizontal transmission such as was required for U-boat detection, centimetre waves were almost essential.'

Radar at sea posed special problems. The radar set had to operate in unstable conditions and in the teeth of high winds. Moreover, the limited space on a warship affected the placing of radar equipment. Obviously the mast was the highest point in the ship, but radar had to compete with equally essential radio communications and direction-finding equipment. These factors inevitably lengthened the period of development.

But this is jumping ahead in our story. The first requirement was to provide the vulnerable battleship with an aircraft early warning system. It was soon seen that it could also be used to locate surface vessels. Secondly, radar could control the fire of the ship's guns— both against aircraft and against surface vessels. In 1938 a major breakthrough came with the introduction of the high-power (50 centimetre) early warning Type 281 set. A modified Army gunlaying set meanwhile served as a fire-control system and was installed on the cruiser *Carlisle*.

A team of scientists under J. F. Coales, who left Cambridge to join the Signal School, was responsible for developing and modifying the 50-centimetre sets. By 1940 three of these sets were in the development or production stage. They were the Type 282 set for short-range anti-aircraft fire, the Type 283 for long-range anti-aircraft fire and the Type 284 for surface gunnery. In May 1940 200 of the Type 284 sets were ordered—before the design had been finally completed —and they were being fitted into ships by the end of the year. These three sets, states Capt. S. W. Roskill, the naval historian, 'initiated a revolution and were the progenitors of all the great family of director-mounted gunnery radars.'[5] They were responsible for radar-controlled gunfire during the vital years of the war.

But the most urgent naval problem in 1940 was how to detect the surfaced U-boat. Wright, it has been seen, was already convinced of the importance of short-wave radar. Yet it was the scientists at TRE, all, as already described, fervent believers in centimetric wavelengths, who persuaded Wright to send a small team of scientists under Dr. S. E. A. Landale, who had joined the Signal School just after the outbreak of war, to TRE at Swanage to learn about the latest centimetric techniques which were then being developed. 'What was required by the Navy,' states Landale, 'was equipment to enable their corvettes and small escort vessels to detect enemy submarines on the surface at as great a range as possible as they approached a convoy in darkness or fog, and we decided that it was hopeful that surfaced submarines could be detected at a range of about 5,000 yards from these small vessels if centimetric techniques then available were applied.'[6]

In September 1940 naval officers and scientists were invited by TRE to witness trials with a centimetric equipment on the cliffs at Swanage. The set was able to follow a submarine seven miles out to sea. At once the Admiralty decided that the Signal School should develop a 10-centimetre equipment for naval use. Speed was absolutely vital. The set not only had to be reliable but its construction made as simple as possible. This was not easy because the Admiralty expected the component parts to be of standard issue pattern. 'But', writes Landale, 'these items were obsolete and cumbersome and in every way unsuited to the development of such equipment, and red tape had to be cut in all directions and components used in commercial radio had to be adapted, and, of course, many new and advanced techniques employed.'

TRE was indispensable to the naval team. In particular, Skinner developed the detector, then 'a very strange and now seemingly primitive crystal device.' The aerial system was suggested and made workable by Lovell. The development of the magnetron will be described in Part 3, but mention should be made of the valuable assistance provided by the research department of the General Electric Company at Wembley under E. C. S. Megaw. Due to the percipience of Wright, contracts for shortwave-valves had been placed with this firm as early as 1938.

Having learned all they could about centimetric radar, Landale and his team returned to Portsmouth to 'build literally with their own hands' the equipment which became known as the Type 271 set. This set was ready by February 1941. Capt. Basil Willett of the Signal School decided, on his own initiative, to accept the risk that the trials might prove unsatisfactory. He ordered components for 150 sets and made in the laboratory twenty-four copies of the original prototype. He also gave instructions that no modifications could be accepted unless essential and capable of being introduced without any delay in production.

The set had to be fitted into a corvette rather than into a destroyer because of the difficulties of transmitting power to the aerial and obtaining good reception from it. Suitable cables had not yet been devised and wave guides (tubes for conducting microwaves) had been insufficiently developed. The first set was fitted in the corvette *Orchis*, due for completion on 23 March 1941.

A cabin housing the set was built on the deck of the corvette with the aerial mounted on the roof. 'Corvettes,' says Landale wryly, 'are very wet and in rough weather the discomfort, inconvenience, and inflow of water whenever the office door was opened had to be experienced to be believed.' In order to overcome the rolling and pitching of these small ships a special aerial system was designed by Lovell.

During April 1941 comprehensive trials were carried out by *Orchis* in the Clyde. 'The difficulties were enormous', continues Landale, 'because propagation on these wave lengths was not understood. Aerial systems had to be screened from the weather, and the effect of the screening was unknown; the effect of the ship's vibration, its rolling and pitching, and the dynamic effect of gunfire, had to be overcome.'

Nevertheless, the scientists' belief in the potential value of the Type 271 set was fully justified. Submarines on the surface were detected up to 5,000 yards and a destroyer up to a distance of 12,000 yards. That July, twenty-five corvettes had been fitted with the new sets produced by the firm of Allen West; by the end of the year over 100 sets were completed and fifty ships equipped.

The first U-boat kill with the aid of the Type 271 set was on 14 April 1942 and the ship was HMS *Vetch*. The number of sightings and attacks by escort vessels was already rising.

The Admiralty scientists now began to fit other types of warship with centimetric radar. A Type 272 was designed specially for destroyers in order to withstand the violent pitch and roll of these vessels. Again lack of space was a problem. The aerial was mounted on the mast and connected to the radar cabin some forty feet away by a special polythene cable. It would have been possible to stabilise the aerial against pitch and roll, but this was a complicated business and had the Navy waited for these refinements there would have been no centimetric equipment for at least two years.

Capital ships did not present such a problem because there was more space. The set was either put in a cabin well up the mast or on a high deck, and a dish-shaped aerial was used.

The Admiralty scientists, having been shown the way by TRE, now seized the initiative, cutting red tape and keeping equipment simple. There is no better testimony than Landale's summing up : 'the short time that elapsed between the idea and the application of the first 10-centimetre sets was undoubtedly due to the determination to make them as simple as possible, and reasonably reliable. Later on, when more sophisticated applications were required . . . the time interval between the specification of staff requirements and the installation of equipment became ever and ever longer.'

The time factor therefore was all-important. From the very beginning of a project an appreciation had to be made as to how much time could be allotted to the various stages—research, development, production and finally to training of personnel. In the case of fire control radar, there were the additional factors of close and constant co-operation with the Gunnery Division of the Admiralty for policy, with the Director of Naval Ordnance for mountings and guns, with the Admiralty Research Laboratory for predictors and computers, and with HMS *Excellent* for trials and training of personnel.

In conclusion of this section on radar, an outline must be given of the requirement for high-powered valves which, by the end of the war, had stimulated the formation of one of the first inter-service organisations. The Signal School had for a number of years been experimenting with silica transmission valves. By the mid-thirties rearmament was in full swing and it rapidly became clear that the arrangements for radio valve production were extremely unsatisfactory. After long discussions between scientists, it was agreed that the Signal School was the farthest advanced of the three services in valve development and should therefore become generally responsible for valve development in all the services. The advent of radar after 1935 put considerable strain on this arrangement.

At last, in 1938, after much opposition from the Air Ministry, the organisation known as Co-ordination of Valve Development (CVD), was formed. It was directed by an inter-service committee, nominally presided over by the Director of Scientific Research at the Admiralty, but, in fact, by Brundrett. He had put forward the original idea and he controlled its operation throughout the war. This committee initiated the development of a valve suitable for generating short waves for radar sets.

Brundrett has described another significant innovation made possible by the CVD committee. 'At the beginning of the war I summoned senior representatives from all the major valve firms in the country and arranged to break down their inhibitions about exchanging information on the development of valves for the benefit of the country.[7] An outstanding feature,' continued Brundrett, 'was the development, in conjunction with GEC Laboratories at Wembley, of the pre-production technique which enabled new devices and service equipment to be used at an astonishingly early stage of development.' Some measure of its success may be seen in the fact that the organisation in a modified form exists today. A less effective arrangement was made for the development of radio components and the reason for the CVD success seems to have been that it had the power to place contracts on behalf of all the services, whereas the components organisation had no such powers.

(iii) High-Frequency Direction-Finders Ashore and at Sea

In the early months of their campaign the U-boats used to lie in wait for shipping on well-known routes. But asdic was so effective that U-boat losses began to mount, and they now operated further out to sea where targets were more difficult to find. Consequently the 'pack' method of operating U-boats was developed. Thus, when a target was spotted by a U-boat, the information was transmitted by wireless to the rest of the pack. The U-boats in the area would then converge on the convoy. At the same time Admiral Doenitz, the U-boat commander-in-chief, kept in touch by wireless with every U-boat at sea from his command post situated at first in France and later in Germany. In his operations room he was able to assess the U-boat commander's reports and make an operational plan which was then sent out over the air to the U-boats. In time, when the most experienced U-boat commanders were being lost at sea or taken prisoner of war, it became more necessary than ever to exercise control from headquarters.

But the considerable amount of wireless traffic which became necessary made it possible for high-frequency direction-finders, more familiarly known as 'Huff Duff', situated at first ashore and later in escort vessels, to intercept enemy radio transmissions from which the

U-boats' positions could be located. The sets could operate upwards from one hundred to three thousand miles.

So far in direction-finding, only aural methods had been used, but after the First World War experiments involving cathode-ray tubes (visual direction finding) began in connection with the investigation of the sources of thunderstorms and the conducting properties of the ionosphere. This work was carried out by the Radio Research Station at Farnborough, and then at Slough, and at the National Physical Laboratory, Teddington. On 5 May 1923, the first test of the cathode-ray direction-finder (CRDF) was made against a known source of atmospherics by R. A. (later Sir Robert) Watson-Watt at the Radio Research Station.

Scientists from the three services attended meetings of the Radio Research Board and were informed of the progress made in these experiments. Some use of direction-finding equipment was made by Army intelligence officers in the Middle East, and one of them, Capt. (later Col.) J. P. G. Worlledge (a friend of Watson-Watt), later helped to introduce radar to the Army. In January 1930 the Air Ministry began to investigate direction-finding for fighter control, but it took six years before visual direction-finding equipment was accepted by RAF Fighter Command. What had happened meanwhile in the Royal Navy?

Interception and source location of radio transmissions, principally by aural methods, was an important item on the research programme of the Signal School between the wars. By 1939, considerable basic knowledge of direction-finding existed. According to Horton who, after retiring as the superintending scientist of the Signal School, joined Fisons to become its vice-chairman, 'it was not the result of a single invention by an individual but was the final outcome of the tenacity of a few individuals working at a time when resources were hard to come by and the scientist a lowly personage in the hierarchy.'

'The technical problems on shore', Horton continues, 'and even more on shipboard, were formidable. This was where the real difficulty lay, not in appreciating the operational value of the thing when done. . . . Progress was really conditioned by the rate of solution of technical problems.'[8] The time factor also was present. Sea trials had to be fitted in with fleet exercises and the co-operation of the commander-in-chief was essential. Horton was instrumental in pioneering installations at Flowerdown, near Portsmouth, and at Gibraltar, and in a number of warships. He believed that Britain was ahead of any other country in direction-finding at the outbreak of war in 1939. This point of view is to some extent confirmed by German admissions after the war that their work on direction-finding before 1939 was inadequate and that they had experienced difficulties in locating the positions of their U-boats during the war.

In 1940 Professor P. M. S. Blackett suggested that high-frequency direction-finders sited on the coast should be used to locate U-boat positions. That summer the Germans had intercepted British submarines by listening into their radio signals, but they had not used direction-finders. On account of the growing U-boat threat, the Admiralty decided to send a merchant vessel into the Atlantic to investigate U-boat radio emissions. Although the Signal School had experimented with cathode-ray direction-finding before the war, no production design existed for interception purposes materially better than aural techniques. At the outbreak of war the Signal School was mainly concerned with aural methods of direction-finding. A new cathode-ray set, known as the FH 4 was now developed by the Signal School, in conjunction with Messrs. Plessey, for use in ships, but over two years elapsed before it became standard equipment. Closely associated with its development were C. Crampton and P. G. Redgement, both established Admiralty scientists.

Shore-based direction-finding stations were built to cover the Western Approaches. Cross bearings on U-boats were easily obtained and their approximate positions fixed. There was, of course, at extreme ranges, say of 1,000 miles, a good deal of error. Bearings were sent to the Admiralty where the course of the U-boats, as they moved into position to attack a convoy, was plotted by a special tracking organisation. This was headed by Capt. C. R. N. Winn, RNVR; he was a barrister in civilian life (now a High Court judge) and well qualified to give evidence rapidly and accurately. The convoy could then be instructed to change course or, alternatively, convoy escorts were alerted to the threat. HF/DF equipment was installed along the north-west African coast after Allied occupation, thus giving additional cover over the Atlantic. However, it was found that the HF/DF stations on the eastern side of the Atlantic provided better fixes than the western side because the American coastline was roughly parallel to the routes taken by the transatlantic convoys, at that time liable to U-boat attack.

When the FH 4 set was ready to go to sea much more accurate fixes could be made. But it was only in July 1941 that the first British escort vessel (*Culver*) was equipped with HF/DF. At first, results were disappointing and not until March 1942 was the first sighting of a U-boat made from HF/DF indications during the passage of the troop convoy WS 17 bound for Madagascar. The U-boat was sunk. In time, however, with the new CRDF equipment HF/DF became as important as radar and because of this it was able to reclaim the best site—at the top of the tallest mast—in anti-submarine vessels. Its great value was that it showed the scale of attack and the bearing of the U-boats. The escort vessels could then dispose themselves to the best advantage before the U-boats began to attack.

In the summer of 1942 three British shipborne sets were turned over to the US Naval Research Laboratory, and on 1 October of that year sets were installed aboard American vessels. S. E. Morison, the American naval historian, has written that in an Atlantic convoy the eyes were provided by radar, the ears by asdic, while HF/DF provided the cats' whiskers for warning at longer range.[9]

(iv) Radio Sonobuoys

A U-boat when submerged could not be detected by the ASV equipment, and there were many occasions when a submarine was known or suspected to be in a certain area but could not be located. Detection from the air of the magnetic field of a submarine was discussed by the Tizard Committee before the war. At RAE, Blackett and E. J. Williams had taken part during the winter of 1939/40 in experiments in the detection of magnetic fields of submarines. Such operations were hazardous, for the aircraft had to fly low over the sea (Blackett and Williams had carried out tests in an aircraft 200 feet above the aircraft sheds at Farnborough). Although the idea was of limited tactical value, it was taken by Tizard in the 'Black Box' to the United States where it was received with enthusiasm and developed as the Magnetic Air Detector. It was used operationally in American coastal waters and in the Straits of Gibraltar with fair results.

The alternative was to detect the submarine by its engines when submerged. An asdic equipment fitted in a buoy had to be dropped from an aircraft. The buoy would be fitted with a directional microphone emitting signals for reception by the searching aircraft. This idea seems to have emanated from Headquarters, RAF Coastal

Command, which made a request for an underwater sound receiver in May 1941. But the manufacture of a complicated and necessarily expendable equipment was at that time outside the resources of this country.

Meanwhile, however, the Americans were independently developing an expendable radio sonobuoy which would be dropped by a search aircraft when it knew that a submerged U-boat was in the area. The underwater sound group at Columbia University's laboratory at New London was in charge of the project.[10]

Very soon the first transmitter model was ready. It was, in fact, an entire frequency modulation broadcasting system on a round chassis less than five inches in diameter and under ten inches long. Part of it had been devised by F. C. Williams at TRE. A special receiver based on the shipborne equipment, but drastically reduced in size and weight, was designed to be put in an aircraft. A hydrophone was designed to catch the noise of the submarine.

The whole equipment was fitted to a small parachute and dropped from a height of 500 feet into the sea. Tests showed that the equipment suffered no ill effects after its descent. Five months after the start of development the sonobuoy was being dropped by aircraft on operations, and production was in full swing by May 1943. The sonobuoys were used to check suspicious signs such as oil slicks, disappearing radar blips, or magnetic air detection indications.

RAF Coastal Command received its first sonobuoys that August, but there were many teething troubles still to be overcome. This was a common experience with new and complicated devices. Further trials were needed and adequate supplies did not reach Britain until May 1944. They arrived at an opportune moment. In December 1943 Doenitz wrote : 'For some months past the enemy has rendered the U-boat war ineffective. He has achieved this objective, not through superior tactics or strategy, but through his superiority in the field of science; this finds its expression in the modern battle weapon— detection. By this means he has torn our sole offensive weapon in the war against the Anglo-Saxons from our hands. It is essential that we make good our scientific disparity and thereby restore to the U-boat its fighting qualities.' The schnorkel submarine was intended to redress the balance.

From July to December 1944, RAF Coastal Command dropped sonobuoys on 118 occasions. They were used in an offensive role in conjunction with an acoustic mine, and the sonobuoy was to provide evidence of the mine's explosion on the target. In the early stages, however, the sonobuoy was too receptive to extraneous noises and the scientists in Coastal Command had to reduce the so-called 'hallucinations' of the equipment. In time, however, this acoustic mine became the principal weapon against the schnorkel. Yet by March 1945 only two out of thirteen attacks against schnorkels, using the acoustic mine, had been successful. At the same time the sonobuoy, while ineffective against U-boats on passage, proved its worth in the protection of convoys because the U-boats travelled fast in order to attack and therefore made more noise. By the end of the war the sonobuoy, used in conjunction with the acoustic mine, was the most promising device by which aircraft could regain ascendancy over the U-boat.

Nevertheless, the sonobuoy was expensive to produce and it could be used only once. If the schnorkel had come into the war earlier and there had been no sonobuoy, a critical situation might well have arisen.

DESTRUCTION

(i) Ahead-throwing Weapons

In October 1916, Admiral Jellicoe, then Comander-in-Chief of the Grand Fleet, wrote in a despatch that the menace of attack by enemy submarine was by far the most pressing question at that time.[11] Again, in the Second World War the German U-boat threatened the success of the Allied cause. But the weapons available to fight the U-boat in the early forties were also the same as those evolved twenty-four years before.*

There were two weapons. First, the depth charge (known as the 'ash can') filled with 300 pounds of explosive and set off by a hydro-statically-operated pistol. This could be set to explode at any of six depths between 50 and 500 feet. Its rate of descent was about ten feet per second. It was dropped or thrown in patterns of five or ten over the stern of a destroyer. Secondly, there was the mine which, in the First World War, sank almost as many U-boats as the depth charge. The reason for this was that German U-boat routes could be fairly easily predicted and minefields laid accordingly. But, as we

---

* In the latter stages of the war rockets fired from aircraft were effectively used against U-boats and will be discussed in Chapter 13.

have noted, the coastline from which German U-boats could operate was very much more extensive in the Second World War.

The system of destroying a submarine, or compelling it to surface, by means of depth charges was far from efficient. When the submarine was detected in the asdic beam, an estimate had to be made in order to bring the ship over the spot where the U-boat was likely to be and then depth charges could be dropped on it from the stern. The disadvantage of the asdic was that as the destroyer closed into the attack and passed over the U-boat no echoes were obtained. There was, therefore, a time lag of about a minute in which the U-boat could take evasive action and escape. The only way in which to cut down the interval was to have an ahead-throwing weapon which could fire projectiles while the asdic was still in contact with the U-boat. Some method of throwing bombs or depth charges *forward* to cover the probable track of a submarine which had been detected was desirable. Such an idea had been put forward in 1916, but nothing had been done to develop an ahead-throwing weapon.

The technique of depth-charge throwing and the composition of depth charges, in contrast to the development of asdic, was sadly neglected in the inter-war years. A multiple small-charge experimental thrower, or mortar, was designed at *Osprey*, but by the outbreak of war little had been achieved.

These experiments were continued under Dr. B. S. Smith. Little progress was made, the difficulty being that as non-contact charges were being used, they had to be exceedingly powerful to have any effect. A large mortar was required, but a weapon of this size would recoil violently into the deck of the escort vessel and cause serious damage. In the spring of 1940 Bullard, then in the Mine Design Department, informed Goodeve of the slow progress of the experiments. Goodeve had, after his useful work on minesweeping, left *Vernon* to form the special section dealing with anti-aircraft devices and special weapons for the protection of ships at sea, later known as the Department of Miscellaneous Weapons Development (DMWD), and already discussed on page 25. The urgent requirements for the air defence of ships at sea prevented any consideration of the mine projector until the end of November 1940.

Goodeve then sent one of his young scientists in uniform, F. D. Richardson, to Whitchurch, Buckinghamshire, where the War Office experimental group, MD1, under Major (later Major-General) M. R. Jefferis, had a testing ground. Richardson, a physical chemist, had worked with Goodeve on Double-L sweep and wiping problems, and before the war he had won a Commonwealth scholarship to Princeton. He was mature and balanced for his age and, given a problem, refused to admit defeat until he had found an answer. During that summer various novel weapons had been developed by MD1 on account of the current lack of orthodox weapons and because of the need for anti-tank weapons should this country be invaded. One of these was the spigot mortar (later known as the 'Piat') invented by Col. L. V. S. Blacker, a retired officer with an ingenious and inventive turn of mind. The spigot completely reversed the method of firing a shell through a gun barrel. Instead of the projectile being despatched by a firing-pin, it was fired by an electrically-actuated peg—the spigot—fitted in the base of the projectile or bomb. Several proposals for a spigot mortar had been submitted to the Ordnance Board but they had all been rejected.

It occurred to Richardson that the spigot mortar might be adapted to fire contact charges against U-boats, and on 12 December, at Goodeve's request, a meeting to discuss the possibility was held by Wright at the Admiralty. An important point in its favour was the lightness of the mortar. Jefferis was now asked to make a preliminary design while a member of Goodeve's department, Lieut. Strickland Constable, was to study the problem of the bomb's passage through the water.

Meanwhile, work continued independently on the multi-barrelled mortar begun at *Osprey* which, after becoming the Anti-Submarine Experimental Establishment, had moved from Portland to Fairlie on the Clyde. The Fairlie mortar, as it was known, was designed on entirely different principles from the spigot mortar adapted by Goodeve. It was a much heavier projector and therefore required either a specially strengthened deck or, alternatively, a complicated recoil mechanism. The Fairlie mortar was to be a 'chromium-plated job', elaborate and highly finished. The spigot mortar, on the other hand, was improvised; it was designed to go into action as quickly as possible. A strong rivalry developed between the Fairlie team and Goodeve's group, which unfortunately generated bad feeling.

Goodeve's team and MD1 now sought to solve two major problems. First, how was the mortar to be fired accurately from a pitching deck? On the official side, the Chief Inspector of Gun Mountings devised a complicated system incorporating an independent training and roll correction. But Jefferis, thinking all the time of speed and simplicity, discovered a way of mounting the projector with sprung beams in which most of the thrust was carried deep into the destroyer instead of merely being taken by the deck. After discussion, his idea was accepted.

Secondly, there was the problem of the fuse. The Chief Superintendent of Armament Design at the Admiralty produced a highly complicated fuse of 127 parts. But for production purposes in the middle of a war this was too complicated. Goodeve decided to pose the problem to the rocket establishment at Aberporth, the Mine Design Department and the Anti-Submarine Experimental Establishment.

Three possible alternatives emerged out of a number of suggestions. In one, the projectile armed itself by hydrostatic pressure through holes in the nose. As it plunged into the sea the shock of impact would set the mechanism in motion. In another, the fuse would be actuated by metal feelers protruding from the projectile like the antennae of an insect. Thirdly, (this was the idea of P. H. Lindley of Aberporth) the fuse would be set off by a propeller which began to turn as soon as the projectile entered the water.

Prototypes of the three fuses were ready within a few days and subjected to tests. A retired naval officer, Cdr. H. D. Lucas, on the staff of the Chief Superintendent, Armament Design, saved weeks of delay by producing working models and there was consequently no need to secure priority in the Ordnance Board's drawing office. Tests took place at the Surrey docks in the Port of London, where the bombs were fired at steel plates covered by a wooden lattice work resembling the hull and deck of a U-boat. The fuse designed by Lindley, and adapted by Lucas, proved to be the most effective of the three.

Now certain ballistical problems had to be solved. The projectile had to dive into the water, sink rapidly and explode on impact with the submarine. In the first design for the bomb (also intended to explode on contact), the fuse was placed in the tail of the bomb, but this proved to be unsatisfactory. The nose was heavily weighted with iron, and Goodeve proposed putting the fuse into the nose. This was only possible with Jefferis's bomb which was designed to be stable while in the air *and* in the water.

It was, of course, essential that the bomb should penetrate a U-boat's deck and blow a hole in the main casing. By chance, Goodeve came across an Italian illustrated magazine which gave him a clue to the depth from the surface of the deck to the hull. A photograph of a workman waist deep on the deck of a submarine revealed that he was in fact standing on the hull. It was now possible to calculate the optimum explosive charge.

The electrical features of the firing mechanism were designed by Sub-Lieut. Francis after consulting the Admiralty Chief Inspector, Gun Mountings, Messrs. Foster Wheeler and Major Jefferis. A switch for the battery of twenty-four spigots, which fired ripples at two-second intervals, was designed by DMWD. A prototype was made at *Vernon*.

By February 1941 the protoype spigot mortar was ready. Its construction was a combined effort of MD1 and DMWD. The musical instrument manufacturers, Messrs. Boosey & Hawkes, using a machine intended for the production of trumpets, also shared the honours. The first trials of 'Hedgehog', as it was called (the bank of spigots resembled the prickles on a hedgehog's back), were held at Whitchurch. They happened to coincide with a demonstration of anti-tank weapons held before the Prime Minister and Lord Cherwell. This was an occasion when a fortuitous meeting accelerated the development of a device. For the naval officer in charge of DMWD exercised his charm on Mary Churchill, who happened to be with her father, in the hope that he would stay to watch the Hedgehog perform.The trick worked and although impatient to return to lunch the Prime Minister was restrained to stay.

A batch of twenty-four bombs was fired in ripples. They described a graceful evolution in the air and fell in a circle about 130 feet in diameter. Churchill's imagination was fired by this performance and when he returned home he instructed the First Sea Lord that Hedgehog should become operational as soon as possible. Further firing trials with live bombs took place at the DMWD testing ground near Weston-super-Mare, where there was a stretch of muddy foreshore into which the bombs could be fired. They were followed by successful trials aboard the destroyer *Westcott* in Liverpool Bay.

By the end of 1941 Hedgehog, with strong backing from Churchill and Lord Cherwell, was in production less than nine months off the drawing board. The Admiralty decided to adopt it at once. Hedgehogs were mounted on specially adapted anti-submarine escort vessels because the latter's armament had to be removed, and in a destroyer or trawler this was a risk which could not be accepted.

In spite of the fact that by the beginning of 1943—still in the critical period of the U-boat campaign—116 ships had been equipped with Hedgehog, only one U-boat was claimed destroyed and three possibly sunk.[12] There were four reasons for this. Firstly, a number of teething troubles required solution; secondly, there is in all novel devices a time lag between the production of a new weapon and its effective use; thirdly, sailors were prejudiced against the weapon. The ordinary depth charge always made a spectacular explosion regardless of whether it had hit its target or not, whereas the Hedgehog bombs only exploded on impact. Finally, Hedgehog was so shrouded in secrecy that little information about its capabilities was passed on to ships' crews. From now onwards, therefore, special training courses in the use of Hedgehog were organised, and with increased knowledge came greater confidence. In fact, the use of Hedgehog almost halved the time between location of the U-boat by asdic and the arrival of the bombs in the water, compared with the old method of dropping depth charges astern. By the end of the war the Navy claimed that Hedgehogs had sunk fifty U-boats.

'Squid', as the Fairlie six-barrelled mortar was called, came into service at the end of the war and was not used operationally. The advantage of Squid over Hedgehog was that it fired off a series of charges set at different depths, whereas Hedgehog had to score a direct hit.

(ii) Airborne Depth-charge Setting

Before discussing this subject a short digression on the operational research section in RAF Coastal Command is necessary.

The name of Professor Patrick Blackett has already occurred several times in these pages. It will recur frequently throughout this book, for he had a finger in many wartime scientific pies. Blackett, like Tizard, Hill and Bertram Hopkinson, was a scientist who had been a serving officer in the First World War; he had been present at the Battle of Jutland. Afterwards he went to the Cavendish Laboratory, Cambridge, to study physics under Rutherford, and he had already become a Nobel Prize winner before the Second World War. His introduction to defence science came when he was invited to serve on the Tizard Committee.

So far, in the RAF, only Fighter Command had an operational research section. In the early months of 1941 it was becoming clear that the defeat of the U-boat was vital if Britain was to survive. Rowe, aware of this, saw Air Chief Marshal Sir Wilfred Freeman,

Vice-Chief of Air Staff, and told him that there was nothing he could do in the war as useful as ensuring that Blackett went to Coastal Command. At once Blackett was appointed as the first scientific adviser to the Commander-in-Chief, Coastal Command, and he formed an operational research section to work principally on submarine warfare problems at the Command's headquarters at Northwood, Middlesex. C. P. Snow, a colleague of Blackett, has said of him that he had a 'gift which made him invaluable in the war, and which this country has not recognised sufficiently, of being able to think of practical problems with a kind of depth of insight known to very few. This saved us many lives and many ships in the last war.'[13]

The new operational research section consisted of a select number of physicists, biologists, mathematicians and engineers. It was kept deliberately small. There were never more than twenty-five members at any one time. Five of them were, or later became, Fellows of the Royal Society. Apart from Blackett, there were E. J. Williams, C. H. Waddington, J. C. Kendrew (the first scientist sent to the Command to find out how ASV was working, and later Nobel Prize winner for studies in molecular biology) and J. H. C. Whitehead.

The section never became entangled in routine statistical work and it lived cheek by jowl with the operational staff. A tribute to its work was paid after the war by one of the commanders-in-chief of Coastal Command, Air Chief Marshal Sir John Slessor : 'A few years ago it would never have occurred to me—or I think to any officer of any fighting service—that what the RAF soon came to call a "Boffin", a gentleman in grey flannel bags, whose occupation in life had previously been something markedly unmilitary such as biology or physiology, would be able to teach us a great deal about our business. Yet so it was.'

The important point about the operational research scientists was that they were able to study problems with a detachment impossible to the staff of the headquarters to which they were attached. This was a new factor in warfare. Thus Blackett soon discovered that depth charges dropped by aircraft had so far proved relatively ineffective when judged by the number of U-boats reported sunk. Blackett's team was eventually able to increase the lethality of the ordinary depth charge to a spectacular degree, and this was achieved merely by simple analysis and deduction.

Blackett set E. J. Williams with whom, as we have seen, he had worked at Farnborough, to solve the problem. Williams was the son of a stonemason in Cardiganshire. He won a £55 scholarship at Swansea Technical College, and his talent for theoretical physics was later stimulated by a year spent at Copenhagen with Niels Bohr. In 1940 he left the University of Swansea where he had been teaching physics and joined the Instruments Department of RAE, where his brother was already employed. Williams had a powerful analytical mind and an individual personality. At Farnborough he would discuss in Welsh over the telephone the theory of bomb sights to the alarm of the operator at hearing a foreign tongue in a secret establishment. Williams died tragically of cancer, aged forty-two, in September 1945. His last task was to visit the Mediterranean in January 1944 to advise on sea warfare problems. Five out of twenty-one years of active work were devoted by Williams to the study of warfare.[14]

At Farnborough, Williams, with Blackett, had worked on a magnetically-actuated depth charge which would explode when passing the U-boat under water. He now called for the aircrews' reports of their attacks on U-boats. The attack on a U-boat from the air was essentially a sudden affair. In a few minutes many hours of operational flying and even more hours of maintenance work might reap a reward or be wasted. The depth charges were normally dropped in sticks, each stick consisting of a number of depth charges which fell in a more or less straight line along the direction of flight of the aircraft. After hitting the water, the depth charges travelled forward a certain distance, sinking as they did so. The rule was that the charges were set to explode at 100 to 150 feet.

In a classic report of operational research literature, Williams attempted to estimate the depth of a U-boat at the time of attack. On an average he calculated that the U-boat would sight the aircraft two minutes before the actual attack. In that time the U-boat could submerge to a depth of 100 feet. Whenever the crew of the aircraft were uncertain where to drop their depth charges there was a big chance that the U-boat would escape. Yet when the hunting aircraft surprised the U-boat on the surface the 100-feet setting of the fuse would cause it no harm. This analysis was not entirely new. A paper suggesting that long-submerged submarines would suffer little from depth charges was produced in the Air Ministry in 1939 but no account seems to have been taken of it. Williams, then, appreciated that the existing rule for depth-charge settings was inadequate both for submerged and for surfaced U-boats. Therefore, the solution appeared to be to reduce the setting to twenty-five feet. Applying the law of probability, he anticipated that the average number of U-boats sunk for a given number of attacks would increase by two and a half.

Williams' argument convinced the air staff at Headquarters, Coastal Command, and in June 1942 the shallow depth-charge setting was introduced. In a short time excellent results were being achieved. The lethality per attack on a visible U-boat rose from two or three per cent in 1941 to about forty per cent in 1944. The Germans believed the RAF were using a new and more powerful type of explosive. Later, a more lethal, torpex-filled depth charge was, in fact, used in conjunction with a useful low-level bomb sight. But the increase in effectiveness was achieved much more easily. As Blackett has written : 'There can be few cases where such a great operational gain had been obtained by such a small and simple change of tactics.' Moreover, a costly proximity fuse, which would have been no more effective than the 25-foot fuse setting, was not required.

Operational research, therefore, was valuable because it stressed that existing weapons should be understood before asking for new ones. Professor J. D. Bernal has summed up the achievement of operational research thus : 'We are apt to be impressed by the spectacular and the complicated : the particular secret weapon on the giant plane; whereas in the actual course of the war it was the new way of doing things that turned out to be the most important. The submarine . . . was beaten not so much by any particular weapon used against it, as by a study of the actual experience of dealing with submarines in different ways, and with the rational continuation of these ways in the tactics of submarine warfare. When the conditions seemed to call for a particular weapon the required performance dictated the design.'[15]

(iii) Attack on U-boat Transit Areas

The Bay of Biscay became, as already seen, one of the important, but at the time little publicised, battle areas of the war. It was bounded on the north roughly by the latitude of 48°N and on the south by the Spanish coast. Admiralty intelligence was well informed on U-boat traffic and supplemented its information with HF/DF fixes (page 68). Moreover, cycles of activity were discernible.

German habits were traditionally methodical and when they changed they did so quite suddenly.

The Battle of the Bay was of particular concern to the operational research scientists as well as to the air staff, for two reasons. Firstly, it brought out the fundamental strategic problem of the anti-U-boat war—to provide enough long-range aircraft without imposing too much strain on offensive operations (bombing of Germany, air support to the ground forces) through which air power might shorten the war. At the same time, on several occasions in 1940 and 1941, Hitler declared that he was relying on the U-boats to win the war. The air effort against the U-boats could not, therefore, be cut too fine. Feelings ran high over the allocation of long-range aircraft. Ultimately it was decided that the Bay offensive should be strengthened, but *not* at the expense of aircraft providing cover for convoys or for the strategic bombing offensive against Germany. A small number of long-range aircraft was introduced in the autumn of 1942.

Secondly, Coastal Command Operational Research Section played a notable part in the development of search radar and countermeasures against German radar.

Williams analysed the Bay offensive in two remarkable reports written in the spring and autumn of 1942.[16] They were the first attempts to establish theoretical equations for the density of U-boats in a transit area, ie, the Bay of Biscay. Williams converted the platitude that the number of U-boat sightings must increase with the flying done and with the number of U-boats available for detection into a theory in which the individual factors could be quantitatively measured and estimated. The total number of sightings or radar detections of U-boats was equal to the area swept by the aircraft times the number of surfaced U-boats in the area divided by the total area of operations. This was further elaborated into a number of formulae from which it was possible to discover the efficiency of search methods and the habits of the enemy and from this the value of the radar equipment could be ascertained. All this was vital information in the increasing tug-of-war between detection and evasion.

In his papers Williams showed that as early as 1941, before the arrival of sophisticated radar, every U-boat was attacked by aircraft about four times a year. If the attacks could be made ten per cent more efficient the air offensive would bring the U-boat campaign to an end. He also estimated the tonnage of merchant shipping which was saved by attacking U-boats in the Bay. If the offensive could only be maintained, then, with a reasonable number of 'kills', the U-boat threat would be reduced to nil. In his second paper Williams demonstrated what sort of force was required to attack each U-boat crossing the Bay. He stressed the value of long-range aircraft equipped with ASV. The density method, Williams believed, could be used to enable a balanced force of aircraft to attack once on an average every U-boat crossing the Bay and to discover the most economical number able to achieve this object.

The significant feature of this battle was that all the factors could be subjected to quantitative analysis. It was an ideal 'case' for operational research. Land operations, as we shall see, with the exception of artillery bombardments, were in comparison messy affairs and much less susceptible to analysis. At Coastal and at Fighter Command headquarters scientists could walk into operations rooms. They were able to exploit to the full their independent, civilian status, encouraged by imaginative commanders such as Joubert and Slessor.

A brief summary will suffice to show the success of the anti-U-boat campaign. In 1941 total sinkings amounted to 2,171,754 tons for a loss of thirty-five U-boats or 62,000 tons per U-boat lost. As the average number of U-boats at sea was twenty-four this meant that each U-boat sank 7,540 tons per month. Up to the end of 1942 about 45,000 tons were being lost for each U-boat sunk. Every U-boat sank, on an average, 4,000 tons per month. But from 15 April 1943, to the end of that month, only 5,000 tons were sunk per U-boat destroyed and only 2,500 tons sunk per U-boat per month—a complete failure for the U-boats. From this time onwards the sinkings by U-boats steadily diminished (though picking up for a short time that autumn due to the introduction of the acoustic torpedo). In addition to air and naval forces directed by skilled operational staffs, much of the credit must go to the scientists engaged in the battle. Moreover, Doenitz's pronouncement 'that the U-boat has no more to fear from aircraft than a mole from a crow' was proved to be as untrue as Goering's equally celebrated remark that no bomber would penetrate into the Reich.

(iv) Planned Flying and Planned Maintenance

Modern aircraft, unlike a car, require constant maintenance, thorough frequent inspections and repairs. Coastal Command, more than the other commands, because of its ceaseless, gruelling patrols, depended on good maintenance.

Early in June 1942 Lord Cherwell learned that Coastal Command aircraft were flying on the average only one sortie per week. He reported this disconcerting fact to the Prime Minister, and within a few days Joubert was instructing the Operational Research Section to make an investigation. E. J. Williams, who had succeeded Blackett as Sir Philip's scientific adviser, appointed a member of the Operational Research Section for the task. He was Dr. Cecil Gordon, before the war a geneticist at Aberdeen University, and known familiarly as 'Joad' to aircrews. Gordon was of South African origin; a man with strong views who, on occasion, clashed with those in authority.

Gordon devised a system of planned maintenance similar to one already working in RAF Flying Training Command. Within a few days the Chief of Air Staff informed the Prime Minister that the number of sorties could be increased without having to call on crews from other commands, in particular Bomber Command. A series of investigations on planned flying and maintenance were now organised. A system was evolved whereby the servicing of aircraft was arranged in accordance with the operational flying programme. It is considered to be one of the most important wartime innovations in the RAF.

Planned maintenance grew out of experience in Flying Training Command before the war. In 1936, when the command formed, training of aircrew was a vital element in the expanding RAF. A tight schedule was demanded, and aircraft had to be constantly available. The training programme called the tune, and the maintenance organisation had to play it.

From 1940-42 planned maintenance based on a rhythmic deployment of aircraft was introduced throughout Flying Training Command by Air Commodore (later Air Vice-Marshal) E. J. Cuckney, the Senior Technical Staff Officer. He was assisted by his Engineer Staff Officer, Wing Cdr. (later Air Cdre.) J. A. S. Outhwaite. When the new system had been established throughout the command, and had proved its worth, Cuckney was instructed by the Air Ministry to introduce the system into the operational training units of Bomber Command. This he did in spite of much opposition. The change-over was drastic. The establishment of both aircraft and technical personnel had to be recast in order to conform with the proposed use of aircraft in terms of numbers in use and in the number of flying hours. But few aircraft stood idle on the ground.[17]

The pioneer work of Cuckney and Outhwaite was adapted by Gordon for the special purposes of certain squadrons of Coastal Command. Basically the system was the same, but Gordon, assisted by J. J. Vincent, a statistician, and T. E. Easterfield, a mathematician, approached the problem as if it had been a biological system. The flying-maintenance cycle of No 502 (Whitley) Squadron based at St. Eval was chosen for study.

First, what happened to an aircraft when it was on the ground? Gordon and his team discovered that the shortage of a particular item of equipment or the lack of aircrews was not the reason for an aircraft being unable to patrol more frequently. The maintenance organisation aimed at keeping the maximum number of aircraft serviceable and ready for operations. The accepted figure was to keep seventy-five per cent of the force serviceable. But in order to achieve this, Gordon found that if all aircraft were flown whenever serviceable about one-third of the force should be airborne at any particular time while two-thirds should be on the ground being maintained. In fact, he found that almost one-third of the total number of aircraft was grounded because of maintenance. A *reductio ad absurdum* solution to ensure the serviceability of all aircraft would be never to fly.

Gordon then had to ask the following questions. Could aircrews fly more often without a decline in efficiency or premature operational fatigue? It was found that their efficiency was unimpaired, although obviously they could not fly all the time. Second, was it the policy of the command to conserve a large striking force? From the point of view of Coastal Command it was better to have a high rate of regular flying than to keep a striking force at readiness for action against a high density of U-boat traffic. Finally, if flying was more frequent, could the maintenance organisation cope? The answer lay in increasing the efficiency of maintenance.

Mathematical analysis made it possible to see what proportions of aircraft, maintenance men and aircrew were required for the different types of activity of the Command, i.e., U-boat patrols, convoy escort and anti-shipping strikes. Whereas the enquiry began with the low use of aircraft, it became clear that the real constraint was manpower.

Operational research demonstrated that a fetish was being made of a high rate of serviceability when the aim should have been the proportion of serviceable aircraft flown whenever operations were possible and the flying hours per maintenance man. It was soon discovered that the greater the intensity of flying and, therefore, the greater the output of squadrons, the lower would be the serviceability percentage. This fact exposed the fallacy of judging the efficiency of a squadron by the criterion of aircraft serviceability.

The experiment with No 502 Squadron was very successful. In the three to four months during which planned maintenance was introduced, the squadron exceeded its own maximum flying effort per aircraft by sixty-one per cent, and also exceeded the best average of other squadrons in the command over a single period by seventy-nine per cent. Arising out of this experiment, a system of planned flying and maintenance was devised for the whole of Coastal Command. Now more patrols could be flown and therefore more U-boats sunk.

Eventually, planned flying and maintenance was adopted throughout the RAF and was largely responsible for the total of 99,000 aircrew trained during the war years. It was said of Gordon, who died in 1960, that : 'His original work (on planned flying and maintenance) led to a wide range of studies, the impact of which is still being felt.'[18]

F

PART THREE

THE WAR IN THE AIR

Chapter 5

Development of the Cavity Magnetron

A number of the radar devices used in the air war depended on very short wavelengths. A revolution in radar had to be achieved. This great leap forward in radar was brought about outside a service laboratory; it was an outstanding example of a requirement stated by a service and of the collaboration of groups of scientists in universities and industry to achieve that purpose. Such was the development of the cavity magnetron valve.

The first employment of microwaves in radar made the metre wavelengths employed hitherto suddenly seem old fashioned. We have already seen how decisive was its application to the airborne and surface sets used to hunt U-boats. In the present Part the way in which it improved airborne interception radar and led to the navigational and bombing aid—H₂S—will be described. In Part Four we shall see how radar-controlled anti-aircraft gunfire was made more accurate by microwaves.

Chapter 6 will show that the floodlight system in the Home Chain had a great advantage in that it could be developed quickly because the constituent parts from which it was composed were not new; they were organised in such a way as to do something new. But the floodlighting technique had severe limitations : it was unable properly to measure angles of bearing. In an airborne radar set, the lower edge of the beam swept the ground immediately below the aircraft from which it was being radiated and this restricted its range except when the target was at a distance less than the height of the airborne radar above the ground; finally, the wide range of angles over which signals could be received made these wavelengths extremely susceptible to jamming.

All these disadvantages could be overcome by a radar set operating on a narrow beam which could sweep the sky with a fan of radiation, or point like a long pencil of light through the dark. This technique was foreseen by Watson-Watt as early as 1936 but the general opinion was that it was impossible to generate wavelengths below about 50 centimetres. At the same time the need for long-distance early warning was so great that scientists could not be spared to think about this problem.

In Chapter 4 the initiative taken by the Admiralty scientists to develop high-powered valves was described. They were inspired by the prediction of Wright that the side that developed power on the shortest wavelength would win the coming war. In 1938, a development contract for valves was placed with the General Electric Company of Wembley. The next stage was to get a team of scientists at a university to undertake research on short-wave valves. The Cavendish Laboratory at Cambridge was earmarked, but all available physicists here were already working on the Home Chain and Brundrett, who was not only in charge of the Admiralty scientific and chemical pools but also concerned with all inter-service effort, hurriedly made arrangements to fix up a contract with Birmingham University where Professor M. L. E. (later Sir Marcus) Oliphant was head of the Physics Laboratory which contained an impressive group of young scientists.

Although Oliphant and his group had been initiated into radar at Bawdsey and Ventnor with other scientists from Cambridge that summer, and had learnt of the requirement for centimetre wavelengths, he had not yet been called up. He was now to become responsible for developing one of the most valuable scientific devices in the war—an effective valve for centimetre radar. He had the backing of Tizard who, at an early stage, appreciated its importance. In addition, Brundrett made a similar arrangement with Lindemann at the Clarendon Laboratory, Oxford, and C. T. Keeley, a physicist, established a powerful party there which worked on crystal detectors. A third team from the Admiralty Signal School Valve Group under R. W. (later Sir Robert) Sutton went to work at Bristol University. Many of the scientists engaged in the work on valves were nuclear physicists who were previously engaged in fundamental research. But they were well equipped to do an entirely new kind of job because they understood the practical problems of high-frequency radio in the design of such apparatus as cyclotrons in which enormous electrical currents flow over large surfaces of copper.

At Birmingham, in the early autumn of 1939, the intention was to produce a high-power microwave oscillator.[1] One of Oliphant's team was particularly suited for this task. He was Dr. J. T. (later Sir John) Randall (now Professor of Physics at King's College, London) who had trained at Manchester under Sir William Bragg and had learnt much about valves while spending some years in the Wembley laboratory of GEC. He was then working on a Royal Society research fellowship and was given special permission to devote part of his time to research for the Admiralty. But the territory in which he was to travel was largely unknown. However, a paper had just been received describing an instrument devised by two brothers, R. H. and S. P. Varian, of Stanford University, California. This was the klystron.* In it a beam of electrons was driven along a path involving holes, or resonators, in two tiny metallic boxes electrically coupled together.

Oliphant and his immediate colleagues, Moon, Sayers and others, set to work to develop the klystron. But Randall and a colleague, Henry Boot (now at the Services Electronics Laboratory, Baldock), who were not in this project, appreciated that the klystron of those days was unable to generate a sufficiently powerful electron beam and was also difficult to mass produce. They then had the idea of applying the resonator principle to the magnetron. This instrument had been invented in the United States in 1921. They at once began to draw up a design for an improved magnetron, or cavity magnetron, which was, in effect, a valve no bigger than a child's fist and which would, they hoped, provide a reliable output of hundreds of kilowatts in short pulses. The design was ready in November 1939 and was, Randall believed, better suited for the purpose of radar than the klystron.

Randall's first magnetron was contrived in the traditional methods of sealing wax and string. Air was evacuated from it by a continuously-operated pump and the ends were sealed off by embedding halfpennies in a pool of sealing wax. A bulky electro-magnet was used to provide the magnetic field, and a loop of wire fitted in one of the cavities in the hope of extracting high-frequency power by this means. After various delays, due mainly to the difficulties in obtaining components in the early days of the war, the magnetron was first tested on 21 February 1940. It worked immediately. Two ordinary car lamps which were harnessed to the apparatus were quickly burnt out. Larger lamps were connected, with the same result each time. Only when low-pressure neon lamps were used was it possible to

* Derived from the Greek for *incoming waves on a beach.*

ascertain that a wavelength of just over nine centimetres was being produced at a power of 400 watts—roughly one hundred times as much as the power output of the klystron.

There was yet another important stage of development. With the complicated oscillatory possibilities offered by its construction, the magnetron could suddenly jump from the main mode of oscillation to another in random manner. Dr. J. Sayers, now Professor of Electron Physics at Birmingham University and currently concerned with the British space research programme, devised a system for curing this by strapping alternate segments together with short pieces of wire so that they oscillated in phase. The strapped magnetron proved to be the most valuable for service application.

Meanwhile, industrial development had gone ahead rapidly under Megaw at the research laboratories of GEC at Wembley. Here, a special technique for sealing the end plates to the valve was originated. Important contributions were also made by the British Thomson Houston company, whose works at Rugby were conveniently close to Birmingham. This smooth co-operative effort of industry and university groups, unknown in peacetime, was made possible by the CVD Committee under the general direction of the Admiralty. In fact, the Director of the GEC Research Laboratory, C. C. Patterson, became chairman of one of the sub-committees. By that summer the cavity magnetron was shown to be a practicable instrument of war.

We already know of its application at sea and in the air in the U-boat war. The events leading to its fitting, first in a night fighter and then in a bomber, will be described later. Power outputs were still further increased and by 1941 wavelengths of three centimetres were being produced though, as described already, they did not become available to the RAF until late in the war.

Two facts should finally be noted. The first is that it was not until some time after the war that there was a detailed understanding of how the magnetron worked. This alone is a tribute to the intuitive genius of the scientists concerned. The second is that the German scientists believed that centimetre radar was impracticable and they abandoned research in this field several months before an H_2S set with a magnetron was discovered in a crashed aircraft near Rotterdam in February 1943. Thus, they never caught up with the Allies in the development of this war-winning device.

Chapter 6

Radar and Radio in Defence

(i) Home Chain

It has been said that : 'On a winter's afternoon (26 February 1935) in the heart of the country, a device was born which was in large measure to decide the fate of Britain and the World.'[1] Few will doubt that the Battle of Britain was decisive, but did victory in the Battle of Britain depend in large measure on radar? Any who contest this claim could reasonably say that without the Hurricane and Spitfire aircraft, or without the skill and courage of the famous few, the battle could not even have been fought. Just so; but the few were few indeed and when it is remembered by what a narrow margin the battle was won, we need not hesitate to believe that it was radar that enabled the few to conquer the many in this momentous battle.

Was radar really born on that winter's afternoon? The answer is surely 'No', for what was demonstrated was not new. It is equally certain that something important happened, for from that day there began a period of intensive activity, costing some twenty million pre-war pounds, culminating in a revolution in methods of defence against mass air raids by day. To understand the significance of the experiment performed near Daventry, we must go back to the years before 1934.

In the pre-Hitler days, there was certainly an understanding that successful defence against hostile aircraft called for an early warning of their approach. Research work to this end was an Army responsibility. For many years attempts had been made by the Air Defence Experimental Establishment to detect and locate aircraft by tracking them as sources of sound. It is doubtful whether anyone except perhaps those engaged on the work had the slightest hope that success would be achieved. Visitors to demonstrations could hardly fail to note that stringent measures were imposed to ensure that there would be no traffic or other competing noises. Even so, ranges of detection, as distinct from location, were only about ten miles under good conditions. Such ranges were obtained with huge concrete mirrors 200 feet in diameter; because Germany had been defeated beyond hope of recovery in our time, these mirrors faced France!

In June 1934, with the threat of a resurgent German Air Force becoming apparent, A. P. Rowe, then on the staff of the first Director of Scientific Research, Air Ministry, H. E. Wimperis, was worried by the prospect of another war. It had been part of his duties to keep in touch with the War Office work on the detection of aircraft by sound location, and he decided to make an informal survey of all that the Air Ministry was doing about air defence. He collected all the fifty-three Air Ministry files bearing in any way on air defence and saw no hope in any of them.[2] Using the official machine (it is important to note) he wrote a memorandum to his scientific chief summarising the unhappy position and suggesting that the Secretary of State should be warned of the true state of air defence. There seem to be no recorded details of the discussions Wimperis had, but they must have been concerned with an action of a kind now common but then so very rare. Wimperis sought the aid of scientists outside the Air Ministry and, in November 1934, the Tizard Committee came into being, a committee which was to transform the whole outlook for air defence, providing hope where only gloom had prevailed.

Early in 1935, a sub-committee of the Committee of Imperial Defence was set up to deal with defence against aircraft. Rowe, one of the two joint secretaries of the committee, has recalled[3] how readily expenditures, vast in departmental terms, were approved by a nod across the table from Sir Warren Fisher, then Permanent Secretary at the Treasury. Moreover, this non-departmental committee enabled all the fighting services to be made aware of the great progress being made with radar.

What is radar? If, standing facing a cliff about 1,100 feet distant, we give a short, sharp shout, sound will reach the cliff in one second and return in the same time. In this way we can measure the distance of the cliff by timing the travel of the sound to the cliff and back. If the shout at the cliff had lasted more than two seconds, the shout would be confused with the echo and distance measurement would be impossible by simple stop-watch timing. The principle of radar is to transmit a 'shout' of electromagnetic energy (radio) and time the reflection of the 'shout' from an object such as an aircraft. Because radio waves travel at the vast speed of 186,000 miles per second it follows that the 'shout' of radio waves must be extremely short if distance is to be measured by timing an echo from an object.

Radio waves were discovered by Hertz, who demonstrated that they were reflected from conducting objects such as metal sheets. Hertz, however, could see no practical use for his discovery. By the early 1920s it was known that somewhere above the earth's surface there was a vast layer, the Heaviside layer, which acted as a reflector of radio waves of the wavelengths then commonly used. Using a technique of short pulses, or 'shouts' of radio waves, evolved by two Americans, Dr. Gregory Breit and Dr. Merle A. Tuve, E. V. (later Sir Edward) Appleton found the height of the layer to be about sixty miles. This was in 1924. At this early date, therefore, it had been demonstrated that the distance of an object—in Appleton's case a vast one—could be determined by timing the passage of a pulse of radio energy from a transmitter to the object and back.

In a sense, this was radar, but it does not seem to have occurred to anyone that reflections could be obtained from a tiny object, such as an aircraft flying at a distance of many miles from a transmitter. We need not blame them for this, since even today it seems incredible that aircraft distant 100 miles and more receive enough energy for reflections to be sent back to the source of the radio pulses. If, however, it is unreasonable to expect applications to defence to have been noted in the mid-1920s it is indeed astonishing that a decade should pass before those with a need joined those with a technique to evolve radar, and so save this country from defeat. Radar involves awareness that an aircraft will reflect radio waves and there is no lack of evidence, in more countries than our own, that this awareness existed years before 1935.

In June 1932, Watson-Watt showed[4] that aircraft interfered with radio signals and re-radiated them, and he deduced that an aircraft would act as a reflector of short-wave radio pulses. When the striking results of early radar experiments became known to government scientists, a member of the radio department of the RAE said there was nothing new about the discovery since it had been known for a long time that aircraft interfered with experimental television sets. Asked why nothing had been done about it, he replied, 'It was not on the programme.' It is appropriate to our theme to consider the astonishing fact that not one worker in the radio field saw the defence significance of the reflection of radio waves from aircraft. Certainly we may say that it was not their job to do so, but we may be thankful that the accidental discoveries of X-rays and penicillin were made by scientists possessing wider horizons. Further, we may wonder why those engaged on the location of aircraft by acoustic methods were not aware of the reflection of radio waves from aircraft and were not constantly thinking of seeking alternatives to the hopeless task they were pursuing. Departmentalism is a curse in the world of science, as in so much else, and, in the light of later events, it now seems not unjust to say that those engaged on the location of aircraft by acoustic methods worked in blinkers. It will be described later how, when the alternative of radio appeared as a solution to their main problem, not all of them rejoiced.

It was not radar then that was born on that winter's afternoon of 1935, for what was demonstrated was merely an interference effect caused by the presence of an aircraft and there was nothing new about that. What was born was a new field of applied research, the application being to a vital defence problem. In the world of universities, it is still fashionable to regard pure research, performed without any apparent application, as the only respectable kind of research. Cancer research makes nonsense of this view, but perhaps its persists because research work may be supported for years without criticism of lack of results simply because it is labelled 'pure'.

The story of the beginning of applied research on radar and of the building of a coastal chain in time for war has been told so often that it will suffice to give a brief summary of events. Before the first meeting of the Tizard Committee in January 1935, Wimperis thought it well to get the facts concerning the oft-recurring claim for a death-ray which would incapacitate aircraft or their crews at a distance from a 'black box', the contents of which could only be disclosed on payment of a large sum of money. Not one of the claimants, and they came from many countries, was prepared even to discuss or demonstrate his 'black box' before receiving some of the taxpayers' money.

Wimperis, then, wrote to Watson-Watt, Superintendent of the Radio Department of the National Physical Laboratory asking him to comment on the possibility of a death ray. The problem was to discover whether it was possible to concentrate in an electromagetic beam sufficient energy to melt the metal structure of an aircraft or incapacitate its crew. Watson-Watt passed the problem to his assistant A. F. Wilkins who, in half an hour,[5] calculated that although the energy needed to produce an effective death ray was far greater than could be anticipated in the foreseeable future, it should be possible to detect the presence of aircraft by the re-radiation of incident energy. From this moment it may reasonably be said that radar, as it later came to be called, never looked back.

Naturally the Tizard Committee wanted a demonstration of re-radiation from an aircraft and this was held on 26 February 1935. Watson-Watt and Wilkins had arranged that equipment in a trailer sited a few miles from the Daventry broadcasting station should attempt to show whether an aircraft disclosed its presence when flying through the Daventry beam. Rowe was present as the Air Ministry observer and reported that the presence (but, of course, not the location) of an aircraft had been detected at a distance of eight miles. In these early days, surely the chief credit must go to Watson-Watt, not for giving Wimperis the answer he did, for it seems that the elementary sums were done by Wilkins; not for invention, for ideas of greater novelty were to come later from other men; but for the faith and vision he showed at the outset, leading to his joining the Air Ministry after persuasion by Wimperis. At that time there was no radar but only a demonstration of what, after all, many had seen and yet had not seen. From the earliest days, Watson-Watt had no doubt that a vast new field in applied science had been opened.

Whence came the name 'radar'? In the earliest days it seemed that direction-finding would not be possible and that positions would need to be determined from two or more range measurements. Watson-Watt and Rowe discussed a name for the new method of (it was hoped) locating aircraft. Because tall radio masts were unavoidable, the letter 'R' gave nothing away. The letters 'DF' were intended to be misleading since DF (direction-finding) seemed unlikely. For a few years, therefore, the work was known as RDF. Later, the Americans chose, with British agreement, the neat, reversible word radar; no one seems to have envisaged that, in the years to come, meeting the wishes of the Americans would lead many to believe, particularly in America, that the work had an American origin.

The site chosen for the first experiments was the barren isthmus of Orfordness, but after almost exactly a year the work, first under Watson-Watt and then under Rowe, moved to the luxurious grounds of Bawdsey Manor, or Bawdsey Research Station as it became known, some twenty miles to the south. Before giving the results obtained during those momentous days, let us be clear about the objectives. The ultimate objective, of course, was to obtain a continuous three-dimensional record of the positions of hostile aircraft attacking by day, at so great a range from the coast that the few precious fighter aircraft could be kept on the ground until they could be directed to intercept the approaching enemy. This meant the determination of place position with an accuracy sufficient to enable fighter aircraft to see and to engage the enemy: it meant finding the approximate height of hostile aircraft, for accurate plan position would be of little use if the enemy was two or three miles distant from the fighters, and it meant determining the approximate strength of the hostile formations, since if the indications were the same for one aircraft as for a hundred, the meagre resources of Fighter Command would often be wastefully used. This last was a factor of great importance since otherwise the enemy could have drawn the fighter aircraft into the air by raids of single aircraft, leaving mass attacks until the fighters were largely grounded.

Criticisms have been made, including those of Lindemann, that the early radar work was slow. Let the facts speak for themselves. The first meeting of the Tizard Committee was in February 1935. By 13 May of that a year a team under Watt had been assembled, special equipment had been constructed and 70-ft. masts erected. On 31 May all was ready for the first tests. On 15 June, under poor conditions for radio reception, the Tizard Committee saw an aircraft followed by radar to a distance of seventeen miles. Thus, after two weeks' work, the range obtained from the 200-ft. concrete acoustic mirrors had been roughly doubled. In July, a range of forty miles was achieved. Forty miles! This was hope indeed, but let it not be thought that the whole problem was solved in two months. In principle, however, it was solved in four. In July, only range could be measured and it is doubtful whether position-finding from two or more spaced stations would ever have been satisfactory if hostile aircraft formations were scattered over the North Sea. By September, however, the problem of direction-finding had been solved, thus adding an unexpected realism to the letters RDF and enabling, in principle, one station to obtain plan position. By mid-September, also, the height of an aircraft flying at 7,000 feet was measured with an accuracy of about 1,000 feet, which was good enough for interception.

By the autumn of 1935 it was clear that a cheap experiment conducted by a handful of scientists had succeeded but that a practical defence scheme based on radar would involve a vast effort in manpower and money. Far higher masts (in the event, 350 feet) would need to be built, provision made for several wavelengths in order to counter jamming, costly transmitters of higher power and complicated receivers would need to be developed and made by industry. But the recording, at coastal radar stations, of the positions of hostile aircraft formations would be of little use unless the data were sent rapidly and accurately to the users, ie, to Fighter Command, to group headquarters and to fighter stations. All this meant more costly equipment and a large-scale laying of special lines of communication.

From May 1936 to April 1939 were three years of intense activity spent in erecting the coastal chain, including magnificent work by Metropolitan Vickers on transmitters and by A. C. Cossor on receivers, the training of RAF personnel and the installation of a whole complex devoted to the rapid use of the data from the coastal stations. On Good Friday 1939, a continuous watch was begun on the coastal chain, stretching from Ventnor to the Firth of Tay, never to cease until the war was won. By that September, the chain often reported ranges of 100 miles and more, and when a year later, mass raids began, it was common to observe enemy aircraft getting into formation above the aerodromes of France and Belgium. The approximate strength of hostile formations could be ascertained and plan position, height and speed of approach obtained with an accuracy sufficient for day interception by fighter aircraft.

Perhaps the only major set-back of the pre-war years was the apparent failure of an exercise in August 1937 due to insufficient care in calibrating the chain stations, and to the fact that the method of correlation and filtering of the data had not been perfected. Looking at the results, a Hitler or Goering might well have prohibited further work. It is to the eternal credit of the users, the Air Staff and Fighter Command, that no despairing voices were raised by them. Indeed, it was decided to create radar defence systems in Malta and Egypt.

Radar served Britain, as nothing else could have done, in her great hour of need. And when it is remembered that the radar chain only became available in the year which saw the beginning of the war, it is indeed fortunate that, from the very beginning, no important Air Ministry voices were raised in opposition to it.

What were the factors which helped or hindered the availability and utility of the radar coastal chain in time for war? Pride of place must be given to an almost incredible technical blunder on the part of the Germans. A system of stations with 350-ft. masts stretching along the whole of the British coast facing Germany could not be disguised and it is not surprising that, having by 1939 a radar system of their own, German military intelligence deduced that the British stations were concerned with air defence. The British stations, however, looked, and were, so very different from their own that in the summer of 1939 they carried out several reconnaissances along the East Coast with a specially equipped Zeppelin airship.[6] For reasons which will probably always remain a mystery, the radar transmissions were not received and the Germans got nothing. They admitted that in the Battle of Britain they were taken by surprise. Being unaware of the magnitude of the part radar was playing in the battle, they did not jam the stations and bombing attacks upon them were few, half-hearted and soon abandoned. Germany paid a great price for failure in the first electronics reconnaissance in history.

Lastly, are there lessons to be learned from the lack, before late 1934, of contact between those with a need and those with a technique which would meet that need? How absurd it now seems that when Wimperis went to the Air Ministry, he was told that radio was not his concern. How absurd it now seems that the hopeless long-range sound research was allowed to continue, for it is often well to declare a vacuum which needs to be filled. Indications of re-radiation from aircraft had been observed for years before 1934: why then had objective work to await a letter from a defence department? Would it not have been wise, as it would be wise today, for the existence of major problems to be aired in universities, industrial research organisations and in all government research establishments? For air defence, it might have meant telling the Germans that we had no long-range warning system but, fortunately, this is what they believed anyway. Again and again it can be seen that unimaginative departmentalism, induced by defence or commercial secrets and by possessiveness, is a main enemy of progress in any sphere of effort.

Page 101: (above) Radar Fighter Direction Aerial System; (below) Ground-controlled Aircraft Interception Equipment.

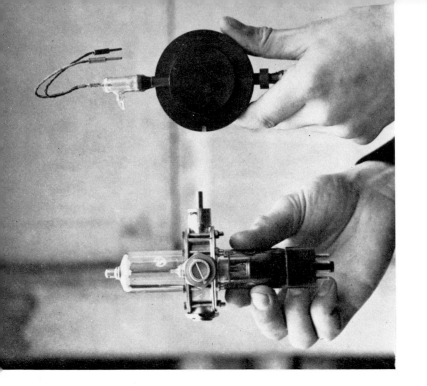

Page 102: (*left*) Sir John Randall; (*right*) the Cavity Magnetron.

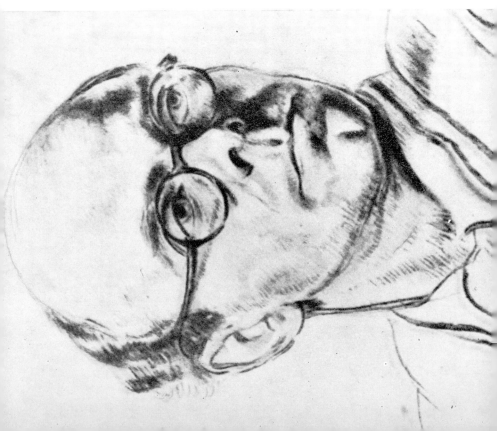

(ii) Detection of Low-Flying Aircraft

The weak link of the coastal chain was that, with the wavelengths used, it was unable to detect at useful ranges the approach of low-flying aircraft. There was a gap which the radar beam was unable to cover just above the surface of the sea. It follows that aircraft skimming the waves, ships, or surfaced submarines could not be detected. In theory, the problem was not difficult to solve. The greater the ratio of the height of the aerial arrays to the wavelengths used, the easier it would be to detect low-flying aircraft and surface vessels. But the radar transmission and reception masts were already extremely high and any further extension would present a difficult problem for the engineers. The best solution was to have an equipment using very much shorter wavelengths. Hence the work on centimetric wavelengths was of great importance to the development of surface radar. Meanwhile, for the immediate future, an alternative solution had to be found.

This solution came from the efforts of a small group of War Office scientists attached to Bawdsey from 1936 onwards for the purpose of developing radar for the control of anti-aircraft gunnery (see Ch 8, (ii)), and for the detection of ships at sea at night, or in mist and fog. The work on a coastal defence equipment began in 1938 and the leader of the group was an Australian-born scientist named W. A. S. Butement, who had already evolved the latest system for radio communication between tanks. More significant for the purposes of radar, Butement had, in conjunction with a colleague, P. E. Pollard, devised in 1931, on his own initiative, a system for the radiolocation of ships at sea, while attached to the War Office Signals Experimental Establishment at Woolwich. The War Office had told them that there was no requirement for such an apparatus, but allowed the two scientists to conduct experiments in their own time. Details of their work will be found in Chapter 8. For the present a brief summary is sufficient. They were able to obtain with their somewhat primitive equipment reflections from a radio mast in the establishment compound and went on to detect a sheet of galvanised corrugated roofing iron at a distance of over 100 yards. They informed the War Office, with suppressed excitement, that with an enlarged equipment they would be able to detect ships at sea. Again they received the dusty answer that there was no requirement for their device. Details of the experiments were sent to the Director of

G

Scientific Research at the Admiralty, but curiously enough not to the Air Ministry. The former, while interested in the possibilities if pursued, doubted whether the idea was practicable, principally because there was then no adequate method of generating sufficient power to enable an adequate range to be obtained. Lack of money for research and lack of interest (rearmament had not yet begun) caused the experiments to cease.

Seven years later the threat of a Second World War had changed the climate of opinion and Butement found himself at Bawdsey; this time the War Office had a requirement for a coast defence radar. In fact, the requirement was a modest one. It was merely to provide a sufficiently accurate indication of bearing to enable a searchlight to be put on its target and thus allow an optical bearing to be determined; in other words, to provide a more accurate measurement with radar than could be obtained optically. Butement then worked out an equation to show how range of detection was related to power. 'This', Butement writes, 'turned out to be "range varies as the eighth power of the power". This was for a few weeks very depressing because, in the interim, E. G. Bowen had, in May 1939, developed a $1\frac{1}{2}$-kilowatt pulsed transmitter operating on a wavelength of $1\frac{1}{2}$ metres and this had been used by W. Eastwood (who a little later joined my team) together with a receiver and Yagi aerial to detect medium-sized ships at only one or two miles range.* Based on this information, the range of ten miles which was desired would need about 400,000 times the power, or 600,000 kW, an impossibility at that time.

'On closer study it became clear to me that something could be done in a number of areas to improve sensitivity, and all these improvement "multiplied together" would give the improvement required.

'This meant developing a sharply-beamed antenna system for use with a much higher powered $1\frac{1}{2}$-metre transmitter (20 kW) and a sharply-beamed antenna system for the receiver, which itself was much improved. It also meant using the shortest wavelength (highest frequency) possible as the radar equation showed. It is therefore interesting to see how our more professional and mathematical approach seven years later (ie, after the Woolwich experiments) had confirmed our judgement in 1931, in our use of the highest fre-

* See page 55.

quency possible (600 megacycles per second),* and a beamed system. (Our use in 1931 of a common aerial for transmitter and receiver was, of course, not duplicated until the middle of the war.)'

Butement now evolved what became known as the 'split beam' method, whereby continuous and accurate following of the target could be made.

About May 1939, the first prototype of the coastal defence radar based on Butement's idea was ready for trial. There was a ready-made target, the 'Butterboat' which left Harwich every evening for Denmark. The 'split beam' method of direction finding worked. At once A. J. Oxford, a member of Butement's team, rushed into the small workshop/laboratory, grabbed a brace, and drilled a hole in the door of the cabin on which the receiving aerial array was erected, the whole being set on a gun mounting so that all could be rotated together. This provided the aperture of a peepsight. Another member (W. Eastwood) nailed a length of timber on the cabin roof and fixed a piece of wire hanging down from it. The latter was quickly bent so as to subtend the ship, between its masts, while the radar indicated by the split beam method that the radar was 'on target'.

'For the next hour', continues Butement, 'to our delight, we observed that while following the target on the radar the bearing was always "between the masts". A few quick sums showed that we had a probable error in bearing measurement of ten minutes of arc, which was adequate to control gunfire without the use of searchlights at all.

'There was a very interesting sequel to this experiment which occurred a few days later (20 June 1939). Winston Churchill arrived to inspect the Establishment. He was then a member of the Air Defence Research Sub-Committee of the Committee of Imperial Defence and so took an especial interest in our coastal defence apparatus.

'I had the task of explaining the *modus operandi* of the "split beam method" of bearing measurement to him and of demonstrating its effect. Half way through my explanation he grasped the principle and finished my exposition for me. Surprised, I said to him "that's quite correct in principle, Sir" (he had made an unimportant

* 'This seems inconsistent with our use seven years later of a wavelength three times as long, ie, 1½ metres, but the Barkhausen and Kurz system had never given high power, and special tubes would have been required, whereas tubes for 1½ metres were ready to hand after slight adaptation.'

but incorrect assumption). He turned on me sharply and said "Well Sir, what but the principle matters in a case like this?"

'I felt a little deflated and proceeded to demonstrate the split method to him. We had a flying-boat as target, but in our desire to do justice to the range potential of the equipment had ordered it further out than in previous experiments; the range was some twenty-five miles. Four of us crowded into the small rotatable cabin, Churchill with a cigar (he chain-smoked his eight-inch cigars; I saw him light one from another!), Watson-Watt, a lieutenant-commander who accompanied Churchill, and myself. I adjusted the radar until we were "on target" as indicated by the radar. I then said "If you will look out of the peephole you will see the target on the cross wires, Sir." Churchill looked out; he paused and exclaimed "I can't see a —— thing". This was most disturbing to me. His naval aide said "Let me look, Sir" and put his eye to the peepsight. I then said "I'll bracket the target going left, on, right on, left and so on." This I did and the Commander promptly said "No wonder you couldn't see it, Sir, the aircraft was obscured by the hair line." (We had forgotten that we had the target at greater range than previously.) Churchill immediately elbowed the commander out of the way and set his eye to the peepsight; he paused as I repeated "the left-on-right" procedure, and he exclaimed "Marvellous". We all got out of the cabin while Churchill "measured" the size of the aerial array, holding his hands before him as he viewed it as some people measure a fish. "We must have this on His Majesty's ships. I will see to it." Next day Admiral Somerville arrived to view the equipment.'[7]

Within three months Britain was at war with Germany, and Churchill was once again First Lord of the Admiralty. Professor J. D. (later Sir John) Cockcroft and a party from the Cavendish Laboratory, Cambridge, were hurriedly sent on instructions from Admiral Somerville, then in charge of naval radar, to the Orkneys and Shetland Islands to set up a radar chain to detect surfaced U-boats passing through from the North Sea to the Atlantic. These radars, which were coastal defence sets hastily adapted under the direction of Cockcroft, became known as CDU sets, the 'U' standing for anti-U-boat.

During that bitter winter a number of sets were installed around the north-east coast of Scotland, and Cockcroft has written that 'without the drive from the top (ie, from the First Lord) this rapid work would have been impossible.'[8] The Fair Isles station detected submarines at ranges up to twenty-five miles, but it was soon discovered that the stations were best used in giving warnings of low-flying attack on Scapa Flow naval base. Compared with the local Chain Home station, the wavelength was much shorter and able to detect low-flying aircraft at much greater ranges.

As the coastal defence radar was designed to detect objects moving on the surface of the sea, very little modification was required to enable them to detect low-flying aircraft. In August 1939 the Air Ministry ordered a number of sets which became known as CHL (Chain Home Low—for low-flying aircraft). The first was operational at the end of November in the Thames estuary (where low-flying aircraft were laying mines), and in the Spring of 1940 were extended further along the east and south-east coastline.* Had the Germans been more radar-conscious they would have flown their bombers below the height at which the British radar screen operated. Such a simple tactical measure could well have altered the outcome of the battle. Indeed, there is still no adequate solution to the problem of detecting very low-flying aircraft.

Later, in 1941 and 1942, the Germans used fighter bombers operating in daylight at tree-top height and on many occasions they came in undetected by radar. By then, however, the Luftwaffe had switched its main effort to the Eastern Front.

Nevertheless the CHL sets played an important part in these tip and run raids, while at one critical period during the Battle of Britain they held the line when three Chain Home sets were put out of action by air attack. It was not long before a hybrid version of Butement's original set appeared which combined coastal defence and the detection of low-flying aircraft.

The coastal defence set was also adapted for another very important task : the direction from the ground of a night fighter aircraft towards its quarry, and this will be described in the section on ground controlled interception. 'Thus', concludes Butement 'the first beamed radar was used in many forms for a variety of tasks and can be fairly said to have stemmed directly from those early experiments in beamed radar conducted in 1931.'[9]

We must now look at two radio aids which played an essential role in air defence.

* In fact, the first sixty models of CD radar originally destined for the Army were converted to CHL sets to supplement the CH stations. None was available to the Army until the end of 1940.

(iii) High-Frequency Direction-Finders

Information received by radar was of little use if the fighter controllers were unable to hold uninterrupted conversation with the fighter pilots or were unaware of their position at a given moment.

A radio direction-finder had been evolved by Bellini and Tosi shortly before the First World War and subsequent experiments with this direction-finder, conducted by F. E. Adcock, a scientist working at the National Physical Laboratory, had revealed that transmissions were affected by natural phenomena such as dawn and sunset. In seeking to remedy these defects, Adcock evolved a system of direction-finding which, in principle, was the same as that used in the Second World War.

One man was largely responsible for the introduction of HF/DF in the RAF. He was a signals technical officer—Sqdn. Ldr. L. J. Chandler—and he designed the Chandler-Adcock short-wave direction-finder in collaboration with the Marconi Wireless Telephone company. It operated on a wavelength of 50-70 metres and had a range of approximately fifty miles—the effective radius of action of fighter aircraft of those days.

The equipment then had to be fitted into an operational system. In trials, held during a joint Army-Air Force exercise in August 1932, it was noted that the direction-finder could give the position of the aircraft just as accurately as when the pilot gave his position on seeing the ground. The following August, Chandler recommended that high-frequency direction-finders should be set up in each fighter sector of Air Defence Great Britain. Bearings obtained from three-minute interval transmissions of aircraft were to be plotted continuously from a central plotting station, which would give the patrolling fighter its position by radio telephone.

The task of installing the direction-finder in fighter sectors now went ahead. In January 1935 HF/DF trials with fighters began, and by the autmun of 1935 four stations were operating in south-east England. At the same time the international situation was becoming more tense. Sqdn. Ldr. R. (later Air Marshal Sir Raymond) Hart, Deputy Chief Signals Officer at Headquarters, Fighting Area, Uxbridge, was given the job of discovering the effectiveness of HF/DF, airborne radio and the Observer Corps. HF/DF was found to be a reliable means of control. But the Home Chain was not yet in existence. Hart and his colleagues, unaware that radar existed, were worried about the lack of an early warning system. Hart's report was an additional spur to the work at Bawdsey.

The next important step towards fighter control was a series of experiments in interception technique which were inspired and directed by Tizard. In 1936, a small team assembled at Biggin Hill which included Sqdn. Ldr. (later Air Vice-Marshal) R. L. Ragg, a navigation expert; Flt. Lt. (later Air Vice-Marshal) Sir Walter Pretty, Sector Signals Officer and Dr. B. G. Dickins, an Air Ministry scientist. These experiments, which were one of the earliest examples of the new science of operational research, took place over a period of eighteen months to two years and were of great historical importance. Firstly, they developed the interception technique, based on direction-finding, which was used in the Battle of Britain. (Radar was not used in the tests. The team assumed that by some means, bearing, distance and altitude of enemy aircraft would be given them.) Secondly, it was the beginning of an era of close collaboration between scientist and serving officer which was to grow throughout the war and which has remained with us to this day.

In 1937, by which time Hart was acting as liaison officer at Bawdsey, the latter was linked with Biggin Hill and it passed on the radar information to the operations room. HF/DF could now be used exclusively for fighter control. More efficient types of equipment were at last available, including the cathode-ray direction-finder. In September 1936, twenty cathode-ray installations were planned to be built, and in the following year the HF/DF system began to spread into other RAF home commands. Completion date was fixed for 1939.

Meanwhile, Chandler was evolving an automatic direction-finding technique installed in aircraft and known as 'Pip-Squeak'. Pip-Squeak automatically switched on the high-frequency transmitter in the aircraft for fourteen seconds in every minute. The pilot was able to use his radio for normal reception and transmission for the remainder of the minute. Although pilots had, in the early days, resisted the new idea, by 1939 their initial apathy had been overcome.

Pip-Squeak was in existence when war began in September 1939 and pilots were trained in its use. With radar, it 'became the key to all the interceptions made in the Battle of Britain.'[10]

The importance of the high-frequency direction-finder as a vital element of the fighter defence organisation was appreciated only just in time. It was fortunate that a serving officer, Chandler, and a civilian scientist, Tizard, were at hand to perfect the equipment and to adapt it to the communications system.

(iv) Very High Frequency (VHF) Radio Telephony

The exploitation of high-frequency wavebands on account of the increasing use of radio was becoming a serious problem in the years immediately before the outbreak of the Second World War. The speech of pilots to their controllers on the ground was liable to distortion and interference. The answer was to provide pilots with VHF two-way radio-telephony.

The problem of interference had grown since aircraft radio was introduced into warfare in May 1915 with aerial observation posts for artillery. By 1928, VHF had been recommended as a subject for research at RAE, but, in fact, the development stage did not begin until January 1935. A set was to be ready by 1940. This was the first time that the RAE radio engineering staff had been given complete responsibility for planning, in addition to technical development. But snags arose and in mid-1938 RAE reported that the task might still take four years to complete.

With international tension increasing, Fighter Command could not afford to be caught in the middle of changing over its communications system from HF to VHF. In January 1939 Watson-Watt, now Director of Communications Development at the Air Ministry, instructed his deputy, Air Cdre. Hugh Leedham, a radio expert, to investigate the VHF/RT situation. On the basis of his findings it was decided to concentrate on a less powerful set—the TR 1133—which would be ready within a year. The Chief of Air Staff now ordered that four sectors in each of the important Nos. 11 and 12 Fighter Groups were to be re-equipped. Hornchurch, North Weald and Debden should operate on both HF and VHF simultaneously.

The first TR 1133 sets were ready for delivery in August 1939 and trials took place at the end of that October. Results exceeded expectation. An air to ground range of 140 miles was obtained at a height of 10,000 feet. One aircraft could speak clearly to another at a range of 100 miles. Even so, it was hoped that a more advanced VHF set—the TR 1143—would be fitted into Fighter Command aircraft by May 1940.

In spite of the urgency, the delivery of both sets was delayed. After Dunkirk, squadrons were ordered to change back to HF, and although sixteen squadrons had been equipped with VHF by September 1940, the Battle of Britain was fought with HF network to which the pilots were well accustomed.

The lesson brought out here is that in the development of war equipment it is better to have the second best in time than to wait for a more advanced equipment which appears too late. The Germans, as has been seen, never learned this lesson.

The defence of Britain against night attack had had to take second priority to defence against attack by day. The problems requiring solution were also more difficult.

(v) Aircraft Interception at Night

We have seen that a very important and unanticipated by-product of the development of airborne radar led to the radar detection of ships (ASV). The problem of an airborne radar set locating a night bomber must now be described. At the time this appeared to be almost insuperable. Consider the situation confronting the night-fighter pilot and his observer. First of all the strain of flying itself, of adapting the eyes to the dark; of taking off and landing at night and of flying over a blacked-out landscape with no landmarks to identify; then the ceaseless flow of information and instructions from the controller on the ground which had to be digested and acted upon. From the scientific point of view, the problem was to produce a short-wave radar set small enough to fit into a night fighter. Thus, in the early stages of the night battle it seemed that only in bright moonlight, when a hostile aircraft could be identified at a distance, did the night fighter stand a chance of success.

Tizard knew well enough that when the day bomber threat had been defeated night attacks would begin. But priority had to go to perfecting the early warning system against daylight attack. So it was that at the outbreak of war no system of detection for the night bomber was available. Only a handful of scientists (under E. G. Bowen as already noted) could be spared to devote their attention to night air defence and hardly any RAF personnel were trained in the use of the primitive airborne radar apparatus that existed. Bowen had to make the radar pulse so narrow that the night fighter could home on to a bomber until the pilot could see it with his naked eye. By June 1939, under Bowen's supervision, a $1\frac{1}{2}$-metre experimental aircraft interception set was fitted into a Fairey Battle which, with its aid, was able to home on to a bomber provided the latter was under a range of two miles and not at a distance greater than the height of the interceptor above the ground. The reason for this was that some of the energy from the interception set was radiated straight downwards and the earth returned a signal so much greater than any aircraft could do, that indications of enemy aircraft greater than the distance between the aircraft and the earth, ie, greater than the height of the aircraft, were completely swamped. Nevertheless the equipment worked well enough for the Commander-in-Chief, Fighter Command, to place an order for thirty Battles to be equipped with aircraft interception sets by 1 September 1939.

At the outbreak of war the Air Ministry scientists moved from Bawdsey to Dundee. The nearest airfield, Perth, was not the best for Bowen's handful of scientists, who were not only responsible for research and development, but for production, installation and air testing. Moreover, the Battles were being replaced by Blenheims, of which six were equipped with radar by 3 September 1939, and thirty by the end of that month.

In November 1939 Bowen's team was moved again, to St. Athan, in Glamorgan, where it was still further away from the home base, thus further complicating the situation. The purpose of the set was, as just explained, to guide the night-fighter pilot on to his target until he was within visual range. It was therefore very important that the minimum range should not exceed the maximum visual range. But this was the major weakness of the early set and it proved difficult to rectify. Two solutions were proposed, one by the Air Ministry Research Establishment, as Bawdsey Research Station was now known, and one by Electric & Musical Industries Ltd. The former provided a small team under W. B. Lewis, a colleague of Cockcroft's at the Cavendish, with a masterly grasp of the details of electronic equipment and techniques. He was made deputy superintendent of TRE by Rowe over the heads of others, and later became Director of the Atomic Energy Establishment at Chalk River, Canada.

Lewis's team worked out a system which reduced the minimum range to 800 feet by modifying the existing equipment. This equipment, known as AI Mark III, had to be fitted into 100 Blenheim aircraft, and in November 1940 it provided the first kill for a radar-directed night fighter. The EMI solution, however, proved to be superior. One of their scientists, A. D. Blumlein, produced a new modulator giving very short pulses for a minimum range and a power pack with the same transmitter and receiver. (Special micropup transmitter valves were produced by GEC.) The minimum range obtained with this equipment was under 500 feet and was a great improvement over the Air Ministry set. Indications of elevation and direction were difficult to interpret on the early Aircraft Interception sets, but during the summer of 1940 this was rectified by changing the polarisation of the aerial system on the fighter from horizontal to vertical. This equipment, known as AI Mark IV, was the main aircraft interception set from about March 1941 until the advent of centimetric aircraft interception equipment in the spring of 1942, and was available for the tail-end of the enemy's main night offensive against Britain.

In the autumn of 1940 the enemy, frustrated by the day defences, despatched his bombers by night against the industrial centres of Britain. Now interception techniques with airborne radar had to be evolved and with complex and untried equipment. Airborne radar was not enough. The crew were unable to navigate at night if they were to intercept as well. They had to be given their route and manœuvred into position to intercept and attack from the ground. Hence the necessity for a ground-controlled interception equipment. Its evolution is described later, on page 117.

Meanwhile, it remains to describe how the Air Interception equipment was improved with the introduction of centimetric radar.

We know that the 1½-metre AI set suffered from ground clutter, and was unable to detect an enemy aircraft if the latter was at a greater height than the fighter above the ground. The beam had to be narrowed so that the earth's reflections did not interfere with those from an aircraft. This could only be achieved with a wavelength of a few centimetres. The problem was recognised at an early stage in the development of AI. In 1939, for instance, Rowe had foreseen that AI would have to be on a 10-centimetre wavelength to be effective. For the time being nothing could be done until the development of the magnetron. The 1½-metre AI was not only inaccurate, but it was particularly susceptible to jamming. Finally, the vehicle for the radar was unsatisfactory, for the Blenheim, originally intended as a bomber, was too slow and the Beaufighter, due to replace it, developed an abnormally large number of teething problems. Beset by all these perplexities the scientists under Rowe at Worth Matravers bent their energies during the anxious summer of 1940, while many wondered whether Britain would survive, upon the night air battle to come.

P. I. Dee, now Professor of Natural Philosophy at Glasgow University, was the driving force behind centimetric AI. Dee, a tall, dark figure with a somewhat caustic view of life, was a nuclear physicist who was working at the Cavendish Laboratory before the war. He was one of the first academic scientists to be initiated into radar, but at the outbreak of war he was diverted into working in the Royal Aircraft Establishment on parachute mine devices. Watson-Watt persuaded him to join the Air Ministry Research Establishment and early in 1940 he arrived at Worth Matravers looking, Rowe has written, 'something like his alleged ancestor, the Wizard of Upton.*[11] Reputedly, Dee was scared of working on radio and had kept away from it. Microwaves did not worry him so much and soon he became a leading innovator in their development. At that time (April 1940) there was no valve at TRE working on a shorter wavelength than 25/30 centimetres although there were vague hopes of a valve for a 10-centimetre set from Birmingham or perhaps eventually from GEC. Dee went at once to Birmingham to investigate and found Oliphant had a 9-centimetre klystron working on a pump. The klystron with its power supplies was far too large to go into an aircraft, and such a narrow beam would have to be revolved to sweep the skies. Methods for receiving the energy reflected from a target aircraft, and for using this energy to display the position of an aircraft, had to be developed.

In order to have something to experiment with Dee, on his own initiative, took away drawings and had a klystron manufactured at the Mond Laboratory, Cambridge, and in June 1940 it was delivered to Worth Matravers. Like Randall's first magnetron, it was a clumsy apparatus which required its own pumping plant to create the near vacuum needed in the working space of the valve. Nevertheless, through this makeshift equipment an echo was obtained from a boy bicycling up the narrow lane from Worth Matravers to St. Aldhelm's Head. This was a dramatic step forward in radar history. Then, in August, reflections were obtained from a Battle aircraft at a range of two miles from these cliffs.

By that time Oliphant and his team at Birmingham had produced the much lighter strapped magnetron which, as we have seen, stabilised frequencies and increased the power to about 5 kW on a 10-

* Dr. John Dee was magician-in-chief or 'scientific' adviser to Elizabeth I.

centimetre wavelength; it was also sealed, which meant that the vacuum could be maintained without a pumping plant. GEC Laboratories then produced a model of the valve suitable for mass production.

Much remained to be done before an acceptable centimetric equipment could be fitted into a night fighter. Every extra pound reduced the climbing power of the fighters. And the radar, installed in the nose, had to be able to scan above and below and to the left and right of the aircraft. It had to provide more accurate angular data than other types of airborne radar, and it had to give these data at ranges of several hundred feet as well as at a range of a few miles.

In March 1941 a 10-centimetre AI set was flown in a Blenheim and picked up the target aircraft at a range of two miles flying at a medium altitude. This was the first time an AI range was obtained which was greater than the flying height of the aircraft. The scanner which made this possible had been largely evolved, not by a physicist or engineer but by a physiologist, A. L. Hodgkin from Cambridge, and the design was by Messrs. Nash and Thompson. Also working with Hodgkin on centimetric AI were three physicists : the late H. W. B. Skinner (in his neglect of himself and his appearance he was the popular conception of the absent-minded scientist), W. E. Burcham, now Professor of Physics at Birmingham, and R. A. Smith, now Principal at Heriot-Watt University, Edinburgh.

There were two major problems, however, which had to be solved before centimetric AI became fully effective. Normally, in radio equipments, one aerial system is used for transmission and another for reception. But the miniature aerial of the AI set was an integral part of the scanning system which made such heavy demands on the limited space available. A special switch was therefore devised in which the same aerial system alternated with great rapidity between transmission and reception. The GEC Research Laboratory, the Clarendon Laboratory Group and TRE were jointly responsible for the development of this device.

The second innovation was the crystal mixer. The provision of power for the centimetric radar transmitted has been described. It was also necessary to devise a special receiver. Dee and Skinner broke down the problem into two parts. First, the detector. In the more powerful radio receivers the high-frequency signal was reduced to a lower frequency for amplification by being 'mixed' with a locally-generated frequency. The 'mixing' caused a signal within the receiver whose instantaneous frequency was the difference between the instantaneous frequency of the incoming signal and the temporarily fixed but adjustable frequency generated by a local oscillator. The 'mixing' was done by the detector now renamed the 'mixer'. Skinner devised what became known as crystal mixers—a delicate tungsten wire was fixed in contact with a silicon crystal. Secondly, the development of local oscillators in the magnetron was carried out by the Admiralty scientists under R. W. Sutton.

The significant point to be noted here was the collective effort of four separate groups from the services, universities and industry in the development of centimetric AI—TRE, the Admiralty Signal Establishment, the Clarendon Laboratory and the General Electric Company. Nothing remotely like it existed in Germany.

Much work had to be done from the autumn of 1940, when an aircraft was detected up to a range of six miles from a centimetric system at Worth Matravers, to the first operational AI Mark VII set fitted into a Blenheim in April 1941. Faster night fighters were also being developed (five squadrons were equipped with Beaufighters by March 1941; before then contacts frequently had to be broken off with Blenheims). Early in 1942 four squadrons of the latest Beaufighter night fighters were equipped with AI Mark VII. About 100 aircraft were claimed destroyed before this set, in turn, was replaced by the improved AI Mark VIII with which the Mosquito fighter was equipped.

In fact, centimetric AI was not available for the main German night offensive against Britain during the winter of 1940/41. The losses imposed on the enemy in that battle, in addition to anti-aircraft guns and single-engined 'cat's eye' fighters, were caused by a combination of Blenheims and Beaufighters equipped with 1½-metre AI Mark IV and assisted by Ground Controlled Interception sets. There was a spectacular improvement in the use of radar over the period January to May 1941.[12] Early in May, however, the Germans broke off the battle, withdrawing their bomber units to the Eastern Front, and so the improved radar equipments were never fully tested. Fighter Command was confident that had attacks continued the night offensive would have been defeated in the same way as the daylight offensive the previous summer.

Centimetric AI sets, however, played a valuable role in the final German night-bombing effort (the Little Blitz) in the winter of

1943/44 and they were employed in the Mediterranean and North-west European theatres of war.

(vi) *Planned Position Indicator and Ground-Controlled Interception*

It should now be possible to appreciate the formidable difficulties of air interception by night. A solution of the problem required a knowledge on the ground at one and the same time of the position, track, speed and height of both the enemy bomber and the night fighter. A controller on the ground equipped with this information was able to tell the night-fighter pilot by radio telephony the direction and height at which he should fly in order to intercept the enemy and, if necessary, to tell him to reduce speed in order to avoid overshooting the bomber target.

The problem was solved by two devices—the Plan Position Indicator (PPI) which was installed in a new radar set known as Ground Controlled Interception (GCI). The work of the fighter controller, once he had received early warning of the approach of enemy raiders from the Home Chain, was greatly simplified by this equipment. In front of him was the screen of a cathode-ray tube resembling a domestic television set. Imposed on this screen was a map of the surrounding area up to distances of about fifty miles from the controller. The respective positions of hostile bomber and fighter were shown by bright spots on the tube face; they were, in fact, small arcs of circles the centres of which the controller had to estimate. The flight of the bomber towards its target and the flight of the pursuing fighter were represented by the spots on the screen and the positions of the aircraft could be read from the tube face which, in addition to the map, was marked in grid square. These positions were plotted on a larger-scale map and, by calculating the speed and direction of flight of the enemy, the night fighter could be directed towards it by the shortest route.

While the Home Chain provided adequate information for daylight interceptions, it was not designed to have the accuracy needed for interception at night, and the coverage over land (while bombers were flying for example to the Midlands) was inadequate. P. E. Pollard who, like Butement, joined the Army cell of scientists at Bawdsey was, in 1938, responsible for the idea of the PPI, or radar 'lighthouse', as it was known in its earliest form. E. G. Bowen, too, pointed out that a plan position indicator would be essential for radar detection of aircraft up to ranges of forty miles.

At the beginning, the PPI was a simple arrangement based on a rotating aerial array (the adapted CHL described on page 115). As it rotated, so the radar beam rotated and, in alignment with it, a line from the centre of the radar screen to its circumference rotated so as to sweep over the whole area of the tube about every twenty seconds. This line provided the range scale and its brilliance on the tube was kept at a low value. When the rotating beam encountered an aircraft, a bright spot appeared on the rotating line and formed a small arc at the indicated range of the aircraft from the radar station. Since the direction of the rotating beam was known at all times, the direction of the located aircraft was also known. Such was the PPI which, in more sophisticated forms by the end of the war, was to be an integral part of radar on land, at sea, and in the air and, next to centimetric radar, was probably the most important wartime advance in radar.*

At first it was proposed to harness the PPI to the Home Chain. This was a failure. Harold Larnder, who with his Operational Research Section in Fighter Command had been concerned since early 1940 with the problem of controlled interceptions, suggested in mid-August that a CHL set with a modified aerial could be used with advantage. The CHL set, it will be remembered, had a small wavelength and the beam could be swung over a large area. TRE now took up the challenge and a team under G. W. A. Dummer (later a senior principal scientific officer at the Royal Radar Establishment and an expert in micro-electronics) combined PPI with a continuously rotating CHL equipment. The radius of the PPI was increased from sixty to ninety miles.

W. B. Lewis, D. Taylor and F. C. Williams, later to become renowned for his work on computers at Manchester University, set to work to assemble the first Ground Controlled Interception equipment at Worth Matravers out of CHL components but with the first PPI. They were helped by Fighter Command Operational Research Section and the Royal Aircraft Establishment. It soon became necessary to enlist the co-operation of a night-fighter squadron to discover how the equipment worked operationally. The nearest squadron was at Middle Wallop and one of the young pilots, Flt. Lt.

* The Germans did not think of PPI until too late. With it, they could have used very much less precise radar equipment.

Page 119: (above) Cathode-ray tube of High-Frequency Direction Finder (FH4) showing the line of bearing of an intercepted signal; (below) Plan Position Indicator tube showing location approximately off Lowestoft.

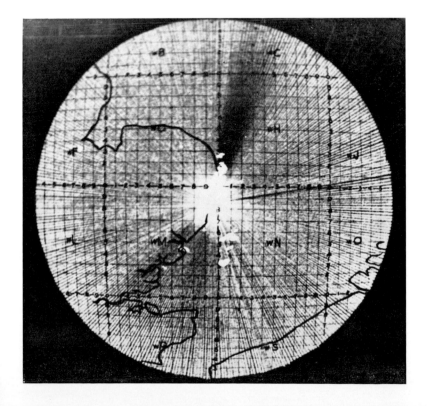

Page 120: (*above*) Rugged valves for proximity fuses, reading L to R early and final models: (*below*) proximity fuses, L to R, 5m to 50cm.

(later Grp. Capt.) John Cunningham, shortly to become one of the most celebrated night-fighter pilots and after the war a fine test pilot, was much appreciated by the scientists for his eager and sympathetic collaboration.

But the early trials were unsuccessful; it was not easy to manœuvre the night fighter into a suitable position to intercept. 'The first task therefore', Rowe has written, 'was to gain the confidence of the night-fighter pilots by using the GCI indications to bring them from the English Channel (over which they had been patrolling) to a position over their home aerodrome. Once this had been demonstrated, the fighter pilots poured over from Middle Wallop to see the new brand of magic, after which they came to believe that, though they might not know where they were, there was an "eye" on the ground that could watch them and lead them home.

'So it came about that scientists in flannel bags controlled night-fighter aircraft against the enemy.'[13]

On 16 October, a GCI station was set up at Durrington at the foot of the South Downs behind Worthing. For it Taylor devised a direct height-reading display which could be used on any particular aircraft as its spot on the PPI came up in the course of each rotation. GCI in its final form was a combination of a CHL set continuously rotating, the PPI visual height-reading and appropriate lobe design.

Six GCI sets were operational by the end of 1940 but results were extremely disappointing in the early stages. The reason was only too clear. Whereas the coastal chain had been evolved before the war when there was time to rectify faults and train personnel, the GCI and AI sets were flung into the thick of the night battle. Equipment had to be made capable of operating under arduous conditions and RAF personnel trained as rapidly as possible. TRE was not defeated by the new problems; a team was formed under Dummer for the purpose of designing training devices. Thus the lesson was learnt that the scientists had to follow their devices into the field and maintain them until the RAF became proficient in their use. In time, this was to change the character of TRE which, instead of continuing to be a breeding ground of new ideas, found itself becoming mentor and maintainer of equipments for the RAF.

However, in the first half of 1941 the night fighters, if they cannot claim to have defeated the night bomber, were at least getting the measure of this threat. And if the battle had continued they might

H

have imposed an unacceptable rate of casualties. The figures for claims are indicative. In January, the night fighters claimed three aircraft to the guns' twelve; in February the fighters claimed four and the guns eight; by the end of March the fighters claimed twenty-two and the guns seventeen; the climax and the end of the battle came in May when the fighters claimed ninety-six and the guns thirty-one, ten were destroyed through other causes.[14] The interception successes were divided almost equally between the 'cat's eye' fighter and the GCI/AI fighter, but the latter obtained nearly twice as many contacts as the former, though they flew less than half the number of sorties. The GCI/AI technique of night fighting had undoubtedly proved itself.

(vii) Identification—Friend or Foe

Although the work involved in identification, Friend or Foe (IFF), did not achieve the same recognition as some of the other devices in the radar family, it was nonetheless indispensable to the prosecution of the air war. What happens when air operations begin? Formations of friendly aircraft are despatched to attack targets in enemy territory. At the same time the enemy air force strikes at targets in this country. Friendly bombers may be returning to base at the same time as the enemy is coming in to attack. Crews of anti-aircraft defences are itching to fire their weapons. Or an assault landing has taken place on an enemy coastline, and the troops in the beach-head are on the alert. How do they distinguish between enemy bombers seeking to attack them and friendly aircraft passing overhead? How are Allied aircraft to be identified? It requires little imagination to see the complexity of the problem.

The need for identification had arisen very early in the history of radar. In 1938, for instance, the Commander-in-Chief, Bomber Command, was so worried by the problem that he declared that unless it could be resolved he would oppose the introduction of radar and arrange for its development to be stopped. What was the use, he said, of being able to detect aircraft if, when the radar operator saw them on his screen, he was unable to tell to which side they belonged?

A special electronic device was therefore devised at Bawdsey by A. F. Wilkins and R. H. A. Carter, which enabled the radar operators to identify their targets with certainty. It was but a hasty improvisation, and in 1938, in response to the threat against radar by the Commander-in-Chief, Bomber Command, a crash programme was developed by D. H. Priest and R. W. Taylor. The outcome was the first operational identification system, devised by F. C. Williams, whom we have already met in connection with GCI, and this was used on exercises early in 1939. No sooner than this was done than an improvised version called IFF Mark II was put into production and installed in RAF aircraft at the beginning of the war. Each aircraft carried a set which periodically received one of the pulses from the radar chain and re-radiated a much more powerful pulse on the same frequency in response. This meant that the blip on the screen from the radar station was altered every few seconds. IFF Mark II worked in all the frequency bands then currently in use.

Such a system was satisfactory so long as all radar stations worked within a limited range of frequency. But the frequency spectrum used by radar began to increase and it became necessary to develop a special type of identification system independent of the main radar chain. Special interrogating transmitters had to be built and since these were necessarily in low power, a very much more sensitive type of IFF set had to be installed in aircraft. This new system was known as IFF Mark III and Dr. B. V. (later Lord) Bowden played a major part in its development. 'It was conceived', states the official historian in *Design and Development of Weapons*, 'from the outset as being comprehensive and universal, and was based on the principle of complete separation between the function of location—the true radar function—and that of identification, at the detecting station.'[15]

An important factor had to be taken into account—the possible entry of the United States into the war. The Tizard Mission had disclosed IFF Mark II to the Americans, and early in 1942 Bowden's team demonstrated the new Mark III, although still in the development stage, to a delegation of American Air Force officers in a monster programme of tests, involving ships and aircraft, at Pembroke Dock. Despite the lack of gear and the inexperience of the operators, the Americans adopted the system and it went into universal use.

So much for the bare bones of the story. There is also the human aspect which is extremely illuminating in the story of the evolution of scientific devices. For the problem of identifying friend from foe arose on the morning of 3 September 1939, when no sooner had

Neville Chamberlain, the Prime Minister, drily announced that Britain was at war with Germany than the air-raid sirens began to wail and the whole country went into hiding for half an hour. Few were told of the subsequent discovery that the warning came because a French aircraft had flown off course and had been identified as hostile. A week later several Blenheims were shot down over the Thames estuary while returning from a reconnaissance over the North Sea. Cases of mis-identification continued to arise. During the invasion of Sicily in July 1942, gliders carrying British and American paratroops were shot down into the sea. Even as late as 1944, during the landings at Normandy, fatal misunderstandings arose.

Tragedies such as these led to a great drive to install in all British aircraft IFF Mark III which, at its best, was extremely reliable. It was so good, in fact, that the air defence of Malta came to depend on it entirely and RAF, Malta, held a court of enquiry into any failure to identify a friendly aircraft.

Bowden recalls how the human problem of identification was borne home on him in a particularly poignant way. One Monday morning, about a week after he had been put in charge of the IFF work at Swanage, the Commander-in-Chief, Fighter Command, sent for him, 'He told me', writes Bowden, 'that on the previous Saturday night a Stirling, after bombing the Ruhr, had been shot up; it got lost and flew back over Bournemouth with its electrical gear out of action. It was misidentified as hostile and two Beaufighters went up to intercept it. One of them shot it down and was immediately afterwards itself shot down by the other Beaufighter. The Commander-in-Chief said to me, "You are in charge of this system, aren't you?" to which I replied "Yes, Sir" and he said, "What are you going to do about it?" And I think it was at that moment that for the first time in my life I realised the fundamental difference between science and engineering and between war and both of them.'[16]

A similar story but with a happier ending was told by Rowe. The pilots of two aircraft which had flown near one another were talking in the mess. One said, 'You were lucky, I nearly opened fire on you.' The other pilot said, 'You were luckier, I did.' A special system based on IFF Mark II was devised as a result, by which British night fighters could be identified and directed, but for intruding aircraft it was called 'Cockerel'. Meantime development of the new Mark III went urgently ahead. 'I think', recalls Bowden, 'the first contract which was signed in America was for 85,000 sets and I well remember going myself to discuss the problem of building them with Dr. Harold Wheeler of the Hazeldine Electronics Corporation. I tried to explain how to build them. He tried to prove to me conclusively that they wouldn't work ! They did.'

Precise equipment such as radar depends to a large degree on the way in which its is used and none more than IFF, particularly in the adequate maintenance of the equipment, both in the air and on the ground. Every component of the IFF system was vulnerable to inadequate maintenance because, obviously, everything had to work before the system was any use at all and no one person was responsible for more than one part of the system.

Furthermore, there were many who had, as Bowden says, 'metaphysical objections to the idea of identification and feared that the enemy would inevitably equip himself with airborne sets which would disguise him completely. They therefore mistrusted the whole thing and it was necessary to overrule their objections to its use.' However, with the winning of Allied air superiority towards the end of the war in Europe, the problem of identification became less urgent and it became reasonable to assume that almost anything that was flying was an Allied aircraft.

In the Pacific theatre of war, IFF Mark III played a fundamental role and the American Navy depended on it to a remarkable degree.

Throughout these evolutionary stages, the scientists were forever straining at the limits of the possible. They had to make use of the best valves which were already in existence. Measuring apparatus was developed which, at the time, they did not really understand themselves and they were compelled to use equipment which they neither understood nor knew how to control. 'We could not allow', says Bowden, 'the best to become the enemy of the good and we had to provide the RAF with something to be going on with at almost any cost.' This was a characteristic feature of wartime scientific work which had been noted before; highly-finished apparatus was no good if it arrived too late. IFF was vital in the destruction of enemy bombers in the German night offensive against this country, but it was probably more important in the Pacific than anywhere else. It was also much maligned and when badly maintained was ineffective. The whole history of IFF confirms Winston Churchill's statement that new techniques of war are often more important when they are first introduced and least efficient.

Chapter 7

Radar and Radio in Attack: Bombing Accuracy

(i) The First Radio Navigational Aid—Gee

Before the war, trained bomber crews were, in theory, supposed to go ahead of the main force and drop flares while those following up only had to bomb the visible markers. In the late twenties, Rowe asked Wing Cdr. (later Marshal of the Royal Air Force Lord) Tedder how the leading bomber aircraft were supposed to find their targets. His reply made a deep impression on Rowe, confirming the latter's worst fears : it was simply : 'You tell me.'[1] Priority was given to systems providing early warning and defence against air attack, because the deficiencies of the RAF in this respect were foreseen. But Bomber Command did not realise its deficiencies and the advice of the Committee for the Scientific Survey of Air Offence was not asked for, nor was it followed, if offered. The creation of a favourable climate of opinion for an invention is often harder than making the actual device. When, during the early months of the war, daylight bombing operations became prohibitive because of the casualties suffered, the bomber force was compelled to operate by night. The deficiencies of navigation and target location now became even more apparent. Still, the aid of the scientists was not invoked.

Not until the summer of 1941 was the relative ineffectiveness of Bomber Command's attacks on Europe established after a visit by Lord Cherwell to the Central Photographic Interpretation Unit at Medmenham. Whilst there, he inspected a considerable number of photographs taken during operational missions and was appalled to note that a high proportion of bombs seemed to have fallen in green pastures. A more systematic analysis carried out by the new Operational Research Section at Bomber Command confirmed Cherwell's observations and established, for instance, that from May 1940 to May 1941, 49 per cent of all bombs fell in open country and that, typically, on a raid on 15/16 May 1940, only twenty-four out of

126

ninety-six aircraft could establish that they had even located the target.

Even so, in 1940 some senior RAF officers, in particular Air Marshal Joubert, were apprehensive, not only about the relative ineffectiveness of Bomber Command's attacks, but also about the bomber losses resulting from poor navigation back to base. At one of the TRE 'Sunday Soviets' that June, Watson-Watt was present and, remembering that in 1937 one of his staff had made a proposal which might now prove helpful, suggested that he should also be called in. He was Robert J. Dippy, who, prior to 1936, had been employed for two years in the Research Laboratories of GEC at Wembley in developing time base circuits for television equipment. This expertise he continued to develop at Bawdsey in the cause of radar.

One evening, during the pre-war Bawdsey era, Dippy visited a cinema in Ipswich and, the film proving tedious, cogitated on television problems. He had been interested by a recent press article on the difficulty experienced by pilots when approaching airports in bad weather. He realised that if an aircraft carried a cathode-ray tube on which the time base was initiated by a radio pulse transmitted from one side of the airfield, then the distance along the time base of a pulse received from the other side of the airfield would be a function of its position relative to the sides of the airfield, provided that the two transmitters operated in a prescribed succession.[2]

On returning home from the cinema, Dippy wrote up his idea and shortly afterwards submitted it to Watson-Watt who, however, felt the defensive problem to be so urgent that effort could not be spared therefrom to develop Dippy's scheme. Watson-Watt[3] has since expressed his apologies for the delay in bringing Dippy's idea 'out of the ice-box' but still doubts if its earlier development, at the expense of defensive systems, would have been prudent. Rowe[4] did not then know of the Dippy proposal. However, on taking over the Bawdsey team from Watson-Watt in 1938, he asked them to put forward ideas for radar in the offensive, but the only response came from E. G. Bowen with his 1½-metre proposal. Rowe wrote to Watson-Watt at the Air Ministry urging that 50 per cent of their effort should be devoted to the offensive. There was no reply.

Other British scientists had submitted not dissimilar proposals, and there is a German patent for a system essentially the same in principle but operating with continuous wave (CW) transmission instead of with pulses. Yet none of these suggestions matured, presumably because the environment was neither favourable nor demanding.

Following the meeting in June 1940, Dippy formulated a system which would not only operate at a greater range than first intended but would also provide an aircraft with its position relative not just to one line but to a pattern of lines forming a grid. The system became known as G (for grid) and subsequently as 'Gee', and was based on the following principle.

If two separate fixed transmitters transmit pulses simultaneously, then a receiver which receives the two pulses simultaneously must be on the right bisector of the line joining the two transmitters, as in the original approach aid conceived idly in the cinema. For a specified time interval between the reception of the two pulses, the receiver must be on one of two hyperbolae, one on each side of the bisector, and if the two pulses can each be identified, the ambiguity between the two hyperbolae may be resolved. A different time interval will prescribe another pair of hyperbolae and so a family of confocal hyperbolae may be prescribed. (See Fig. 1 full lines generated by Tx's 1 + 2.)

A second pair of fixed transmitters can similarly generate a second family of hyperbolae and the two overlapping families will constitute a grid in which, however, the 'squares' will be trapezoidal. Such families of hyperbolae may be superimposed upon a map so that

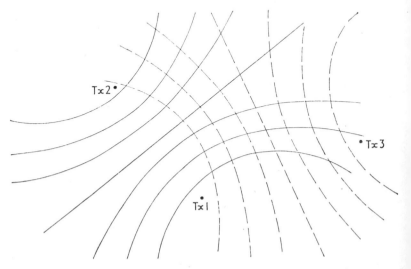

Fig 1   Diagram of 'Gee' System

hyperbolic grid references may be converted into fixed points relative to the ground. One of each pair of fixed transmitters can be made common, working with each of the other two in turn. Fig. 1 shows a second set of hyperbolae generated by transmitters 1 and 3.

Two particular features of the system contributed to its success. One, in response to a challenge from W. B. Lewis, and concerning the time base control, rendered the system less susceptible to jamming, and the other enabled an accurate determination of the measurements to be made at leisure, following the instantaneous setting of the controls (rather as in shooting the sun with a sextant).

The accuracy of the system is a function of the distance between the ground stations and at the maximum range, eg, covering the Ruhr, was of the order of a few miles. Nevertheless, the effectiveness of Bomber Command was rapidly improved by Gee, while its increased accuracy at short range over the United Kingdom proved a welcome homing aid to returning bombers, often in poor weather conditions, and especially when damaged aircraft limping home urgently wanted to land.

In June 1940, as already recorded, the need for better navigational aids for Bomber Command was unofficially discussed with the scientists and Dippy was authorised to elaborate his ideas. The need for greater accuracy was firmly established during the subsequent months by the analysis of bombing results derived from Lord Cherwell's observations, and in May 1941 an operational requirement was tabled.

Henceforward developments proceeded very rapidly. In August 1941, service trials with twelve handmade sets installed in Wellington aircraft took place, followed in the same month by operational trials. From the latter, however, one aircraft failed to return and, as it might have fallen into enemy hands and its secrets revealed, further operations were postponed until a larger bomber force had been equipped.

On 8 March 1942, operational use of Gee recommenced using production equipment based on the experimental sets designed for the service trials. Eighty Gee-equipped aircraft led a force of 270 other bombers against Essen using the eastern chain of ground stations—other chains were being set up by then—sited to give cover over Holland and the Ruhr.

Not surprisingly, after five months' operation of Gee, the enemy was jamming the system to such an extent that it was restricted to short ranges and was no longer usable over Germany. Some circuit modifications to the Gee receivers were expeditiously adopted, affording a temporary respite, but further countermeasures ensued and it was not until an improved set, incorporating a diversity of radio-frequency channels, became available that Gee took on a further substantial lease of operational life.

Nevertheless, throughout its total existence (subsequent chains of ground stations were set up to cover the Western Approaches and the English Channel and used by Coastal Command and ships of the Royal Navy) Gee proved to be an important aid as supplementary to other systems (see the next section on 'Oboe') and, in its own right, was an invaluable aid in returning to base where, of course, the jamming was ineffective.

Gee then, represents an invention conceived out of time, but born and nurtured in an environment in which it rapidly developed and flourished. The need found the invention awaiting it, unlike some other cases when the demand provoked the invention. One of its triumphs was on 6 June 1944 (the landings in Normandy); its use by ships and aircraft during the poor visibility of those critical hours gave rise to the suggestion that D-Day should instead be called G-Day.

It has been said[5] that Dippy, whose health later suffered, was frustrated by official indifference and that this led to his ill health. Dippy denies this, asserting that Bomber Command was at all times keenly interested and that he was constantly amazed by the manner in which potential difficulties were smoothed over. Certainly Dippy drove himself so hard in the 1940-41 period that when an extremely bad attack of chicken-pox was followed some months later by three successive attacks of influenza, his resistance broke down and he withdrew temporarily from the technical scene.

We know that since the Gee system depends on the careful measurement of time differences, the inherent accuracy of the system is limited. F. C. Williams was also present at the TRE meeting in June 1940. Among the many fertile ideas that derived from this ingenious scientist was a scheme, tabled shortly after the meeting but not taken up at the time, which became known as 'H'. In this an aircraft would transmit pulses of radio energy which would be received by two ground stations and re-radiated in an amplified form. These re-radiated pulses would be received by the aircraft which, by use of a time base, would be able to measure the time taken for the pulses to accomplish the double journey. From a knowledge of the velocity of radio waves, the distance of the aircraft from each of the two re-radiating ground stations could be measured. Such a system was inherently more accurate than Gee since it measured times of transit, ie, range, and not differences in times of transit.

However, the H scheme was not adopted at the time for two main reasons. As the aircraft had to transmit, it revealed its radio presence over enemy territory. A hostile fighter equipped with a suitable radio receiver could therefore home on to the transmitting bomber. This reservation later applied to other radio systems used by bombers and thus came to be no longer over-riding.

The H system also required that a large number of aircraft should interrogate the ground based re-radiators (beacons) simultaneously and this posed technical problems not immediately solvable. For these reasons, the 'passive' Gee system was initially preferred, though H was subsequently developed and proved to be an important weapon in the radio armoury.

(ii) Oboe—The Most Accurate Bombing Aid

When, in the autumn of 1940, the Germans launched their night offensive on Britain it was discovered that the raids were led by pathfinder aircraft fitted with special radio equipment to enable the pilot to fly along a radial radio beam from a transmitter in enemy controlled territory, so aligned that it would take him over the target. From other beamed transmission across this track the pilot could calculate his ground speed and determine when to release his bombs.

The setting up of these beams required great accuracy and had to be undertaken in advance of the raid. The RAF were therefore able to determine the position of the beams and in many cases hurriedly to redeploy the anti-aircraft defences and, later, to employ sophisticated radio techniques which gave false signals to the German raid leaders without the pilots being aware that their radio system was in any way being interfered with.

The relation of all this to 'Oboe' lies in the fact that the squadron chosen to 'plot' the position of the German beams was the Blind Approach Technical and Development Unit based on Boscombe Down near Salisbury. It was re-named the Wireless Investigation Development Unit (WIDU) and undertook other tasks in addition to enemy beam determination.

One of the X-*Gerat* beam transmitters was located on the Cherbourg peninsula and the WIDU made a number of sorties in an effort
to bomb it. The technique was to fly the aircraft along the beam
towards its source until it ran into a cone of silence vertically above
the transmitter. On proceeding in the same direction beyond the
transmitter, another 'back' beam was detected and from careful
timing measurements an estimate of the mid point of the cone of
silence, ie, the transmitter, could be made. A very careful navigational manœuvre was executed so calculated to bring the aircraft over
the transmitter after a certain time, when bombs were released. Such
techniques, perhaps not surprisingly despite the carefully executed
manœuvres, proved abortive and the transmitters remained live.

The assistance of TRE which was already working closely with
WIDU in support of their monitoring functions, was now sought in
the hope that radar techniques might be used to determine the
ground speed and range of the aircraft and so enable a bomb release
point to be calculated and transmitted to the aircraft. Accordingly,
a radio beacon was installed in the aircraft and interrogated by a
radar station at Worth Matravers. Range and ground speed were
measured and a bomb release point calculated but, alas, without
success. The abortive exercise, however, inspired a few of the TRE
staff to ponder the possibility of a system which would be independent of German beams and which could be directed over any target.

Some CHL aerials had been designed to determine the azimuth
of a reflecting target with great precision as described on page 105
and this system was now used to guide an aircraft along such a
predetermined radial direction. If the aircraft strayed off course, it
was automatically detected and an audio-modulated signal transmitted to the pilot on another channel—dots, if on one side, dashes,
if on the other—to enable him to correct his track. The system was
known as the 'Howler-Chaser', but one of the scientists considered
the tone generated was not unlike that of an oboe and this latter
name stuck, though the system which ultimately bore it was very
different from that which was so christened.

The Howler-Chaser, of course, provided only directional information to the aircraft. At the same time, experiments were being conducted to determine the accuracy of radar range measurement.
Aircraft were flown over easily recognisable features, such as the end
of Boscombe Pier, Bournemouth, the navigator signalling by radio
when he was vertically above the feature so that a radar operator

might determine the range of the aircraft from the radar at that precise moment. These flights were necessarily conducted at low level and therefore at short range but a consistency of eighty-five yards was easily achieved with ill-adapted equipment and, since range determination by radar techniques is inherently capable of quite precise measurement, a comparable consistency and improved performance might be attained at greater ranges with specially designed equipment.

TRE collaborated with WIDU on this problem, though on low priority during the end of 1940 and the beginning of 1941. It was, of course, in early 1941 that the relative ineffectiveness of Bomber Command's efforts became conspicuous.

At that time, Alec H. Reeves, who some few months earlier had joined TRE from the Standard Telephone organisation, began to turn his attention to the problem of offence. Reeves was a dreamer. On entering his office one would find him leaning back in his chair with his feet on the table and a faraway look in his eyes. 'I never ceased', wrote Rowe, 'to be amused at the time it took him to bring his thoughts back to an awareness that he was not alone.' Reeves was already an expert in pulse techniques, having filed a number of patents for pulse communication modulation (PCM) techniques which were not fulfilled until after the war when, with the development of the transistor and its economic use as a fast switch, PCM techniques were exploited. It is but recently—the mid-1960s—that Reeves' pre-war work has been publicly recognised on both sides of the Atlantic.

Reeves reviewed the current work with the Howler-Chaser and F. C. Williams' proposed H system. The use of three radio channels in the former system—for directional information, for range determination, and for communication with the aircraft—he condemned as exposing the system to a threefold threat from enemy radio countermeasures, and the H system, he considered, would introduce too great a complication in the necessary aircraft equipment for immediate solution. He wanted to win 'this war, not the next'. In so far as H was subsequently developed and used operationally in conjunction with Gee, his criticism proved invalid.

In a paper written about May 1941, Reeves proposed a system which had something in common with Dippy's Gee. Two ground transmitters, interlocked by a land line, would send out pulses so related in time as, when simultaneously received by an aircraft, would define a single hyperbola, approximating at long range to an asymptotic straight line, lying over the target. A bomber aircraft slightly to one or other side of the hyperbola would receive the pulses non-synchronously and this condition could be electronically detected and converted into an aural output of the form common to beam-trained pilots.

One of the ground stations would utilise its pulse train in conjunction with a pulse repeater in the bomber to determine range and ground speed and would transmit a bomb release signal on the same pulse channel (shades of PCM !). Naturally, Reeves discussed these ideas with officers from WIDU and, in particular, with one of their number, Sqdn. Ldr. H. E. Bufton.

Bufton made two important comments on Reeves' proposal. In the first place he believed that to fly a bomber from the British coast in what was virtually a straight line all the way to the target was merely inviting attack; in the second place, he pointed out that in configurations where the angle subtended at the target by the two ground stations was appreciably less than a right angle (and this would invariably be the case) the direction of greatest error in positioning the aircraft would be in a direction parallel to the line joining the two ground stations. To the extent that this error could be absorbed by dropping a stick of bombs along this direction, Bufton's criticism pointed to a direction of flight at right angles to that proposed by Reeves. Indeed, both comments pointed in this direction and accordingly Reeves gave the matter further thought.

A comparatively easy compromise could, he suggested, be effected by arranging for the aircraft to fly at constant range from one of the two ground stations. When one aircraft departed from this circular track it could automatically be sent signals proportional to the departure again, a presentation common to pilots trained in beam flying. At Reeves' insistence, the modulation transmitted to the pilot made use of the same radio link as was used for range measurement.

The second ground station could now, assuming the aircraft to be on the prescribed circular track, operate quite independently and measure range and ground speed to determine the point of release of bombs. (See Fig. 2).

In May 1941 a team of scientists at TRE was set up under Reeves who had as his right-hand man, Dr. F. E. Jones, and it must be stated emphatically that the success of the scheme thereafter depended on the combination of these two very forceful personalities. There was at this time little confidence in the scheme beyond TRE and WIDU, especially as Reeves coupled with it, even in these early days, certain ambitious extensions of capability.

It was of utmost importance, therefore, that a demonstration be arranged, and to this end two CHL radar stations, one at Worth Matravers and one at West Prawle, in Devon, were taken over and modified. At the same time aircraft were equipped with modest additional equipment though not, it should be noted, aircraft from

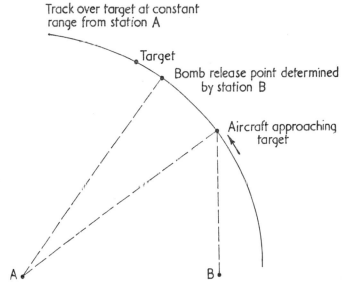

Fig 2   Diagram of 'Oboe' System

TRE's experimental unit. The beam-flying technique was so specialised that its commanding officer would have nothing to do with the demonstration. Fortunately Air Commodore (later Air Vice-Marshal) O. G. Lywood, under whose control lay the WIDU, agreed that his aircraft might be used and so the link established between Reeves' Oboe team and Bufton and his men was maintained.[6]

A programme of flights over a camera obscura located at South Cerney, near Cirencester, was arranged, the aircraft's track being controlled by the Dorset ground station. At the moment when the aircraft was judged by the Devon ground station to be vertically above the camera, a signal was communicated to the navigator of the aircraft who caused a 'flash' bulb in the bomb bay of the aircraft to be energised. The operators of the camera obscura plotted not only this flash but the track of each aircraft run, and an inspection of the record proved most impressive in the consistency with which all the tracks and flashes were superimposed one on another.

So successful and impressive were these experiments that it was decided to mount bombing trials, first on a range at Stormy Down, near Porthcawl, and later, on a range near Pwllheli. At a distance of 110 miles from the control stations, aircraft flying at 6,000 feet dropped bombs within an average of forty-five yards of an arbitrary point on the bombing range. On some days the bombing runs were carried out above cloud and the range operators could scarcely believe their eyes when the bomb explosion splashes continued to appear in exactly the same area as when the sky was clear.

These trials were impressive although mounted with hurriedly contrived equipment primarily designed for other purposes. This equipment operated on a wavelength of about $1\frac{1}{2}$ metres and it was appreciated that a wavelength such as this would easily be jammed by the enemy were it to be employed in any operational system. The availability of equipment within this waveband certainly enabled these demonstrations and trials to be staged, but Reeves and Jones always intended that any operational system would employ rather more sophisticated techniques on the newly developed wavelengths of about ten centimetres and, in parallel with the trials, the design of such equipment went on.

Striking though the bombing trials had been, many service and civilian officials were highly critical of the Oboe systems propounded by Reeves. They pointed to the limitations of the demonstrated system. Only one aircraft could be controlled at a time by each pair of ground stations and each aircraft required a ten-minute run-in to establish the required track; thus a maximum of four to six aircraft per hour could attack a target. The straight and level run in would, it was said, render each aircraft an easy target to anti-aircraft guns and enemy fighters. Reeves countered these criticisms by pointing out that, with the accuracy achievable, a very few aircraft could wipe out a small and critical target and that in later stages of development a single pair of ground stations suitably equipped could, with multiple control positions, simultaneously direct up to twenty aircraft.

One high-ranking official in the Ministry of Aircraft Production wrote : 'I regret having to do this, but I am sure it is time to say quite bluntly that these disquisitions from TRE on Oboe are becoming ridiculous. If they came as inventions from the outside public, and not from official sources, they would be rejected without hesitation.

'I see with grave concern that TRE now proposes to incorporate Gee with Oboe.* I repeat now, even more strongly, that it would be disastrous to permit the protagonists of this fantastic Oboe the chance of causing a sensible and practical system like Gee to share the disrepute into which Oboe, even if raised to Mark XX, will inevitably fall.

'If I had the power, I would discover the man responsible for this latest Oboe effort and sack him, so that he could no longer waste not only his time and effort, but ours also, by his vain imaginings.'

This letter was passed by its recipient, a deputy director in the Ministry of Aircraft Production, to Rowe, with the laconic note : 'I gather from the above that . . . . is inclined to doubt the value of Oboe.'

Others, however, had confidence in Reeves and these included Bufton, whose opinion as an operational pilot of great skill Reeves valued highly. Another was Rowe, who drafted more staff to support Reeves. Criticism, such as that contained in the letter quoted, only served to spur him on to prove his points.

The operational range of a system such as Oboe would be limited to little more than line of sight, so that even with high-flying aircraft—say at 30,00 feet—a range of only 250 miles would be obtainable. This meant that aircraft directed from British-based ground stations would be able to strike at the Ruhr and its vital industrial targets, and with the accuracy of which Oboe's protagonists were so confident, a worthwhile destructive effort might, they claimed, be achieved. Reeves had, meanwhile, already conceived a scheme whereby the range of the system could be extended to 600 miles by flying 'repeater' aircraft along a portion of the path between each ground station and the bomber, relaying pulses from the ground station to the bomber and the returning pulses from the bomber back to the ground station. Suffice it to say that although, later on, a ground station at South Shields was specially commissioned in

* This refers to a proposal, adopted operationally, to use Gee to navigate to a suitable point some ten minutes' flying time from the target and adjacent to the Oboe track.

order to stage such a repeater operation and a repeater aircraft specially fitted, only one operation was carried out.

Towards the end of 1941 a new requirement arose which, though it delayed the development of Oboe by absorbing many of the staff engaged upon it, served to defeat some of the critics and so accelerated the official requirement for its use.

That autumn the German warships *Scharnhorst* and *Gneisenau* were undergoing repairs in Brest. The harbour was heavily fortified and the ships so docked that low-level airborne attacks were difficult and dangerous to carry out. High-level attack by night was thought to offer a greater chance of success, provided there was an effective system of control.

A Lorenz-type beam transmitter was set up at Helston, in Cornwall, and oriented so as to lay its beam over Brest. Aircraft from a Stirling squadron in Bomber Command were fitted with special receivers to interpret the beam signals, and pilots, trained in beam flying, drafted into the squadron. A CHL station in Cornwall was specially equipped to determine the range and ground speed of the aircraft, each of which was fitted with a special transponder.

Over thirty sorties were made during December 1941 and January 1942 without loss, even though each flight involved the aircraft flying straight and level at 17,000 feet over one of the most heavily defended strips of land in the world. This achievement, which incidentally inflicted some, though not crippling, damage to the two warships, served to confound the critics of Oboe who had alleged that the straight and level run-in would be suicidal.

However, the need for high-flying aircraft, primarily to achieve the required range and also to increase the immunity from anti-aircraft attack, still remained. A pressurised version of the Wellington aircraft—the Mark VI—was under development and one of the early models was installed with the $1\frac{1}{2}$-metre Oboe equipment. Its performance as an aircraft was never entirely satisfactory, and after the crash of a Wellington severe limitations were imposed on its high-level performance.

Dr. B. G. Dickins and G. A. Roberts, civilian scientists in charge of the Operational Research Section of Bomber Command, conceived the idea of using the new light Mosquito aircraft to carry and drop target-marking flares which would then provide aiming points for the heavier bomber force with their greater bomb loads. These flares were contained in bomb shells which exploded at a relatively low altitude and ejected self-igniting flares which further descended on parachutes. During this last phase they were necessarily subjected to wind drift, but it was considered that subsequent Oboe-controlled Mosquitos would drop fresh markers at the correct point so that the effect of wind drift would be corrected from time to time.

Such a proposal would be heresy to Reeves and his team; that the phenomenal accuracy of which Oboe was capable was to be so discarded was repulsive in the extreme; it was rather like using a micrometer to crack nuts. Reeves clearly recalls a walk on the Malvern Hills with Roberts when the latter, anticipating Reeves' instinctive dislike of such a proposal, tactfully and warily broached the subject, pointing out that the combination of the high-flying light Mosquito bomber with a target-marking capability might prove a more fruitful application of Oboe than any alternative, and Reeves was persuaded.

The early days of 1942 were spent in equipping Mosquitos and training pilots, in mounting ground stations on the east coast, and in training technical staff and operational controllers, for the Air Ministry had decided that the 1½-metre system should be brought into operation even though its life would be short on account of the ease with which the enemy would be able to jam the system.

Not everyone in the Air Ministry was convinced of the wisdom of employing Mosquito aircraft on Oboe and, following a meeting, the commander of No 109 Squadron (formed from the former WIDU) was given a week in which to carry out a trial installation and flight test of an Oboe-equipped Mosquito. The squadron engineer officer with his staff, and with assistance from TRE scientists, worked solidly for six days to complete the installation, only to find that the seventh day's weather prohibited any flying. Nevertheless, the squadron commander, so great was his faith in the system, reported back to the Air Ministry that test flights had, in fact, been successfully carried out—a modern equivalent of the story of Nelson turning his blind eye to the signal at the battle of Copenhagen.

One fundamental problem still remained. The latitude and longitude of surveyed sites for the ground stations in Britain were easily ascertained, but the co-ordinates of targets on the Continent were available only from French and German maps which were drawn up in a different geodetic reference framework from that of the British counterparts. Calculated distances between a British ground station and a Continental target were subject to a small but un-

known error. Some cross-check had been provided by a Capt.
Brown who, from the cliffs of Dover, had accurately determined
from the firing flashes the bearings of German cross-Channel guns.
The location of the these guns relative to the French maps was
obtainable from other sources. The extrapolation of this data to the
Continental hinterland was naturally subject to error and so it
became necessary to carry out an Oboe calibration exercise.*

On the night of 20 December 1942, the first Oboe sorties were
carried out over enemy territory using small bombs to attack a
German army headquarters in Belgium. Within forty-eight hours
the positions of all the bombs which had exploded (some, it was
discovered after the war, had not) were available to the Oboe
controllers and a small correction factor was subsequently introduced
into range calculations. The following night four Oboe aircraft hit
the Krupps works at Essen, and on Christmas Eve a successful attack
was made on a power station in Cologne.

Oboe was first used for target marking in March 1943 and the
story of its subsequent success prior to and following the invasion of
Europe, which was followed up by mobile Oboe ground stations, has
been told elsewhere. In the course of nearly three years, the losses of
Oboe aircraft were less than 0·2 per cent of sorties.

The 1½-metre system lasted much longer than anyone had the
right to expect, and the improved system employing the 10-centi-
metre waveband and several other sophisticated features were available long before the death knell of the original system had been
sounded. Indeed, when enemy countermeasures were first experienced, Reeves immediately began work to enable the system to
employ twin pulses and corresponding 'latched' receivers; modifications were quickly introduced and the life of the early demonstration
equipment prolonged.

This is no place in which to record the contributions made by so
many others, the Americans, for instance, to the sophistication and
perfection of the technicalities of Oboe. But without the inventive
genius of Reeves, backed by the forceful development urge provided
by F. E. Jones, Oboe would almost certainly have never come to
light. Rowe has said : 'I sometimes think that none but Reeves would
have evolved Oboe.'

In the case of Gee, we saw that an operational requirement

* It is worth noting that the accuracy of Oboe was such that discrepan-
cies in the geodetic grid were revealed.

created an environment in which an earlier idea was encouraged to develop and flourish. With Oboe, the same need for a more accurate, offensive use of Bomber Command drew from the scientists new ideas which, with the critical assessment and enthusiastic support injected by an operational pilot, took a quite new form uniquely adapted to the need. Reeves has also said, 'The man who made Oboe work (as distinct from getting Oboe made) was Bufton.' The original proposals were ambitious and were subject to much criticism. The advent of the right aircraft, the Mosquito,—to be used in a different role from that originally foreseen, a target-marker rather than a carrier of a heavy bomb load—proved to be an important feature of the operational system, though it may remain an open question as to whether the effectiveness of the Mosquito with its light bomb load dropped on small key targets might not have been greater than the mass area raids on towns and cities, led by pathfinders and marked by Oboe-guided flares.

(iii) H_2S—A Self-contained Airborne Bombing and Navigational Aid

The exposure in 1941 of the relative weakness of Bomber Command's attacks on the Continent brought forth, as we have seen, both Gee and Oboe. These systems, however, depended on a link between aircraft and ground stations based in Britain and their operational range was limited to little more than line of sight—only to the fringes of western Germany. True, with the Allied invasion of Europe, ground transmitters were established on the Continent and the effectiveness of the system extended further east, but in 1941 no such forward bases were available.

What was needed was some accurate navigational system, self-sufficient within each aircraft, so that the crew could determine their position independently of their home base.

Those attending a 'Sunday Soviet' at TRE in October 1941 dispersed sadly, without discovering a single promising idea; though no one, it would appear, seems to have recalled some interesting observations made by E. G. Bowen in 1937.[7]

Following the development of ground-based early warning radar in the pre-war Orfordness and Bawdsey days, Air Interception sets of smaller power and dimensions were developed, suitable for airborne installation so that fighter aircraft flying by night and in restricted visibility might detect enemy raiders and give chase. We have already seen that ground echoes imposed a limitation on the use of the equipment, since enemy raiders could only be detected at ranges less than the height of the fighter above ground. During flight trials of this equipment, which operated on wavelengths of 7 metres and, later, of 1½ metres, Bowen had observed that he could discriminate between radar echoes from agricultural and from urban terrain. Indeed, he made good use of his observations in identifying echoes from Harwich and used them as a navigational aid when crossing the coast line and returning to the nearby airfield. A difference between radar echoes from land and from sea had already been observed but this new phenomenon was much less marked and might well have escaped the notice of a less perceptive observer.

Bowen was anxious that this phenomenon of discrimination between different types of terrain should be investigated further and in a note,[8] he recommended that : 'To do this work effectively, different equipment would be necessary, working on a *longer* wavelength.' An exact analysis of the phenomenon, available only subsequently, reveals that its magnitude is a function of radio wavelength and would be more pronounced at *shorter* and not longer wavelengths. The emphasis on the more pressing defence role at that time precluded an immediate investigation and it may well be that Bowen's recommendation of a longer wavelength deterred others at the October 1941 Soviet from reviving Bowen's work.

At the meeting was Dee. He and his colleague Skinner were using centimetric wavelengths for developing more effective AI sets in order to remove the limitation imposed by the downward 'spill' of energy towards the ground which we have already discussed. At these shorter wavelengths, the energy could be more efficiently directed with aerial systems easily accommodated within the nose of an aircraft. The use of these new wavelengths would bestow an immense advantage upon the Allied forces because the enemy would be unlikely to detect the radiation and even if he did detect it would be unable to jam it.

Dee and Skinner, with others, had installed experimental centimetric AI sets in a few aircraft and were experimenting with duplicate equipment in the Leeson House stables at Langton Matravers, some 250 feet above and overlooking Swanage Bay. Dee recalled that he was able to detect ships moving in the waters between Swanage and the Isle of Wight and the Needles under conditions not dissimilar from an aircraft looking forward and downward at surface targets ahead. The element of luck was present here in that the site chosen for research happened to be the right one and enabled a town to be 'seen' as from the air. Dee immediately arranged for the aerial system in one of his experimental Blenheim aircraft to be slightly depressed so that instead of 'looking' directly ahead, it would 'look' slightly downwards. On 1 November 1941, a trial flight was made and a clearly discriminated radar echo from Southampton was obtained. Subsequent flights at 8,000 feet revealed clear echoes from towns thirty-five miles ahead. When the still wet photographic prints of the radar display were placed before Rowe, he remarked, 'This is the turning point of the war.'[9]

Alan Hodgkin suggested that the aerial should scan from side to side and that the polar diagram should be arranged to be wide in elevation and narrow in azimuth; these changes greatly enhanced the use of the set by making it less critically dependent on the direction of flight of the aircraft.

At this stage Lovell was charged with the development of the system based on these principles, which came to be known as H_2S.

The aerial eventually took the form of a paraboloid mounted in a transparent perspex blister below the fuselage and which could be rotated round a vertical axis; a circular area of ground below and about the aircraft was thereby illuminated by a sweeping sector of radiation. (Fig 3, page 144)

The invention of the Plan Position Indicator, described earlier, enabled a map to be traced on the cathode-ray tube which, in so far as different types of terrain were concerned, could be compared with an ordinary map and the aircraft's position determined in relation to identifiable features on the ground such as towns, lakes or rivers.

Echoes from the ground immediately below the aircraft are, of course, the first to return to the aircraft and the time base is not initiated until that moment. The adjustment needed to achieve this is an accurate measure of the height of the aircraft above the ground beneath—another valuable feature of the system.

Under Lovell, development proceeded and an equipment was installed in a Halifax aircraft and flown towards the end of March 1942. The programme, however, suffered a severe set-back that July when half the H_2S research team perished when their aircraft crashed. Included among those lost from this team was A. D. Blumlein of EMI, a pre-war pioneer of television techniques whose contribution to H_2S was proving invaluable. The loss of such experienced men and the almost unique installation in the crashed aircraft undoubtedly delayed development.

Meanwhile the promising results achieved in early flights had attracted the attention of Lord Cherwell and, through him, Churchill. The programme accordingly enjoyed a high priority. Even so, a number of factors, not primarily of a technical nature, delayed development and this was very frustrating to those whose confidence was spurring them to tireless efforts.

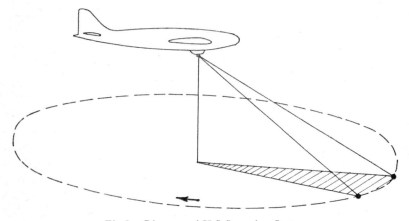

Fig 3   Diagram of H_2S Scanning System

The Americans began to develop a similar system but quickly gave it up. They were, it must be remembered, protagonists of daytime formation bombing techniques using visual methods, and although they ultimately adopted Gee, Oboe and H_2S, they were not in the first place keen on any non-visual aid. Valuable time was wasted by British scientists in identifying the reasons for the marked discrepancy between results achieved on the two sides of the Atlantic and the lack of American confidence at this time was seized on by some RAF officers prejudiced against techniques which threatened to supplant the normal visual methods of bombing.

Another factor which delayed development arose when Cherwell insisted that H_2S was necessary only in the final stages of a bombing mission in order to identify the target and aim the bombs. He therefore maintained that the low-power microwave generator, the klystron, was sufficient. He did not appreciate that a device which only worked for ten minutes might just as likely not work at all. Cherwell's recommendation was readily acceptable to those who argued that while the klystron could be destroyed if the aircraft crashed or seemed likely to fall into enemy hands—indeed, it was fitted with a detonator which would operate on impact in a crash or at the control of the aircrew—the magnetron with its metal anode block would not be so easily disposed of. Repeated attempts with various forms of explosive failed to destroy details of the construction of the magnetron and of the wavelength on which it operated.

The magnetron, we know, was of vital importance to the Allied cause. To make a gift of such significance to the enemy might well tip the scales against Allied victory and there were many who opposed its operational use beyond the shores of Britain—an argument used, as we shall see, for the delay of other devices.

In 1942, on instructions from Headquarters, Bomber Command, Air Vice-Marshal D. C. T. Bennett, the newly-appointed commander of the Pathfinder Force, spent several days at TRE's airfield at Defford, flying with a number of experimental H_2S sets. He was dissatisfied with the klystron equipment which normally only gave a useful range of ten miles and very much less when the aircraft was taking evasive action against enemy searchlights, radar-controlled guns and night fighters. On the other hand, ranges of twenty to thirty miles were obtainable with magnetron-equipped sets and the resulting echoes were sufficiently intense to be useful even when the aircraft was taking evasive action. In conditions of steady flight the information provided by ground echoes from some 3,000 square miles was invaluable to the navigator, and aircrew soon became confident in navigating long distances from base to the target area and back, since the usefulness of the equipment was not merely confined to the target area itself.

Eventually, before the end of 1942, on account of the force of Bennett's recommendations, the decision was made to proceed with the magnetron equipment.

Another factor which hindered the development of H_2S arose from its use over the sea as well as over the land. There was, indeed, a pressing need for a navigational and bombing aid to enable the offensive to be pressed beyond the ranges of Gee and Oboe. At the same time, as we know, the effectiveness of Coastal Command's attacks on surfaced submarines in the Atlantic was decreasing because the enemy was using a listening device which

enabled submarines to submerge before being sighted. The availability of ASV on a new and, to the enemy, unknown and probably
undetectable wavelength would, it was expected, restore the
supremacy of the command.

Clearly the same principles are involved in distinguishing built-up
areas from open country as in detecting surface vessels on the sea.
There are, however, subtle details concerned primarily with the
aerial design and configuration which are not altogether recon-
cilable within one standard equipment, and the conflicting priorities
proved to be a source of some delay in the production of sufficient
numbers to play an important part in either role.

Nevertheless these difficulties were sufficiently overcome to enable
a force of thirteen H_2S-equipped aircraft to lead a raid on Hamburg
on 31 December 1942 in appalling weather conditions and to mark
the target sufficiently well for a strong follow-up force to inflict
heavy damage on the city. Raids as far afield as Turin followed in
due course.

By mid-1943, the U-boat menace in the Atlantic had been contained by the use of H_2S/ASV installed in Coastal Command
aircraft fitted with Leigh lights.

The relatively few H_2S sets available to the RAF required, as
with Oboe, their use being confined in the early days to pathfinding aircraft which marked the target with flares. Out of 53,000
sorties in 1943, over 32,000 were led by H_2S-equipped aircraft and
20,000 by Oboe.

There was some doubt over the value of H_2S in 1944 when it
was alleged that enemy fighters were equipped to home on to the
H_2S transmitters. Limitations were imposed on the use of the equipment and the set earned in some quarters of Bomber Command
an undeservedly poor reputation. Aircrews were superstitious and
the enemy might have exploited their apprehensions. Dee personally went the round of squadrons and scotched the rumour.

H_2S was, of course, only practicable with the advent of centimetric radar and it was Dee who, while developing an improved
AI set, saw its possibilities. Bowen's early observations are of interest
in retrospect, but Watson-Watt has said that it 'cannot be claimed
that (they) led at all directly to the ultimate triumph of H_2S but
they were certainly pioneer observations of differences which
could only be adequately exploited and explored by the very fine
moving pencil of H_2S.'[10]

(iv) Radio Countermeasures

Radio countermeasures have two objectives: first to jam the enemy's early warning radar or his radar-controlled anti-aircraft defences and, secondly, to prevent or distort the passage of information and instructions over his fighter control system. The ultimate object is to keep down bomber losses to an acceptable level. In the early days of the war radio countermeasures did not rate very high on the priority list of scientific research. The Air Ministry was reluctant to start a jamming war for fear of retaliation. When the RAF began to go over to the offensive, the need for jamming the German radar, or for making 'spoofs', and feint attacks, became more apparent. One of the earliest attempts at a radio countermeasure was in 1940/41 when bomber crews believed (in fact, erroneously) that by switching on their IFF sets they embarrassed the German radar-controlled searchlights.

It was essential for the prosecution of radio countermeasures to obtain technical details of the enemy's radio and radar installations. This, for instance, required the capture of the German apparatus known as *Würzburg*, used to control anti-aircraft fire, and was the object of the successful Commando raid on the radar station at Bruneval on 27 February 1942. The technical details once understood, it was possible to discover how the defence system was organised and operated. This daring raid, in which a member of TRE —D. H. Preist—took part, has been described in other books. In particular, the work done by photographic reconnaissance was very important. But perhaps not enough has been made of the German reaction. They at once realised that their radar would henceforward be subject to jamming and decided to change the wavelength of every radar station from the northernmost part of Norway to North Africa and made them capable of frequency variation—an exceptionally difficult task.[11]

In 1942 RAF Fighter Command used a radio countermeasure called 'Moonshine', in which a few decoy aircraft simulated a large force of aircraft to the enemy radar chain. Apart from creating geographical diversions, this device could be employed to get enemy fighters into the air at the wrong time.

By 1944 a host of airborne jamming devices were in operation known by such unlikely names as 'Mandrel', 'Airborne Cigar', 'Fidget', 'Boozer', 'Tinsel', 'Monica' and so on. A special group in

Bomber Command was formed to operate them. Each device had a separate task : to jam radar-controlled guns and searchlights, or air interception equipment or radio-telephone broadcasts, or to give warning of the approach of night fighters.* Perhaps the best known of them was the most simple—'Window', the name given to resonant strips of tin foil dropped from aircraft and which were designed to throw into confusion radars controlling anti-aircraft guns and searchlight, and later, one of the German airborne interception equipments. The growth of the idea of Window is especially relevant to the theme of this book.

It has already been observed that the development of a particular device usually stimulates the growth of countermeasures. At the same time it may happen that a new invention is so zealously fostered that research on countermeasures may be discouraged, or even suppressed, in order to give the device the appearance of being insuperable. The development of radar is a case in point.

In 1935, R. V. Jones, now Professor of Natural Philosophy at Aberdeen University, and who had been a student of Lindemann, was researching at the Clarendon Laboratory, Oxford, into the infra-red spectrum of the sun. Although the Tizard Committee had rejected infra-red in favour of radar, Lindemann insisted that trials to discover whether infra-red was worth developing should take place; the committee agreed and Jones became responsible for the work. The trials, in fact, merely confirmed tests made by Dr. A. B. Wood, nine years earlier, that the amount of infra-red from the exhaust gases of an aircraft engine was inadequate for detection purposes. Nevertheless Jones, surprisingly enough, was asked to develop an airborne infra-red detector and he joined the Air Ministry as a scientific officer, though continuing to work at the Clarendon. After a visit to Bawdsey in June 1937, it occurred to him that the radar chain, even on a clear night, might be as impotent as infra-red if dipoles, or reflectors, were sown *en masse* over the North Sea : 'trying to detect an aircraft flying through (them) would be like trying to see through a smoke screen.[12]

* The lavish use of these devices defeated their object and the enemy night fighters found it easy to home on to the radio transmissions. This was one of the reasons for the heavy casualties of Bomber Command in the spring of 1944. Eventually Bomber Command was persuaded that one of the best counter-measures to the enemy defences was radio silence. The loss of the enemy's early warning system after the invasion was another important factor in the reduction of casualties.

That autumn Lindemann told Jones that an attempt was being made to stop the work on infra-red. Jones was convinced that this was a mistake and emphasised the vulnerability of radar to jamming. Lindemann was so impressed by his argument that, some time in 1938, he asked Churchill to raise the matter at a meeting of the Air Defence Research Sub-Committee of the Committee of Imperial Defence, of which the latter was a member. Churchill did so and while Tizard and Watson-Watt agreed that radar could be disrupted in this way, they were clearly reluctant to embark on trials to prove it.

Radar was then in its infancy and some in the know were sceptical of its possibilities. Consequently those who were most closely concerned with its development found it hard to admit that countermeasures might rob radar of its accuracy. It was just 'not done' to suggest that radar would, on occasion, not work.* Rowe, however, took a more realistic view, and when he took charge at Bawdsey in succession to Watson-Watt his main worry was that the coastal chain would be rendered useless by deliberate jamming. Aware that it was the antithesis of the scientific attitude, but nevertheless of the essence of war, he gave one of his staff (E. C. Williams) the job of trying to jam radar stations by flying up and down the coast using special equipment.

Nothing further was done to develop the idea of Window until June 1940, when a system was being sought which would 'bend' or disrupt the radio beams which were guiding German night bombers to targets in the Midlands. Lindemann recalled the idea of sowing dipoles though now it was as a possible means of throwing the German bombers off target by dropping the strips to one side of them. He discussed it with Jones who was now working in Scientific Intelligence in the Air Ministry. The idea of upsetting the German radio signals was brought up at several meetings of the Radio Countermeasures Committee but was found to be impracticable.

Nevertheless, early in 1941, Lindemann, using his great authority, succeeded in obtaining trials in which dipoles were dropped to produce false echoes in radar, and they worked. By that autumn more attention, as we have seen, was being paid to the effectiveness of the bomber offensive against Germany. On 5 September, the Radio Operational Research Officer at Headquarters, Bomber

* It is of interest to remember that the Americans decided to have a separate laboratory for radio countermeasures.

Command, (the Operational Research Section had not yet been formed) pointed out to Watson-Watt, then Director of Communications Development at the Air Ministry, that the enemy radar used for searchlights and anti-aircraft guns operated on a wavelength of 53 centimetres and might therefore be countered if each aircraft carried bundles of aluminium strips 26 centimetres long which would be thrown out when near the ground defences. He asked that experiments should be carried out without delay. In the meantime Jones had produced a report which stated that the German radar could be obliterated 'either by deliberate jamming or by sowing a dense field of spurious reflectors.'

Another scientist who appreciated the importance of radio countermeasures and who later became principally responsible for their development was Dr. R. (later Sir Robert) Cockburn, who had recently come to TRE from Farnborough. He convinced Rowe of the urgency for starting research on problems involved in conducting a radio war. Rowe told him to form a radio countermeasures group. Dramatic point was given to Cockburn's argument a few weeks later when the German battleships *Scharnhorst* and *Gneisenau* escaped from Brest up the Channel. A major factor contributing to their success was the intensive jamming of the British radar screen along the south coast.

The circumstances in which the name 'Window' was chosen were fortuitous. Before submitting a code name to the appropriate branch of the Ministry of Aircraft Production, Cockburn came to Rowe with a proposal for a name that had some relevance to its purpose. Rowe asked him : 'Cockburn, why try to be clever about a code name?' Then looking round the room, he said : 'Why not call it Window?', this being the first thing his eyes lighted on; the tin foil strips forever after became known by this name. At the end of 1941, it was proposed that metal-backed propaganda leaflets should be dropped, thus serving two purposes. Fortunately this scheme was never put into effect, for the Germans would have discovered in a few days what was afoot. Apart from this, the sheets were too large, which meant that the number of bundles which an aircraft could carry was strictly limited.

Tests continued during the early months of 1942 and that April the Chiefs of Staff agreed that Window should be introduced. By this time, however, Lord Cherwell had entirely reversed his opinion about Window and believed that the aircraft interception equipments of night fighters would be jammed if German bombers used it over this country. These views were shared by the Commander-in-Chief, Fighter Command, Air Marshal Sir Sholto Douglas. Cherwell's volte-face would appear to have stemmed from his friend, Derek Jackson, who had not only been a distinguished Professor of Spectroscopy at Oxford but had also ridden in the Grand National and recently had became one of the two outstanding AI observers in the night-fighter force. On the principle that one who had so successfully accounted for a number of enemy bombers would be the appropriate man to deal with ways in which the air defences could be neutralised, at the request of Cherwell, Jackson was put in charge of the operational trials of Window.

On the other hand, the principle of Window was no longer a secret to aircrews and it even inspired a cartoon which appeared in the *Daily Mirror*. Despite attempts to sow rumours that Window was a failure it was unlikely that the Germans would remain long in the dark. Thus the main reason for not using Window seemed to be invalid and this became even more apparent at the end of October when Jones issued a report which showed that it was almost certain that the Germans knew about Window, and presumably they had not used it because they knew they stood to lose by it. Tizard, like Jones, now believed that there was no reason why Window should not be introduced. The trials demanded by Cherwell went ahead and proved that the ground-controlled interception equipment and the aircraft interception apparatus were easily jammed by Window. The following proposals were then submitted to the Chief of Air Staff : enough Window should be manufactured to swamp the German radar system thereby making the radar control of guns, searchlights and night fighters impossible; at the same time British night fighters should be fitted with the new American centimetric radar as rapidly as possible, thereby making them proof against Window. These proposals were approved by the Chief of Air Staff.

Experiments went ahead during that summer primarily with the object of discovering the effect of Window on the British air defences and, secondly, of deciding the best method of distributing Window by Bomber Command. They were carried out by the Air Defence Research and Development Establishment and TRE. On 4 November a meeting was called by the Chief of Air Staff to discuss the next phase. Curiously enough, the Operational Research

Section of Bomber Command was not over-enthusiastic about Window, partly because it believed it would have to be restricted to jamming radar controlling the anti-aircraft guns; secondly, because it thought Window might interfere with H_2S; and, thirdly, because it anticipated that the new tail-warning device called 'Monica' would provide greater benefits to the protection of bombers than Window.* These views were represented at the conference by Harris's deputy, Air Vice-Marshal Saundby. Fighter Command continued to oppose the scheme and Window was therefore again postponed for another six months, during which time trials and countermeasures against the enemy's use of Window were to continue. Only Jones, who held that the depleted German bomber force was too heavily committed on the Eastern Front to be a menace to Britain, was in favour of the immediate use of Window. Cherwell continued to favour the anti-Window faction and before one meeting when, according to Jones who had been giving his opinion, 'as I was leaving his room (Cherwell) fired a parting shot : "If you go into the meeting and say that, you'll find Tizard and me united against you". I could not help saying, "If I've achieved that, by God I've achieved something"—and even the Prof chuckled.'

Fresh calculations were now made to find out the amount of Window that would need to be used for jamming. Estimates were made by Jackson of Fighter Command and by Jones. Dickins of Bomber Command Operational Research Section examined the two estimates judicially and decided on a release rate which not only promised success but which also could be maintained by the bomber crews. Portal called the next meeting on 2 April 1943 to decide whether or not to introduce Window. As it was now considered practicable to drop Window all along the bombers' route, Dickins was much more enthusiastic about the scheme and he told Harris, who was to attend the meeting, that 'there is now a good possibility of saving one-third of our losses on German targets by using this countermeasure. The Command has nothing to lose and possibly much to gain by using it.'

The fears of Fighter Command were also somewhat allayed on account of the fact that the new centimetric radar, proof against Window, was being installed in their night fighters. Nevertheless

* The Operational Research Section at Bomber Command did not get on with TRE and there was no love lost between the two organisations.

Page 153 : (*above*) A Bailey bridge across Caen Canal, July 1944 : (*below*) aerial system for Wireless Set No 10

Page 154 : (*above*) A Flail Tank in action; (*below*) a DUKW amphibious
vehicle.

the meeting revealed that the country's aluminium supplies would be unable to meet the drain if Window were used, while the automatic Window launcher would take another eighteen months before it was ready for service. A member of the bomber crew would have to perform this task for the time being. In spite of these handicaps the meeting agreed to recommend that Window should be introduced on 1 May. Measures were taken to speed up Window production and to ensure that the strips were the correct size. The production of launchers was also hastened.

But the introduction of this device was still further delayed. The Chiefs of Staff now agreed that Window should not be used until after the invasion of Sicily. Cherwell, although at last realising that it was time Window was used, advised Churchill not to let its introduction harm Allied plans in the Mediterranean. 'Meanwhile', state the official historians of the Strategic Air Offensive, 'British bomber losses between 1 April and 14 July 1943 amounted to 858 aircraft. German bomber losses in the same period were, it seemed, twenty-seven aircraft. It appeared to Sir Charles Portal that if Window had been used in these months, Bomber Command might have saved 230 bombers and crews and the Germans might have saved sixteen.[13]

Yet another conference was necessary. This was held on 15 July and was attended by the Prime Minister, Portal and Herbert Morrison, who was reponsible for civil defence. The Chiefs of Staff provided figures for the bombers which might still have been flying if Window had been introduced that April. Morrison, with Watson-Watt's backing, believed it to be his duty to oppose Window and wanted German bomber bases to be attacked. Portal then exposed the deficiencies of aircraft in the depleted German bomber force. At last, Churchill took the matter into his own hands. Jones, who was acting as Portal's expert witness, had the satisfaction of being in at the end of the argument. 'I felt', he has written, 'that it had almost been worth the intervening struggles to hear Winston say "Open the Window".'

The Sicily landings safely accomplished, Window was used for the first time on the night 24/25 July in a major attack on Hamburg. The effects of the device went beyond expectation. General Galland has told how the defences based on radar were utterly confused. The air situation was, he declared, 'veiled in a fog.'[14] A German radar operator said excitedly, 'They are coming in thousands.' At Headquarters, Bomber Command, the operational research scientists calculated that in the first raids in which Window was used losses were reduced by rather more than one-third, thus confirming the forecast of the previous September.

Window, supported by other radio countermeasures, became an integral part of the bomber offensive. Perhaps one of the most successful feint operations took place early on D-Day, 6 June 1944, and this will be described on page 228. Meanwhile the technique of Window-dropping improved and methods of launching it and accelerating its production became the responsibility of a special Window Panel under Jackson. Altogether some twenty million pounds of Window were dropped over Europe and the development of counters against this simple device occupied many of Germany's best scientists.

The fears of German retaliation with their own brand of Window proved groundless. They did use it (known as *Düppel*)* over England during the winter of 1943/44 but it was largely ineffective; they fared no better with it in the Mediterranean theatre. In any case the German bomber force, as Air Ministry Intelligence insisted, was spent. It is of interest to note that the same arguments that had been expounded at British conferences were also used by the Germans for and against the use of *Düppel*. Goering, in particular, forbade the idea to be mentioned and papers relating to it were withdrawn from circulation.

What lessons are there to be learned from the sad story of Window? Firstly, that between 1937 and 1940 several of those most closely connected with radar, were, probably for emotional reasons, able to suppress any attempts at testing the idea. It might be argued, as Jones has pointed out, that this was justified by events and that it was more important to persuade the Air Staff that radar *would* work than that it could be upset. At the same time none of those who knew about Window and wanted it tried out was in a position to do anything about it. Then there was the ambivalent attitude of Cherwell who, although stimulating trials in the first place, was against using it, almost up to the last moment. Finally, too much attention was paid to the possibility of German retaliation which, in the event, proved to be minimal because of the size of their bomber force.

* *Düppel* is equivalent to jamming.

PART FOUR

THE WAR ON LAND

Chapter 8

Air Defence

The Army, by the very nature of its role in the inter-war years, was the least technical of the three services. It was the last of the three to acquire a director of scientific research and even when one was appointed in 1938, the creation of the Ministry of Supply the following year absorbed all the scientific establishments working for the Army. This created a gulf between user and scientist which it was frequently difficult to bridge in the war years.

Responsibility for technical equipment, as opposed to weapons, lay, until the creation of the Ministry of Supply, with the Royal Engineer and Signals Board. All its members were service officers. In 1934 the Director of Mechanisation (an appointment created in 1927) took over its direction and administration. The board was divided into three committees responsible for field engineering equipment, air defence and signals respectively. From 1937, committees on radar and camouflage were added. Each committee was served by a civilian scientific establishment—the Experimental Bridging Establishment at Christchurch, Hampshire; the Air Defence Experimental Establishment at Biggin Hill and the Signals Experimental Establishment on Woolwich Common. The scientists, although closely connected with the activities of the board, had no say or status in Army affairs, and Rowe recalls how astounded he was, when serving on the Sound Locator sub-committee of the board, at the humble and subservient manner of the head of one of the scientific establishments.

(i) The Tachymetric System of Fire Control*

The speed of a modern aircraft made automatic and continuous tracking essential in order to determine its future position. An anti-

* Fire control and the development of proximity fuses were equally the concern of the Royal Navy but for the sake of convenience are discussed in this Part.

aircraft gunner needs to know two facts : the future position of his target and the time of arrival of the shell at the target. Estimation of the future position of an aircraft is the job of the predictor. There were, between the wars, two systems of prediction by mechanical methods based, of course, on the use of optical instruments : the tachymetric system in which a speedometer of some kind is used to discover the vertical or lateral angular velocity and which is multiplied by the time of flight; and the goniographic method which is either based on a measurement or an estimate of the *ground* speed and angle of *course*, or is based on the air speed and the angle of *orientation*.

By the end of the First World War, when anti-aircraft gunfire was notoriously wild, a primitive predictor known as the Brocq (after a French inventor), operating on the tachymetric system, was in use. During the early 1930s the Vickers mechanical predictor, working on the goniographic system, ie, providing course and speed, came into service. When the Army began to rearm a few years later, it was decided to buy, in addition, the Sperry predictor from the United States. This instrument controlled the heavy (3·7 and 4·5 inch) anti-aircraft guns.

Prior to this, a group of scientists had begun to work on naval fire-control problems at the Admiralty Research Laboratory at Teddington. At that time in the twenties, electronics were in a comparatively elementary state and consequently the fire-control group, under J. M. Ford, appreciated that it would take time before an all-electric predictor could perform adequately. In June 1927, Ford devised an hydraulic transmission system—probably the most advanced form of automatic control then in existence. It was known as the ARL Type B oil unit. This magslip (magnetic slip-ring indicator) method of transmission was soon used extensively for controlling guns and searchlights.

From 1920 the War Office had appointed a liaison officer to keep in touch with developments in optics, predictors and rangefinders at the Admiralty Research Laboratory. Holding this appointment in 1935 was Major (later Colonel) A. V. Kerrison, a gunner officer. He had studied mathematics under the astronomer and mathematician, Professor H. C. K. Plummer, FRS, at the Military College of Science, then at Woolwich. He was not only inventive, but became a good scientific team leader. Incidentally, he was also an outstanding Association footballer. Kerrison had been interested in the mathematical aspect of prediction for a number of a years and, before his appointment at Teddington, had written a paper for the Royal Artillery Committee in which he advocated the use of a curved course predictor using a tachymetric solution. As we have seen, the predictors currently in use estimated a target's speed and course. Kerrison's design measured the angular rates of change of the target's position in the sky and computed the future position of the target at the end of the time of flight of the shell. This predictor produced the right answer even when the aircraft was flying on a curved course. As the Army was being equipped with Vickers and Sperry predictors, no effort was available for the development of such an instrument and, although models were built at the laboratory to test Kerrison's principles, further research was stopped.

Kerrison, however, had the opportunity to apply his mathematical system of remote control when, early in 1937, the War Office, then searching for a light anti-aircraft gun, decided to purchase the Swedish 40-millimetre Bofors. Kerrison took charge of a team at the Admiralty Research Laboratory. Their task was to develop a predictor for the Bofors which would operate in conjunction with Ford's hydraulic transmission system. Thus the predictor, which only weighed 500 lb and was portable, could be set up away from the disturbing vibration and shock of the gun, and its computed angles transmitted electrically to gears on the gun which automatically elevated and traversed the gun on the target.

In the autumn of 1938 successful firing trials using the predictor were carried out. The predictor gave increased accuracy, and enabled the number of men operating locator, predictor and gun substantially to be reduced. Kerrison, when senior officers came to watch firing trials, demonstrated the effectiveness of remote control by ordering the guns to bow on their arrival.

Full-scale production of the predictor (known as No 3 Predictor) now began and became all the more urgent on account of the Munich crisis in September 1938. The revolutionary advances in electronics during and since the war make it difficult to appreciate the value of this instrument. In due course a licence was obtained to manufacture Bofors guns in this country, but only a small number were in the hands of regular and territorial units by the outbreak of war. The gun was intended to protect vital points against close-range air attack. It played an important part in the Battle of Britain and in the sieges of Tobruk and Malta. Later it was used to good effect in the battle against the flying-bombs.

Meanwhile the work of the fire-control group at Teddington had expanded and in 1938 took over the development of predictors for the Army. By 1943 the Admiralty Gunnery Establishment was formed and Kerrison, who had by then retired from the Army, became the superintendent. Kerrison also designed an anti-aircraft prediction system for the Royal Navy. This instrument, which involved the use of three-dimensional cams, never reached a sufficiently advanced stage to demonstrate to the Director of Naval Ordnance its superiority to the current system of fire control then fitted to naval vessels. One reason for the decision to stop work on it was the difficulty of producing three-dimensional cams; British manufacturers were consequently not keen to develop them. But another, and perhaps more significant, reason was the Navy's support of 'hose-pipe' methods of fire against aircraft, as opposed to predicted fire. Kerrison, who would have made a fine civilian scientist, believed fervently in his method and, not afraid to speak out, became involved in many a heated argument with senior naval officers. On one occasion before the war he was supported by Winston Churchill who, while watching an extravagant barrage put up by naval gunners at a demonstration, remarked : 'The Navy always travels first class.'[1] Nor was the Army exempt from this attitude. Kerrison recalls his disagreement with General Sir Frederick Pile, Commander-in-Chief, Anti-Aircraft Command, during the heavy raids on London when there was a clamour for volume of fire as opposed to predicted rounds. (At night, tracer provided guidance for the predictor.)

The Tizard Mission took Kerrison's design to the United States in August 1940, and in due course a Bofors gun and its predictor were shipped to Canada, later arriving at Fort Monroe, the US Army base. The Americans decided to adopt the Kerrison predictor for their 37-millimetre and 40-millimetre anti-aircraft guns. According to the American official history,[2] engineers were unable to obtain from the British any drawings of the control system and had to take the predictor to pieces, measure each gear, and then make about 600 drawings before production could begin. This was entrusted to the Singer Manufacturing Company in New Jersey and a special factory was built for the task. Production began in February 1942 after a number of trial models had been made, and by 1944, when work was stopped on account of Allied air supremacy, the factory had produced about 23,000 predictors—more than any other predictor for the US Army.

The Tizard Mission also advised the Americans to develop an electrical predictor, and within six weeks scientists had worked out specifications for a 90-millimetre electrical predictor to operate in conjunction with a radar set. A year later the first model was ready for testing and it became a standard equipment nineteen months after the inception of the idea. As many of the M9's components were standard commercial apparatus it was, although mathematically intricate, easier to manufacture than the mechanical predictor it superseded.* A few of these predictors were developed for British use as the No 10 predictor.

General Pile declared that: 'Of all our equipment, the Kerrison predictor was one of the most potentially useful and accurate instruments. It entailed no guesses on the part of operators (except an initial one of range) and produced a mathematically correct answer if its three operators only did their duty. Theoretically, it should have been ten times more efficient than shooting by sight. In practice, owing to human frailties, it was perhaps twice as effective.'[3] Its development is a good example of one man's persistence in following through an idea. A colleague, Mr. N. H. A. Warren, has written of Kerrison: 'Much teamwork was essential but without the driving force of the enthusiast (his) work would have been ineffective, because it would not have got beyond the screen of bureaucracy surrounding the services. Kerrison was successful in leading a team of engineers to produce effective equipment for the services . . . Modern defence equipment in common with civil projects is now so complicated that it requires a large team for its successful development and many different kinds of skill are required so that the above comments do not apply.'[4]

Previously the only reliable means of locating aircraft had been by the naked eye assisted by the telescope. The provision of radar to fulfil this task was a revolutionary step forward and we must now study its early development.

(ii) Radar for Laying Anti-Aircraft Guns

Radar for anti-aircraft guns was not an essential factor in the defence of Britain but later, in its more sophisticated forms, it did

* It was, in fact, the first electrical computer.

much to increase the accuracy of the guns and economise in expenditure of ammunition.

The anti-aircraft gunner must be able to pick up and identify the bomber in poor visibility and at night. He then needs to know its height, speed, course and bearing. This information must then be fed into the predictor in order to lay the gun. The more continuous the information, the more likely the chances of hitting the target. Extreme accuracy of range, measured to within feet of the aircraft, and angles to within minutes of arc, are required.

The work on acoustic equipment at Biggin Hill, which was under the direction of Dr. W. S. Tucker, has already been described on page 93. Until the discovery of radar there appeared to be no alternative system of detection. However, one of the duties of the Royal Engineer and Signals Board was, as already explained, to keep in touch with contemporary scientific developments and on 4 July 1935 the Director of Mechanisation, Major-Gen. A. Brough, accompanied by Col. Worlledge, the Signals member, visited Watson-Watt at the Radio Research Station at Slough. (Worlledge, it will be recalled, knew Watson-Watt from his service in Egypt.) The object of their visit was to discover whether radar could be used for directing anti-aircraft fire on unseen targets.

The early work on radar had to be, and was, shrouded in secrecy. In February 1935 it appears that radar-aided guns and searchlights had been discussed by Watson-Watt and Rowe but the General Staff seems to have been unaware of the Tizard Committee which had been in existence since the beginning of that year. There was no Army representation on this committee. General Pile has put on record that there was too much secrecy over the development of radar or, alternatively, that the Army was not 'adequately or efficiently represented on the various scientific committees.'[5] However, Brough and Worlledge reported favourably on what they had been told at Slough.

The visit to Slough was the first recognition by the War Office of radar's existence, but, in fact, the possibilities of long-range detection by radio waves had already been appreciated as early as January 1931 by two members of the Signals Experimental Establishment—W. A. S. Butement and P. E. Pollard.

Butement, whose work on radar detection of low-flying aircraft was described in Chapter 5, was born in Australia and came to England in the twenties to study physics, chemistry and mathematics at University College, London. After doing some post-graduate research, he joined the Signals Experimental Establishment as a junior scientific officer. In due course, as we shall see, he was to become responsible for the research, design and development of the principal wireless sets for the Army, before going to Bawdsey to work on Army radar, and later to the Air Defence Experimental Establishment where he was responsible for designing the proximity fuse for shells. He has recently retired from being Chief Scientist of Australian Defence Scientific Research and Development; during this time he made notable contributions to guided missile projects. Butement was a versatile and energetic scientist, and a colleague has spoken of the respect with which he was regarded. He used to expound on many subjects, including religion and medicine, outside his chosen sphere, and Watson-Watt has written that at Bawdsey he 'availed himself freely of the privilege of working at any hour of the night or day without permission from anyone.'

'Pollard and I', writes Butement, 'discussed the possibility of detecting ships for the improvement of coastal defence gun batteries. We considered that the greatly-increased sensitivity of receivers at that time made it possible to detect very small radio signals, and that enough energy would be reflected from a ship to allow detection, if a powerful transmitter were available. We concluded that to conserve power and to give an indication of bearing at least good enough to allow a searchlight to be "put on", we would need to use a beam of radio waves and hence, to keep the aerial system compact, a very high frequency. We therefore set out to develop a transmitter operating at some power on the highest frequency we thought then practicable. We chose a wavelength of 50 centimetres. For our source of power we contemplated the use of the Barkhausen and Kurz principle (first used in 1921) in which a high voltage is applied to the grid of a triode while the anode is kept at a low voltage. We contemplated using the Fitzeau method of measuring range. Fitzeau many years earlier had used pulses of light of equal mark/space ratio, and so arranged a system of rotating shutters that his reception could be blocked at various discrete shutter speeds because the light reflected back from a mirror arrived after the shutter had moved from "open" to "closed" '. We planned to apply this principle of equal mark/space pulses for the range measurement.

'We wrote a very brief (too brief in retrospect) note to the Royal Engineer and Signals Board, but were informed that "there was no War Office requirement" for such equipment. We were, however, allowed to work in our own spare time in the evenings, and to draw from the general stores such apparatus as could be found there.'

Butement and Pollard then constructed a pulsed radio transmitter with which it was possible to measure range. 'In due course we got the apparatus working . . . and found at once that we could obtain reflections from the base of a mast in the centre of the Establishment compound on Woolwich Common. This was perhaps nine inches in diameter. We then set up an ordinary sheet of galvanised corrugated roofing iron, measuring about six feet by two feet, as a target and were delighted to be able to detect this at a range of 100 yards or more.

'We then informed the War Office of our experiments, inviting them to witness a demonstration. We were again informed that "there was no War Office requirement". We persisted, as we felt justified in doing; we then were able only to state it as our opinion that the range of scaled-up equipment on a ship would be enough to justify its adoption. In due course, perhaps as a result of our persistence, perhaps as an unconnected event, our partnership was broken, Pollard being posted to the Air Defence Experimental Establishment.

'Details of our work were sent to other establishments, but it is impossible to say on any evidence available to me that it had any direct bearing upon the radar work which started four years later as a result of the efforts of Watson-Watt, Wilkins, and others.'[6]

Seven years later, Butement found himself at Bawdsey working on coast defence radar, but this time there *was* a War Office requirement.

In October 1936, a small cell of Army scientists was established under Dr. E. T. (later Sir Edward) Paris at Bawdsey to work on applications of radar (or 'Cuckoo' as the Army called it)* to anti-aircraft gunnery and coastal defence. Very close collaboration between the Air Ministry and War Office teams soon existed. In

---

* 'Cuckoo' because of its onomatopoeic qualities which resembled the working of radar—*Cuck* (transmission of wave), *Koo* (the responding echo).

addition to Paris and Butement, the first members of the cell were H. S. Young, a physicist, who, before going to Biggin Hill, had worked at the Admiralty Research Laboratory, and who was also a gunner in the Territorial Army and therefore appreciated the practical problems of gunnery, and Pollard.

The War Office had at last begun to follow up the possibilities offered by radar. But much opposition came from the Director of the Biggin Hill establishment, Dr. Tucker who, as radar became increasingly apparent as being the quickest and most accurate form of aircraft detection, entrenched himself the more firmly behind his belief in the superior powers of acoustic means of detection. When he asked Rowe if it were true that ranges of twenty miles were being obtained by radar and the latter agreed that this was so, he said : 'You have confirmed my worst fears.'

From the end of 1936 the growth of German air power caused the Bawdsey staff to give up their weekends to work. By September 1937 experimental models had been made for a gun-laying set working on a six-metre wavelength. Accuracy to within twenty-five yards had been achieved in good conditions. However, the height-finding capability was much less satisfactory.

By the spring of 1938 the War Office cell had a GL set ready for production and that August the War Office accepted radar as a practical and essential aid to anti-aircraft operations. Production by Metropolitan Vickers and A. C. Cossor now began in conditions of great secrecy. Even at this early stage the possibilities of short-wave radar had been foreseen as the ultimate solution to the anti-aircraft problem and limited experiments were in progress to determine its accuracy.

Much time had to be spent on trials of the equipment and it is interesting to compare this with the development of the successful American short-wave radar—the SCR 584—in which sufficient faith was shown for it to go into large-scale production without the usual time-consuming peacetime schedule of prototypes and trials. Unlike the RAF radar equipment, which could easily be replaced, or the naval sets which could be maintained while at sea, the army sets were required to be very sturdy. This was necessary in order to prevent the line of communication from being congested with expensive spare parts. The GL sets also had to operate in extremes of temperature—in the damp heat of jungles, or in the Russian winter. The story is told of the Russian operators in subzero conditions lighting a fire under a GL II set, fortunately without upsetting its operational efficiency.*

Another factor which presented difficulties was the training of crews to operate the equipment, as Anti-Aircraft Command was destined to be a reservoir of manpower for the Field Force. Officers and technicians were constantly transferred to overseas units almost as soon as they had been trained.

More serious was the scepticism with which the scientist and his mysterious equipment was received. Although the artillery was one of the technical arms of the Army, the scientific and technical knowledge of the average officer was limited, for until then his equipment had not required a very high standard of technical skill. Furthermore, the intense secrecy which surrounded the early radar sets did not help to speed the process of education.

By the end of 1939 a total of fifty-nine GL sets had been delivered to units and was increased to 344 during 1940. This figure may sound impressive but in reality the sets were far from reliable. To some extent this was overcome by the ingenuity of L. H. Bedford, a skilled radio engineer and chief designer of A. C. Cossor—one of the few people outside government service initiated into the secret of radar. Not merely restricting himself to technical problems, he went on to analyse the GL set's performance as a whole. He appreciated that there were two major limitations. One, as we have seen already, was the inability of the set to register height and, secondly, the irregularities of the ground in the vicinity of the aerials caused serious errors. For the first limitation Bedford modified a height finder, which had originally been developed at Bawdsey for the Home Chain, to be used with the GL1 and, secondly, he recommended that wire netting should be spread over the ground from which uniform echoes would be reflected. As a result of Bedford's proposals about fifty GL sets were fitted with the attachment in time for the night 'blitz' on Britain during the winter of 1940/41, while practically the entire stock of wire netting in the country was purchased and laid round the GL sets.

Apart from their inaccuracy, the early 6-metre GL sets could be jammed and they were affected by ground echoes from the sur-

* Technologically, the Russians at this time were far behind the Western Allies. Their radar system was virtually non-existent; and they did not permit British personnel to service equipment sent to them.

rounding countryside. They were too large to be dug into the ground and, consequently, were very vulnerable. The War Office was therefore advised by the Ministry of Supply, in August 1940, to develop a centimetre set for anti-aircraft guns. A small team of War Office scientists under Pollard joined Oliphant at Birmingham University where the work on the magnetron was in progress. The work on centimetric gunlaying sets was later transferred to the British Thomson-Houston Company's research establishment at Rugby.

Centimetric radar for the Army, both British and Canadian, should have arrived much earlier than it did. Fortunately this did not matter with the gradual winning of air superiority, achieved in mid-1944, by the Allied air forces. We saw that a division had been created between the military user and the scientist after the formation of the Ministry of Supply. Later, the Ministry of Aircraft Production became responsible for a substantial part of army radar, but there was no single body which was responsible for army radar as a whole. In this respect the War Office was worse off in comparison with the Admiralty, which had its own signals establishment, and the Air Ministry which maintained close liaison with the Ministry of Aircraft Production. Furthermore, there was no equivalent of the TRE 'Sunday Soviets' at which the operational, administrative, scientific and technical sides could meet on an equal footing and exchange views.

It remains to assess the achievement of anti-aircraft radar. Although the General Staff missed an early opportunity to develop radar, when its possibilities had been proved by another service, they pursued the idea. On the whole, greater resistance to new ideas was met at a lower level where there was a lack of appreciation of what scientists could do. The need for a short-wave set was early recognised, but time was short and the Army's scientific effort, which was small, concentrated on devising a set which would simply provide range. It must not be forgotten that the GL sets had to be far more accurate than the RAF early-warning sets. In spite of criticism from the gunners, they reduced the area of search required for the visual sighting of aircraft and they saved the gun crews from many hours of exhausting stand-tos. Searchlights, hitherto wavering beams clumsily probing the night sky, also, in due course, became radar-controlled and worked in close co-ordination with the night fighters. In 1940, 20,000 rounds were required to bring down a raider and in the spring of 1941 this had been reduced to 4,000 rounds.

The development of centimetric radar (GL III set) for the anti-aircraft guns was not as rapid as it should have been. Cockcroft believed that about six months were wasted because of the false start on its design and another six months were lost because of indecisive policy and failure to place orders promptly. One reason for this was the wide gap between scientist and user. Nevertheless, as the gun radar improved, the number of rounds required to bring down an enemy bomber was reduced. Watson-Watt reckoned that one radar-aided gun was worth at least five which were without this benefit.[7] The outstanding triumph of Anti-Aircraft Command was the part it played—and it was in the end the major part—in the battle against the flying-bomb. This was due to the fact that the latter flew at constant heights, direction and speed which piloted aircraft did not. At last continuous following of the target was possible using the American SCR 584 set and the electrical M 9 predictor in combination with the proximity fuse. Radar had, in the end, solved the hitherto insoluble anti-aircraft defence problem. 'It provided', as Major-General Sir Edward Clarke, Director-General of Artillery, was able to write after the war, 'the means of locating and tracking aircraft accurately, instantaneously and continuously in all circumstances . . . Radar was, in fact, the technical brain and backbone of our anti-aircraft defence system.'[8]

(iii) Proximity Fuses

One of the most powerful anti-aircraft devices which originated in World War II was the proximity fuse.* Even before the outbreak of war, scientists in Great Britain, the United States, and Germany were thinking about the possibilities of influence or proximity fuses to detonate shells, torpedoes, or bombs. Several patents for proximity fuses had been published, but none explained how the mechanism was to be made. Most scientists were convinced that the technical difficulties inherent in development were too great. The pressure of war, of necessity, broke down these doubts. The initial successful development of the fuse took place in Britain. No German proximity fuse was used during the war. Had it not been for the

---

* Also known as the VT fuse. Popularly assumed to stand for 'variable time' or 'vacuum tube', VT was, in fact, merely a code name.

Page 171 : *(above)* A Naval Lighter Pontoon; *(below)* a Landing Ship (Tank).

Page 172: (*above left*) Sir Robert Watson-Watt; (*right*) P. I. Dee; (*below left*) A. C. B. (later Sir Bernard) Lovell; (*right*) Sir Donald Bailey.

Tizard Mission the Americans, similarly, might have failed to develop an effective proximity fuse in time. The Americans were able, however, effectively to mass-produce the fuse.

In Britain, proximity fuses were designed for use in shells, or rockets, or bombs. Proposals were made to actuate the weapon with three different types of fuse. One was a photoelectric fuse, to be used either in a bomb or rocket (originally suggested, it is believed, by Blackett at a meeting of the Tizard Committee, and strongly supported by Lindemann); the second, an acoustic fuse to be used in a bomb and dropped on a formation of enemy aircraft, was designed by P. Rothwell of the Air Defence Experimental Establishment; finally, fuses set off by radar or radio signals were to be used either in a projectile or a bomb. The fuse used in a shell certainly contributed to the winning of the war. The acoustic and photoelectric fuses proved to be impractical.

The inventor of the radio-operated shell (or rocket) fuse was Butement. Butement, it will be recalled, had worked on radar at Bawdsey, but at the end of 1939 he was transferred to the Ministry of Supply and posted to the Air Defence Experimental Establishment, then at Christchurch, in Hampshire. Towards the end of 1939 he wrote a paper proposing the development of a guided weapon (a rocket) to be automatically directed on to an aircraft target; the weapon was to be detonated by a radio-operated fuse. He presented this paper to the Radar Applications Committee chaired by Professor Appleton. The committee concluded that the weapon was too complex for work to be begun on it at that stage of the war, but agreed that further thought should be given to the proximity fuse for development as a separate unit.

Chapter 13 will show how rocket development was considered particularly urgent on account of the serious shortage of anti-aircraft guns and the use which the Germans were making of the dive-bomber against land and sea targets. On 7 May 1940, just over a month after the German invasion of Denmark and Norway, a meeting was held at the Projectile Development Establishment at Fort Halstead to discuss the best method for operating a fuse by radar or radio. Cockcroft, then Assistant Director of Research in the Ministry of Supply, Dr. A. D. (later Sir Alwyn) Crow, in charge of British rocket development, and Butement, among others, were present.

Butement described two possible methods of operating the fuse.

L

In one, the position of projectile and aircraft could be plotted by radar and the fuse operated by the requisite pulse when radar images of projectile and target coincided. In the other, a short-wave radio beam in which the frequency would be varied continuously over a narrow range would be directed on to the target. Under these conditions a projectile approaching the target would receive signals on two different frequencies at any one instant, one from the ground, and one, which left the transmitter later, reflected from the target. Reduction in distance between projectile and target would lessen the difference in frequency between the two signals, resulting in beats of continuously descreasing frequency. The fuse would comprise a short-wave receiver, provided with a low-pass filter designed to stop all signals above a determined frequency, but capable of passing or triggering sufficient current to fire the detonator immediately on receipt of a signal of the specified low frequency. This would take place at about 100 feet from the target. The meeting decided to go ahead with the second, or radio-operated, fuse, principally because they considered that the first method required equipment in addition to the fuse and, secondly, that it would be less accurate and confusion might arise if several aircraft and several projectiles were in view together. Furthermore the radio fuse could operate in darkness or in cloud.

On the following day, back at Christchurch, Butement discussed the project with two of his colleagues, E. S. Shire, a physicist and contemporary of Cockcroft at Cambridge, and A. F. H. Thomson, another War Office scientist. 'It was clear at once', continues Butement, 'that both Shire and I had had further ideas. Thomson interrupted us both and said : "Before you get involved, each write down the essence of your idea." We both did and it was at once obvious that Shire and I were independently clear that no modulation was necessary, or any other requirement, but that the Doppler* effect would provide a signal which would be used to operate a fuse.'[9] Butement and Shire then both wrote short papers explaining their proposals to their 'masters', but there is no doubt that

* After Christian Doppler, the Austrian physicist (1803-53). The Doppler effect has been compared to a train approaching an observer and emitting a whistle. As the train passes the observer, the pitch falls abruptly. Neither pitch, either before or after passing, is the true pitch of the whistle which lies between the two. This apparent shift in pitch (or frequency) is the Doppler effect.

Butement originated the idea in his initial proposal for a guided weapon.

What was revolutionary about the idea was the use of the projectile as an aerial. Already it had been proved that very tough, or rugged valves would survive the recoil after being fired from a high-velocity gun. (These trials were initiated by Cockcroft with Pye Radio, and later with GEC, after the outbreak of war.) How was an aerial to be connected to the shell? Butement's answer was to put the fuse—itself a small radar set—*inside* the aerial which was the skin of the projectile. An insulating ring was required by which the outer surface could be excited. 'No one', states Butement, 'had ever put radio apparatus inside its own aerial before!'

All this was reported to Cockcroft, and after discussion in Appleton's committee and a preliminary test of a prototype fuse against a sheet of tin plate, Electric & Musical Instruments Ltd were instructed to make some proximity fuses for testing purposes. When they were ready, experiments were made by Butement and his team at Christchurch. First, the fuses were taken to the top of a 60-ft tower. 'A Fairey Battle aircraft', writes Butement, 'was detailed to assist and the pilot was ordered by radio by one or more of the research team on the tower to fly at various heights overhead while the researchers noted the effect on suitable instruments. Various heights were chosen to simulate the different distances of nearest approach which would occur when a shell was fired at an aircraft. The pilot was eventually required to fly over the tower so as to clear it by ten feet—a nerve-racking experience both for the researchers and the pilot! These trials showed that the fuse could be effective at well over 100 feet from the aircraft, which was more than adequate.'

The team then moved to the rocket range at Aberporth in South Wales. A number of sample shell fuses were made up and mounted in 3-in. rockets so that trials could proceed without delay. Butement then continues: 'A glider made of plywood was purchased and was covered in aluminium foil to simulate the reflecting properties of an aircraft. The glider was then suspended beneath a barrage balloon and used as a target for the fuse experiments. The fuses were so arranged that if they could have caused a shell to explode on passing near an aircraft, a puff of smoke would be released and could be photographed.

'The fuses were fired on their rockets so as to pass close to the glider beneath the balloon. Half of the fuses caused the puff of smoke to be seen as they passed the glider. Several passed too far from the glider to function and operated as they neared the sea due to reflection from it, and several were ineffective. However, the half of the total number of rounds which were successful clearly demonstrated the effectiveness of the fuse.'

In July 1940, the Admiralty asked for proximity fuses for anti-aircraft weapons* and a conference was held at the Royal Aircraft Establishment Section at Exeter to discuss the progress of the various fuses under trial.

At this stage the Tizard Mission left for the United States with the proximity fuse among its other secrets. Cockcroft was in the party and, as he was well acquainted with all the details of Bute-ment's fuse, was able to expound them to American officers in Washington. The Americans had not at that time evolved a radio proximity fuse. On 27 August 1940, the Chief of the Bureau of Naval Ordnance was informed that 'the British have under develop-ment, which had progressed to a certain state, an influence fuse used in anti-aircraft fire. The influencing force is reported to be radio.'[10]

In the meantime Vannevar Bush, as we have seen, Director of the Office of Scientific Research and Development, appreciating the importance of this new device, asked Merle Tuve, at that time in charge of the Department of Terrestial Magnetism at the Carnegie Institution, Washington, whether he could take charge of a special section (Section T) in Division A of the National Defence Research Committee, responsible for research and development of weapons, to investigate the possibilities of the fuse. The project was to be conducted in the utmost secrecy. Tuve readily agreed. A contract was negotiated between the NDRC and the Carnegie Institution as a result of which Section T's proposals for the fuse took place in Tuve's department. On 19 September, Cockcroft and a colleague, R. H. Fowler, met Tuve for further discussions in the privacy of the latter's home and plans of the radio fuse were lent to the Americans to copy. As British industry was stretched to the utmost, the manufacture of the fuse in quantity would have to be done in the United States.

Believing that the proximity fuse (known to begin with as T 3),

* Battleships were particularly vulnerable to air attack. In December 1941, for example, the *Prince of Wales* and the *Repulse* were sunk by Japanese aircraft off Malaya.

was second only in importance to radar, the Americans began an immense research and development programme. Much had to be done, especially in making the electrical components, such as the tubes and batteries, withstand very high accelerations. As already explained, unlike the British who believed in maximum co-operation (cf, the work on the magnetron), the Americans made contracts with academic institutions and electrical firms to carry out parallel development on each problem. Each group worked on its own in conditions of absolute secrecy and was not allowed to communicate with the others. The entire project was supervised by Tuve and his Section T. This procedure seems to have been successful and the lack of liaison does not seem to have handicapped the work; in fact competition between the respective groups urged the work forward. It is open to question whether the British or the American system was the better solution. Both systems worked. Nevertheless the Americans tended to waste effort (they could afford to do so) and it may be that the British methods were more speedy, eg, the arrival of the first centimetre radar.

To outline the various stages in development: first, an intensive programme for testing the components of the fuse for ruggedness began. During the winter of 1940/41 contracts were made with Bell Telephone Company, the Raytheon Company, the Western Electrical Company and the Hytron Company for the development of particular components. Tests then took place consisting of firing the tubes vertically from a smooth-bored gun, spinning them in a centrifuge, dropping them in bombs and the entire fuse was tested to see how it reacted to an approaching aircraft. Scientists at the Physics Department, Toronto University, developed a battery which not only had to meet the power demands, but keep its vitality over months, or even a year, of shelf life.

By May 1941 the main design was accepted and top priority was given to the production of shell fuses—the prospective user being the US Navy. The fuse was also being considered for rockets and bombs. On 26 April 1941, a bomb was successfully detonated at a height of 150 feet above the sea. Here again use had been made of the bomb fuse research by the British. In the course of 1941, contracts were made with the Crosley and Sylvania companies for fuse component manufacture.

The tests were, of course, time-consuming and required a great deal of preparation. One serious aspect which required solution was the eradication of noisy tubes (microphonics) and their failure due to vibration. Nevertheless by November 1941 the period of development had been completed. After successful trials at sea, on 29 January 1942, the US Navy decided that the radio proximity fuse was sufficiently successful to justify full-scale production. An 80-million dollar order was placed with Crosley Corporation. By that time the United States had entered the war and this event only served to increase the urgency of bringing the new device into operation as rapidly as possible. The US Navy was especially interested.

A new contract was signed with Johns Hopkins University on 10 March 1943. The university provided a congenial atmosphere for work, and by now the number of scientists working on the fuse had grown from 100 to 700. In all, about fifty academic and industrial organisations were involved.

The peak of the tests came on 11 August 1942, when the guns of the US cruiser *Cleveland* in Chesapeake Bay succeeded in hitting aircraft targets. Large-scale production was immediately pressed. The order of priority for customers was the US Navy, the Royal Navy, the US Army and the British Army, in that order. In the event, most of the fuses intended for the Navy went to the Army and this was only made possible by close co-operation between the two services. On 5 January 1943, sixteen months after the beginning of intensive research, a shell with a proximity fuse fired by the US cruiser *Helena* brought down the first Japanese aircraft in the Pacific. Morison has written that the proximity-fused shell became so deadly that the Japanese Air Force was forced to adopt suicide tactics.[11]

The production of the fuse was a triumph of American industrial methods. One example of how the urgency of war requirements increased production will suffice. Before the war the total US production of radio valves was 600,000 per day. By the close of the war the Sylvania Company alone was producing 95 per cent of the miniature rugged valves required for the proximity fuse. More than 400,000 valves per day were being produced in twenty-three different plants. With American production of proximity fuses in full spate, there was no need for the British to duplicate the effort.

The War Office had not yet asked for proximity fuses. But when it was known that the Germans were preparing to launch unmanned aircraft against this country, General Pile, a great believer in the latest scientific techniques in warfare, and who had seen demonstration firings of the shell in 1941, urgently asked that provision should be made to supply his command with proximity fuses. At the end of May 1944 permission was given by the Chiefs of Staff for the fuses to be used over Britain. But they were not used until mid-July 1944, a month after the V-1 attacks had started, and by which time the anti-aircraft gunners had not only been trained to use the fuse but had also been moved out of the London area nearer the coast to deal with the threat more conveniently. Several American scientists, including Dr. Edward Salant and Dr. R. E. Gibson of Johns Hopkins University, lived with the troops and advised them on how to use the fuse effectively.

We have already learned that the flying-bombs were ideal targets for the guns and they became even more effective with the SCR 584 radar, the M 9 electrical predictor and, finally, the proximity fuse. In the first week of operations in which the proximity fuse was used, 24 per cent of the targets engaged were destroyed; in the second, the total destroyed was 46 per cent; and in the third week, 67 per cent. The climax was reached in the fourth week, by which time the launching sites were being overrun by the Allied armies, when 79 per cent were destroyed.[12] Proximity fuses were also used in the defence of Brussels and Antwerp against the V-1s. In one of the final flying-bomb attacks against England, the Germans fired twenty-four bombs from Walcheren Island, off the Dutch coast. They were all shot down within five miles of the English coast by anti-aircraft guns.

Stringent security measures to prevent the enemy from learning details of the fuse had so far restricted its use to Britain and over the sea. By the autumn of 1944 a stalemate had set in on the western frontier of Germany. Among other measures to bring the war to a swift conclusion, the Combined Chiefs of Staff on 25 October agreed to release the new fuse for operations in Europe. The date fixed for the earliest use of the fuse was 16 December—as it happened, the day on which the Germans launched their desperate counter-offensive in the Ardennes. Very large stocks of these fuses were now available as Allied air superiority had by then reduced German air offensive operations to a minimum. It was therefore possible to use anti-aircraft shells on a lavish scale with the proximity fuses set to burst thirty feet above the ground. They were used by American gunners on 21 December against the spearhead of the German advance and caused momentary panic. But post-war investigation showed that the claims made for the proximity fuse in halting the German advance were 'grossly exaggerated.' In fact, the fuses were only employed on a few occasions in the critical stage of the battle and then only because visibility was too bad for visual ranging. But they were used, often with murderous effect, when the Americans, in their turn, began to counterattack.

* * *

The proximity fuse arrived at a late stage of the war, and only just in time for the flying-bombs, in spite of the massive production effort of the United States. It would, of course, have been even more important had Allied air superiority not been achieved, and greater efforts would presumably have been made to bring it into operation at an earlier stage. At the same time the great technical achievement in evolving the components must not be underestimated. Hitherto radio valves had been only sturdy enough to withstand handling and shipment. They now had to be not only highly sensitive but capable of being fired at high velocity from the barrel of a gun. The fuse was a device as closely shrouded in secrecy as radar—and perhaps more so. Secrecy is always a double-edged weapon and Major-General H. M. Paterson, who was a member of the Technical Artillery Branch of the War Office during the war years, maintains that there would have been a greater demand for it by senior army officers if they had known of its existence.

In retrospect, the priorities were perhaps not established early enough, although in the United States the groups working in competition served to accelerate the ultimate development of the shell fuse. Lastly, the development of the fuse was a fine example of close collaboration between British and American scientists. From the first disclosure by the Tizard Mission, none of the British fundamental research was withheld.* In their turn, the Americans co-operated to

* Since September 1943, the US Government has held a patent filed on behalf of Butement and his co-inventors for proximity fuses in projectiles. In April 1965 the US Department of Justice dismissed a claim made by Russell H. Varian, the American scientist and inventor of the klystron, against Butement and his colleagues for prior invention of a proximity fuse. The Patent Board established that priority of the invention should be assigned to Butement, Shire and Thomson. As the design of the proximity fuse was given to the Americans as part of Lease-Lend in reverse, no money was paid to the inventors.

the hilt when their great scientific and industrial potential had been deployed.

Let the final word on the proximity fuse be said by one of its principal customers—General Pile : 'To the scientists who carried out fundamental research we all owe a great deal, but we could never have designed and produced the fuse in this country in time and in sufficient quantities to meet the menace of the flying-bomb. American scientists together with American production methods and above all American generosity, gave us the final answer to the flying-bomb.'[13]

Chapter 9

Mechanised Warfare

(i) Wireless in Tanks

The control of fast-moving mobile forces presented a nice problem for their headquarters, and it was obvious that the answer lay in radio communications.[1] In the First World War, on the Western Front, there had hardly been occasion to make frequent use of wireless, but in the far more mobile campaigns in the Middle East, in particular in Mesopotamia and Persia, signal detachments, composed of Australian troops, were given greater scope in the use of wireless.

In 1931 a complete brigade of tanks was formed for the first time —a temporary measure—but it was the most important experiment embarked on by the British Army since the end of the First World War. The brigade commander, Brigadier (later Lt.-Gen. Sir Charles) Broad worked out a drill for rapid tactical movement which was based on the use of wireless. Although only a few tanks in each battalion were equipped with sets, Broad reported at the end of the exercise that radio-telephony was 'essential to efficient manœuvre.'[2]

This idea was carried a stage forward by Brigadier P. C. S. (later Major-Gen. Sir Percy) Hobart, when the 1st Tank Brigade was formed in 1934. The exercises held on Salisbury Plain that year were of great significance for they established in principle that wireless was the best means of inter-communication and control in an armoured force.

Hobart, originally an officer in the Royal Engineers, had soon become an eager convert to the theory of armoured warfare. He had vision combined with practical thoroughness and he was able to inspire enthusiasm for the new ideas among all ranks of the new brigade. He appreciated the importance of control for mobile formations, and was convinced that wireless rather than visual signals between tanks was the answer. He further believed that wireless was not a preserve for the signals specialists and insisted that all officers should become proficient in its use. Hitherto it had been believed that

182

the instruments were too difficult for general use and were only suitable for communication between battalion headquarters and company commanders. Nevertheless prejudices died hard. Wireless was considered 'an unreliable toy' and in the chapter on 'Command and Control' in the *Field Service Regulations*, published in 1935, it was not even mentioned, which may have been the reason for the failure to make full use of wireless in the brief 1940 campaign in France. But it was fortunate that in the early days of experiment there should have been officers with vision like Broad and Hobart to create the demand for wireless. We must now see how these demands were fulfilled.

Initial design and construction of prototype sets were the responsibility of the Signals Experimental Establishment on Woolwich Common. More than other service experimental establishments, research was hamstrung by financial restrictions because the Navy and Air Force could prove that their units could not function without radio whereas the Army could not prove any such necessity.

In the early thirties the problems facing the designer of a mobile radio set were immense; the various components such as the valves with filaments 'delicate as a spider's web' were very cumbersome and the whole equipment usually had to be carried on the back of a trotting or galloping horse, or the unsprung limber of a horse-drawn wagon.[3]

Moreover, the establishment was rigidly tied to rules for set design which had been drawn up over the years by the War Office from the First World War onwards. Radio equipment was therefore inevitably bound to be bulky and very expensive and, as Butement writes, 'was the direct result of the autocratic control exacted in those days. I was, for instance, told that the No 9 set was to be tailored to a new tank turret measuring 42 in. by 12 in. by 16 in. which had been set up as a part "counterbalance" to the gun.'[4] At the same time, such liaison as was permitted with the commercial radio industry only took place *after* a set had been designed in the Establishment.

After the exercise conducted by Broad in 1931, the scientists at Woolwich had to provide a system of radio communication between individual tanks on the move. At that time piezo-crystals were the only means by which sender and receiver could be stabilised. As each tank radio had to operate on a number of frequencies in order to allow for enemy jamming and for other reasons, a comparatively large number of crystals were required. The War Office appreciated that this was very expensive and that it would throw a great strain on industrial production in time of war.

Butement, who was personally responsible for designing all the principal tank wireless sets before the war, had to solve 'the problem of maintaining a number of transmitter-receiver stations on a chosen frequency so as to be able to operate as a disciplined group.' For several years he attended Hobart's tank exercises on Salisbury Plain—an early example of collaboration between scientist and service officer. 'I always travelled in his tank', writes Butement, 'and together we worked out the whole concept of tank control by radio.' The employment of tanks and armoured vehicles in deep, thrusting movements controlled by radio telephone was a revolutionary concept in warfare and although these exercises were deprived of much of their realism by inadequate equipment, they provided the laboratory in which the principles of the *Blitzkrieg* were worked out—the *Blitzkrieg* methods which the Germans were to use to such dramatic effect in the early summer of 1940. For there were no security restrictions and German military observers were invariably present. The tragedy is that it was the German Army rather than the British who appreciated the significance of these trials.*

Between 1934 and 1937 Butement, during the exercises of the Tank Brigade, devised a new circuit whereby it was possible to ensure automatically that all transmitters and receivers in a given 'net' were tuned to the chosen frequency. In 1936 the procedure became known as 'netting'. At first a modified No 9 set was used; Butement then designed the No 11 set which incorporated the new circuit and with which it was possible to obtain good speech signals of even strength on the move so long as a signal could be received at all. And there was no need to use piezo-crystals, except in special cases. The result was a big saving in money and manpower during the war.

In the No 11 set developed from the start, in contrast to previous practice, in collaboration with Messrs. E. K. Cole, Butement was able to break away to some extent from the traditions of the Signals Experimental Establishment, 'but not without a good deal of trouble with my masters who, however, were gracious enough later to thank me in writing for the "rapid production of an excellent set".' In

* The first exercise for an entire German *panzer* division which demonstrated that movement and control of a large number of tanks were possible took place in July 1935.

addition to the introduction of automatic netting, Butement was able 'to construct the set as a drawer in its case, so that the set as a whole could be withdrawn for valve change and servicing. . . . The only modern tube available, when work started, for the transmitter output was a tetrode which permitted only a moderate output in the space available.' But an adequate number of sets was not available before 1937. 'Later versions of the No 11 and particularly the Australian version (the No 111) were fitted with 807 valves so that a good output was obtained.' One of these high-powered sets was used by General Le Clerc, commanding the Free French force which marched across the Sahara in early 1943 in an epic movement to join up with the British Eighth Army under General Montgomery, and enabled him to keep in touch with his troops throughout the operation.

The Nos 9 and 11 sets also proved their worth in the defeat of the Italian Army in the Western Desert in the winter of 1940/41. One of the principal factors in the British success was, according to Liddell Hart, 'The power of controlled manœuvre made possible by wireless and developed by practice.'

The most useful set produced in the war for mobile armoured forces was the No 19 set, which incorporated two transmitter-receivers and an inter-communication service. The main transmitter-receiver, known as the 'A' set, operated, on a high-frequency band, and provided regimental and squadron communication. The other transmitter-receiver, known as the 'B' set, operating on very high frequency, provided inter-tank communication. The intercom system enabled the tank commander to speak to each member of his crew. Hitherto, when a troop commander wanted to pass instructions to his tanks, he had to use simple flag signals, thereby exposing himself to enemy fire. The idea of the 'A' and 'B' set was evolved by Butement and Hobart in 1934 during the exercises on Salisbury Plain.

The evolution of this set illustrates the clash of values of the War Office as opposed to those of commercial radio firms—in this case Pye. In 1939 the War Office required a new tank radio, and, as usual, its specifications were rigid and required very high standards. A prototype was produced by the Signals Experimental Establishment, and a similar set was designed by Pye. That August, at a tense meeting held in the War Office for radio manufacturers and staff officers, C. O. Stanley, the forceful managing director of Pye who had raised the firm from scratch, pointed out the difference in weight between his firm's set which weighed 29 lb. and the Establishment's set which weighed 50 lb.[5] The Pye set was made with pressed steel plate, normally used for canned food, and thus avoided using the light alloys reserved for the RAF's radio sets. But nothing happened.

After Dunkirk, the British Army required a radio which was light, occupied little space, could operate in noisy conditions and, finally, which was easy to mass-produce. Three tank radios were then in current use. First, the No 9 set, reasonable in performance but too large to go into the turret of some tanks; it was inefficient and expensive to make. Secondly, the No 11 set, high-powered and of reasonable size but of inadequate performance. Both sets operated on the short-wave band and were suitable for medium-range communication, but neither was suitable for mass-production. Thirdly, there was the long-wave No 14 set, intended for inter-communication between tanks in a troop, but too large and with a poor range of frequencies.

A new set must have the performance of the No 9 set combined with the capabilities which the No 14 set should have possessed. There also had to be an intercom amplifier to enable the tank commander to speak to his crew. The set must not be larger than the No 11 set.

The Signals Experimental Establishment now prepared three models for trials. Pye, knowing of this, decided to produce a rival set as rapidly as possible. In July 1940 they began work on 'A' and 'B' sets. The 'B' set was produced first, as a rather longer period of development was required for the 'A' set. Both sets were ready for trial that November. This composite set was the No 19 Mark I set —a rather rough job compared with the War Office set. At the trials, two of the three War Office sets became unserviceable while the Pye sets, or most of them, gave good ranges (though not better than the War Office sets had done before going unserviceable). Pye directly convinced the Minister of Supply of their set's superiority and early in 1941 he ordered 3,000 No 19 sets.

The effect of this very rapid development was seen some months later when almost every No 19 set in the Western Desert went out of action at a most critical time.* A condenser in the power pack rated for a maximum temperature of approximately 70°C was being

* During the First Battle of El Alamein, in July 1942

operated at 105°C. Not surprisingly it broke down. Due to pressure from Butement at the Ministry of Supply and good fortune, a substitute condenser to go in the same space was obtained from the United States, flown to North Africa and fitted into all tanks. This and several other faults were rectified in subsequent marks of the set.

Meanwhile, Pye had been asked to develop a Mark II set as quickly as possible. Trials with the new model were held in March 1941, followed by full-scale production in Britain, and later in Canada and the United States.

Thus there were two extremes of policy. On the one hand, the highly cautious War Office policy leading to expensive but reliable equipment in small numbers because of the price and effort involved; on the other hand, the hasty, rather slap-dash approach of the commercial radio comany, as in the case of the No 19 set Mark I, leading through a series of models to a reasonable equipment.

(ii) Microwave Communications

The war stimulated the beginning of microwave communications in the form of the No 10 set, probably the first very narrow beam speech radio communication system using multi-channel interlaced pulse modulation and operating by relaying signals from hilltop to hilltop (the modern equivalent of the beacon).

Butement, assisted by A. J. Oxford, E. W. Anderson and J. G. Macmillan, was responsible for its genesis. The idea arose, in 1942, after the Japanese had captured the rubber-growing areas in the Far East. The War Office foresaw that there would be a shortage of cable for field trunk communications equipment, and Butement, then Assistant Director of Scientific Research (Radio and Radar) in the Ministry of Supply, was given one weekend that summer in which to provide an answer. He at once followed up some contemporary ideas on the possibility of applying centimetric wavelengths to speech radio and cast back his mind to some research begun by Baudot, inventor of multiple telegraphy, in 1874, but not resumed until just before the war.*

* These ideas had to some extent been anticipated. On 31 March 1931, Standard Telephone & Cables had tested a cross-Channel two-way radio-telephone link on a wavelength of 18 centimetres. In 1933 a permanent R/T link between Lympne and St. Inglevert, operating on a wavelength of 17·4 centimetres, was set up—the first of its kind. But the military possibilities do not seem to have been appreciated.

Butement now proposed a radio link operating on a six-centimetre wavelength. Parabolic mirrors would generate the very narrow radio beams required. (They enabled $\frac{1}{2}$ watt to do the work which would otherwise have required half a million watts.) If the Germans intercepted the signals they would think they were radar emanations which, in the event, was what happened. As the links were to be used for communications within an army corps, Butement suggested that there should be eight speech channels. By the end of 1942 Butement's solution had been accepted, first by Appleton's committee and then by the War Office which gave approval for development.

The layout of the signals terminals naturally depended on where the Allies were going to land in France. Unfortunately, Butement and his team were not told this, as were several other scientists, and he therefore proposed to establish a set at Ventnor, on the Isle of Wight, and another terminal at Beachy Head, in Sussex. Should the landing take place in the Pas De Calais, there was no difficulty about the equipment operating across the narrow part of the Channel. But if Cherbourg was the objective, the greater distance and the varying heights on either side of the Channel might cause difficulties. However, the height of the south coast near Ventnor was very similar to high ground near Cherbourg and the distance was about the same as between Ventnor and Beachy Head. A link was therefore planned between these two points. The Ventnor-Beachy Head stage, meanwhile, worked satisfactorily, which showed that the seventy-odd miles to France could be spanned.

After the Normandy landings, the Ventnor site was shown to have been well chosen and the link went into operation earlier than expected. The severe gale which delayed the build-up in the beachhead damaged the telephone cable laid under the Channel. The radio link between Ventnor and Cherbourg was immediately put into operation and from the latter point a second link connected it to General Montgomery's headquarters, south of Caen.

The speed of the advance after the break-out from the Normandy beach-head across northern France and Belgium to Brussels and Antwerp left the signals organisation in a predicament. There was adequate cable, but it could not be laid fast enough. Montgomery demanded an instant solution. The No 10 set had worked so well over the two-stage link from England to France that the decision was taken to extend it into Belgium.

No provision had been made for operators to use the new equipment. J. G. Macmillan was therefore put into uniform (a strategem often demanded by scientists working in the services) with the acting rank of major and sent to France to train the signallers who, until then, had only handled line equipment. He accomplished this with such success that the No 10 set followed Montgomery to Luneberg Heath where he received the unconditional surrender of the German armed forces in the north. By that time twenty sets stretched back to Brussels, enabling Montgomery to speak not only with any unit in his army group, but with Eisenhower at Supreme Headquarters and the Prime Minister and the Chief of the Imperial General Staff in Whitehall, the latter two speaking through conventional telephone and cable links.

Montgomery, who preferred to work in a small isolated tactical headquarters, soon appreciated the value of the set which he called his 'No 10 thing.' He formed the habit of determining the position of his future headquarters by drawing on the map a circle five miles in diameter and telling his staff to 'find your hill' within it. He later remarked : 'I have no hesitation in saying that I consider the No 10 set to be a very marked and rapid advance in wireless technique. No other army, Allied or hostile, possessed equipment equally effective in its role. . . . The value of being able to retain personal control over my armies . . . cannot be over-estimated.'[6]

The Americans copied the apparatus and it was used by the US forces. Microwave communications since the war have been developed considerably for civilian use; the Post Office Tower in London is the most notable example to date.

It should be noted that in both the devices associated with Butement, the initial stimulus came not from a requirement for increased control and better communications, but because of a possible lack of materials essential for radio sets.

(iii) The Bailey Bridge

Just as with radio, experience in the First World War had provided little stimulus to bridging problems. But with the mechanisation of the Army and a number of different types of vehicle coming into use, military bridges were required to carry much heavier loads. By the early thirties there were three bridges for carrying heavy equipment, or for dealing with gaps where floating bridges were unsuitable : the large box-girder bridge which could cover spans of 130 feet; the small box-girder bridge 60 feet in length and capable of carrying a nine-ton load; and the Hamilton* semi-permanent bridge for the line of communication, able to cross gaps of up to 200 feet, the girders of which could be doubled or trebled to carry very heavy loads. All these bridges took advantage of new welding techniques and high-tensile steel, then coming into general use. A vital factor in military bridging was speed in construction and it was recognised that standard equipment was essential for the different loads to be carried.

New equipment was tested on the River Avon by the Bridging Experimental Establishment at Christchurch, Hampshire. Technical advice was provided by the Structural Engineering Committee composed of a small number of distinguished civil and military engineers. The Experimental Bridging Establishment, like other service experimental establishments in the inter-war years, was run on a shoestring. It had evolved out of the Experimental Bridging Company, Royal Engineers, under Major (later Lt.-Gen. Sir Giffard) Martel who had designed the first box-girder bridge. When rearmament began, there were two officers and about thirty-five engineers and other technicians in the establishment. Despite these handicaps it became extremely busy with a large number of projects connected with amphibious warfare, anti-tank devices, and the solution of water supply problems.

The civil engineering designer at Christchurch, from 1928 until the war, was D. C. (later Sir Donald) Bailey. He began as an unestablished civil servant. Bailey had been trained as a civil engineer at Sheffield University and had worked in the City Engineer's Department there and with the London Midland and Scottish Railway before going to Christchurch. Quiet and unassuming, he had great determination, besides considerable inventive ability which showed itself not only in his work on bridge structures but also in the development of anti-tank mines and other technical equipment. By the outbreak of war, Bailey had become an established civil servant and it was said of him in the early years of the war 'that the loss of his services would be a disaster.' Bailey rose to be head of the Military Engineering Experimental Establishment and, until his retirement, was Dean of the Military College of Science at Shrivenham, where he exerted a benign influence on the modern scientist-soldier.

* Designed by A. M. Hamilton, a well-known civil engineer. His bridges were much used in South-east Asia.

In 1936, while watching box-girder bridge trials, the idea for a new type of structure came to Bailey, involving the use of steel panels instead of girders, which would be easier to handle and quicker to erect.[7] He made a rough sketch for the Superintendent of the Establishment, Col. S. G. Galpin,* which illustrated how one panel could be fitted to another. The War Office, however, displayed no interest in Bailey's idea. Its requirements for bridging had been fulfilled and Bailey, in the meantime, was fully occupied by the other projects undergoing trial in the establishment. Nevertheless, in spite of the great pressure imposed by rearmament, he began to evolve in his spare time a design for a bridge made of steel panels without waiting for encouragement from the War Office.

Essentially, Bailey's idea was to bolt together a number of flat, steel panels or frames (10 ft. by 5 ft.) in a variety of combinations depending on the job to be done. The main girders of the bridge were to be built up from these panels which could be arranged in one, two or three trusses, side by side, and one to three storeys high, with almost any combination in between. The panels were attached to each other by the insertion of steel pins through holes in the overlapping jambs. A roadway was carried by the steel transoms resting on the bottom chord of the girders forming a through bridge. The panels could each be lifted by six men and each of the parts could be packed into the standard 3-ton lorry.

After the outbreak of war the requirement for a heavy infantry tank (the Churchill) led to a demand for a heavy bridge which would carry a weight of some seventy tons. Moreover, the box-girder bridge was unsatisfactory from many points of view. The only portable bridge of the First World War, involving tubular girders, was designed by C. E. (later Sir Charles) Inglis, a structures expert, and subsequently Professor of Engineering at Cambridge. The Inglis bridge, in various sizes, became the principal means for crossing dry gaps in France, and could be assembled quickly under war conditions. Inglis was now asked by the War Office to design a new version of his bridge. The Experimental Bridging Establishment was not consulted.

The Inglis bridge, however, departed from the prefabricated principle of box girders already established before the war and, furthermore, its tubular construction imposed great strain on certain

* Galpin later designed the 'scissors bridge' carried by a tank and used to a small extent during the Second World War.

components of the bridge. When Bailey learned about Inglis' new design he knew that it would be a failure and this, as Bailey modestly insists, was out of no disrespect to Inglis who, in contrast to Bailey at the time, had an established reputation—and whom Bailey valued as a professional colleague and friend. Thus, in December 1939, when Bailey and Brigadier F. E. Fowle, a member of the Royal Engineer and Signals Board, responsible for the Bridging Establishment, went to Cambridge to see Inglis' design, Bailey declared that the top lateral member of the bridge, technically known as the top chord, would fail when under compression, ie, when the bridge was fully loaded, and when the bottom lateral member, or lower chord, was in tension. He pointed out that tubular girders were unsuitable for taking stresses in compression because they could not provide a good strut. The bridge was unsafe, especially when the load was off centre.

Yet such criticism from Bailey and other members of the Experimental Bridging Establishment was ignored by the War Office and development of the Inglis bridge took place at Cambridge instead of at Christchurch. By the following year the Inglis bridge was in production.

In the meantime, however, the British Army had begun to prepare to return to the Continent. A universal general service equipment was required to deal with the great range of spans and loads likely to be demanded on Continental operations and this equipment also had to be easy to mass-produce. But the Inglis bridge, in addition to its structural weakness, involved difficult castings and was expensive to manufacture. It began to run into trouble.

At last the Inglis bridge was tested at Christchurch on 25 January 1941; the upper chord, as predicted by Bailey, failed. Several tests were subsequently made with the same result. The Structural Engineering Committee, then consisting of Sir Ralph Freeman, who had designed the famous Sydney bridge, Professor A. J. S. Pippard and Guthrie Brown, was told the Inglis bridge was unreliable. Now was Bailey's moment. He was told to submit drawings to the Ministry of Supply. On 13 February the Structural Engineering Committee told Bailey to go ahead and design an all-purpose bridge for the Army.

Bailey not only executed the design; he supervised the production of the panel. By 5 May the first prototype equipment, built by Braithwaites, was ready for testing. The speed of this development would not have been possible without Bailey's pre-war calculations.

All the tests were entirely successful. The Bailey bridge was accepted at the beginning of July 1941. Orders were placed for over 200 bridges with 130-ft. span and strong enough to carry a Churchill tank. By that December, ten months after the order given for full-scale trials of the bridge, the first Bailey bridging equipment had reached the sappers. Production of other types of bridge closed down.

The Bailey bridge, declared General Martel, doubled the fighting value of the Allied armoured and motorised forces. Its adaptability was one of its greatest assets. It was developed as a suspension bridge and as a mobile bridge for an assault river crossing. On several occasions it was launched from a tank across a river under enemy fire. It was used as a canal-lock bridge and as a pontoon bridge for spanning the Rhine and other wide rivers. It could carry a load of up to 100 tons. Bailey bridges were seen in every theatre of war and are still used for civilian purposes today all over the world.*

During the war, 650,000 panels were turned out in this country. British manufacturers produced a total of 400,000 parts of equipment, or enough to make 200 miles of bridge. In the United States, twenty miles of Bailey bridge were manufactured for the US Army.

Bailey's success must be attributed to his dogged persistence in working out his design without any official support, and this made possible its rapid development when at last accepted. Yet without the pressure of the Army's requirements in 1940 and, in particular, for a standard bridge, it is open to question how long it would have taken for the Bailey bridge to be accepted. It is important to note that the War Office persisted in supporting the Inglis bridge in the face of expert criticism. But the Bailey bridge won support from another quarter, for 'although the private soldier would carry and fix Bailey panels and components under frightful conditions and seemed to enjoy it, he always hated carrying Inglis' tubes, a strange psychological fact which Inglis, student of human nature though he was, could never have foreseen.'[8]

(iv) Countermeasures Against Land Mines

'The worst obstacle to the tank is the land mine, the possibilities of which have yet to be fully developed,' wrote Liddell Hart in July 1921. Land mines were, of course, no novelty in warfare. In the

* In the 1968 floods in the West of England they replaced damaged bridges.

First World War they had added another obstacle to the hideous conglomeration of barbed wire. In Great Britain, the potentialities of the anti-tank mine made little impact on the military mind. When a staff officer suggested during a conference after an exercise that 5,000 to 6,000 mines might be laid on a divisional front, his prophetic remarks were greeted with laughter. (During the fighting in France in 1944 over a million land mines were laid by the Germans.) Continental armies were more realistic. By the outbreak of war in 1939 the German army possessed two fairly sophisticated devices—the *Teller*, or anti-tank mine and the *Schu*, or anti-personnel mine.

The British Army was largely unprepared to cope with these obstacles, which could be dealt with in two ways. One was to detect the mines and mark out a safe passage through the minefield; the other, to detonate the mines with a mechanical device by rolling over them, by beating the ground with a flail, or by pushing explosives into the minefield to cause detonation.

First, mine detectors. At the outbreak of war the British Army had no mine detector, although one had been produced by the Signals Experimental Establishment for troops operating in Palestine shortly before the war. Forced to improvise in the desert, several highly complicated mechanisms were devised under the guidance of the Scientific Adviser, Middle East Forces. But they required skilled personnel to handle them. By 1941 the Army realised that a standard service mine detector was required. Mines were still being located by the primitive and dangerous method of prodding with a bayonet or even by poking the earth with bare hands. A school of mines run by the sappers in the desert was set up to find out the best way to breach a minefield and to test new ideas.

The designer of the first standard mine detector for the British Army was a Polish signals officer—Lieut. Jozef Stanislaw Kozacki.[9] Shortly before the war, the Polish Army had begun research into the problem of mine detection. After the occupation of Poland by the Germans in 1939, a number of Polish units escaped to France and work on the detector began again in 1940. When France collapsed, Polish forces arrived in Britain. In the winter of 1941/42, after specifications for a mine detector had been issued by the War Office, a design and model was produced by Kozacki and a sergeant at the Polish Signal Training Centre in Scotland. This design, submitted anonymously, was accepted.

In the Polish detector, one of two coils was connected to an oscillator which generated oscillating current of an acoustic frequency. The other coil was connected to an amplifier and telephone. When there was zero mutual coupling between the two coils, no signal was transmitted to the amplifier and no sound came over the 'phone. But as soon as the coil system came in proximity to a metallic object this condition of balance was upset and the telephone reported a signal. The equipment, carried on the man, weighed just under 30 lb. For assault troops, a miniature unit was devised which could be operated while crawling on the ground.

After successful trials, 250 Mine Detectors No 2 (Polish) produced by Cincma Television Ltd were rushed out to the Western Desert in time to be deployed in the spearhead of the advance at El Alamein. They could locate a *Teller* mine at a depth of two feet and a *Schu* mine at a depth of one foot. The detectors enabled the sappers to advance at a speed of 200 yards instead of 100 yards an hour.

The other way of dealing with a mine was, it has been seen, to detonate it.

Martel, while at Christchurch, designed the RE tank which could be used for a variety of tasks such as laying bridges, moving heavy weights, digging trenches, carrying out demolition work, and sweeping mines. Although lack of money prevented further development it was, in fact, the prototype of the Armoured Vehicle RE (AVRE tank) which was widely used in 1944/45 in the northwest European campaign. Martel continued to press for the development of minesweeping by tanks when at the War Office in the late 1930s and prototypes using rollers or ploughs were evolved. Neither was particularly satisfactory. Early in the war the first type of flail, which operated in front of a tank's tracks, was devised by Galpin at Christchurch, but no action was taken by the War Office. At this time more attention was being paid to the tank itself rather than to ways of halting it, and the practical issue of dealing with minefields was side-stepped. As we have seen, the advocates of a device are often reluctant to consider countermeasures which might lessen its value.

The flail tank was a normal tank, though in the early stages gunless, with a jib in front to which was attached a mechanically-operated drum which revolved lengths of chain and churned up the ground. It was born in the Western Desert, where minefields covered by anti-tank weapons had become a serious problem. A South

African, A. S. J. Du Toit, a mechanical engineer and an enthusiastic motorist, was the father of the idea. In 1936 he had driven from Johannesburg to London in thirteen days and four hours, a fact which, he later claimed, showed the potentialities of a mechanised force in Africa. He became transport officer to the First Field Force Brigade of the Union Defence Force and, in Abyssinia, had his first experience of a minefield. In August 1941, while recuperating from dysentery at the base camp in Helwan after duty in the Western Desert, Du Toit listened to a lecture on minefields. At the end, the lecturer invited his audience to submit suggestions for dealing with mines.

After discussing the problem with other officers, Du Toit showed the commandant of the camp a drawing of a flailing device as described above. Appreciating that this might be a valuable contribution to the war effort, the commandant sent Du Toit to South African Army headquarters in Cairo. In due course, after trials in Pretoria, a decision was taken to develop Du Toit's version of the flail tank in Great Britain. Production would take place in Britain rather than in South Africa for security reasons. Initial development began at the Armoured Fighting Vehicle Research and Development Establishment at Chobham. Du Toit's flail was found to be superior to the rollers developed by Galpin and others.

By Christmas 1941 a flail tank known as the 'Baron' had been evolved with the active assistance of Du Toit. At the request of the Ministry of Supply, the flail equipment was developed by the Associated Equipment Company of Southall, Middlesex. Du Toit, A. A. Houston, chief designer of the company, and C. F. Cleaver, a railcar engineer, were responsible for developing the device. Du Toit had intended the tank to be able to fire as well as to flail and the flail was to be driven by the main engine, but this was not achieved at once. In December 1942 orders were given to Messrs. Cullen of Cardiff to begin production, and Du Toit then returned to South Africa.

Meanwhile in the desert, minefields covered by anti-tank guns had become increasingly numerous and clearing them was costly and slow. In September 1942, twenty-four 'Matilda' tanks were adapted by another South African, Major Girling of 30th Corps, at No 7 Base Workshops, Alexandria, based on Du Toit's design. They were used by the Eighth Army under the name of 'Scorpions'. Unlike Du Toit's model, the flail was driven by an auxiliary engine mounted externally and had no gun. The Scorpions were the first specialised armour to go into action, making their début at the Battle of El Alamein where they cleared a path through German minefields. A second batch of thirty-six improved Scorpions (this time the flail was fitted to the Valentine tank) were brought into service and took part in the advance to Tripoli. Scorpions were also used in the Sicily landings.

At home, the Associated Equipment Company improved on the Baron, and fulfilled Du Toit's idea of a fighting tank with the flail driven by the main engine. The standard Sherman tank fitted with a 75-mm gun was chosen to be fitted with flails, and was known as the 'Crab'. While flailing, the Crab was very vulnerable and reserve Crabs had to cover its operations with their guns. But it could travel faster than the Scorpion, the normal speed while flailing being 1¼ miles per hour. An even more sophisticated version was produced during the Normandy campaign with a special hydraulic gear by which the jib was held at a steady height above the ground. This system was known as 'contouring' and was useful when the minefields were laid in sand dunes or in uneven ground.

As with other devices, the usual teething troubles[10] accompanied the development of the flail in England. There was, for instance, a shortage of chain, as the Admiralty had requisitioned all existing stocks. Various alternatives, such as flash-welded links and wire cables, were tried without success and in the end, ordinary roller chain manufactured by Welling's proved to be the most suitable. Spare chains were carried on the sides of the Crabs, as normally chains did not survive contact with more than two mines before the lower links were blown off. One set of chains, however, once blew up forty-three mines. Flailing was not, as can well be imagined, a congenial occupation for the tank crew who had to endure, in addition to the usual hazards of battle, the dust and noise of the explosion; although it is recorded that, apart from the dust, the effect of an exploding *Teller* mine was not noticeable within the tank. Negotiating wire obstacles provided a further problem when the flail drum became clogged. The AVRE now came into its own and, carrying bridging equipment and explosives, overcame obstacles in a minefield.

As a result of the painful testing of the German coastal defences during the Dieppe raid, it was decided for the landings in north-west Europe to concentrate all specialised armour into one division—

the 79th Armoured. If the invasion was to succeed, armour, breaching devices, vehicles and troops specially designed for an assault on a fortified coast were essential.

Major-Gen. Hobart who, as already seen, was an early exponent of tank warfare, became the division's commander. After forming what was to become the famous 7th Armoured Division in Egypt, he was retired in 1939. Churchill wrote that 'the catalogue of General Hobart's qualities and defects might almost exactly have been attributed to most of the great commanders of British history', and took him out of the Home Guard which he had joined, appointing him commander of the new 11th Armoured Division. Hobart had originally been called in to advise, but he soon became indispensable for the direction of this specialised division.

The American Army, it is interesting to observe, made no attempt to concentrate its specialised armour on the same pattern. Although shown the flail tank during the North African campaign, its attempts to develop a minesweeping tank were not a success. On several occasions during the campaign in north-west Europe, the 79th Armoured Division supported the American First and Ninth Armies.

Crabs went into action on the beaches on D-Day, 6 June 1944, in the British sector, flailing and firing alternatively. They proved their worth, clearing a path up to obstacles, at which point an AVRE dropped fascines enabling the flails to cross the gap. The Americans, on the other hand, landed their tanks *en masse* and without special vehicles in front. They suffered severe casualties as a result. The fact that the flail tank could fight as well as performing its special function was of outstanding value and proved the value of Du Toit's original idea. The flail tanks also gave effective assistance at Le Havre, in the clearing of the Scheldt estuary, and during the Rhineland battle.

Chapter 10

Medical Research

The theatres of war where disease was most rampant were the Far East and South-west Pacific and the Commander-in-Chief of the 14th Army in Burma, Field Marshal Lord Slim, has paid tribute to the beneficent effects of medical research. 'The scientific ideas', he has written, 'which helped us most were on the medical side. Without these I don't think we should have fought the war at all because in 1942 and the beginning of 1943 my Army was steadily disappearing from disease, mainly malaria, but with a melancholy list of other diseases like scrub typhus, skin diseases and the rest.'[1]

Measures against Malaria

The Japanese capture of Java—the principal quinine-producing area of the world—compelled Allied research chemists to press forward with the development of synthesised anti-malarial drugs. In the First World War the Germans had been confronted with an identical problem when the Allied naval blockade prevented them from obtaining supplies of quinine. They remembered the lesson and by about 1930 the German firm of Bayer, Meister & Lucius had developed atebrin,* which was widely used between the wars.

When war with Germany became likely, steps were taken in Britain to conserve stocks of German-produced drugs, and when war did come, preventing any fresh information coming out of Germany, a number of problems had to be solved afresh by British chemists. Fortunately, by 1939, Imperial Chemical Industries had already built a laboratory for pharmaceutical research at Blackley, near Manchester.

Professor R. A. Warrington Yorke, a member of the advisory committee to the ICI biological section, remembering the number of

* Atebrin, Atabrine, Atabrin, Quinachrine and Mepacrine are synonymous.

casualties in Salonika due to malaria in the First World War* was insistent that proper countermeasures should be taken. N. (later Sir Neil) Hamilton Fairley was another. In the First World War Fairley served as a medical officer with the Australian forces in the Middle East where he carried out valuable research on typhus fever and bilharziasis, or schistosomiasis. In the inter-war years he worked in Bombay as Professor of Tropical Medicine and as a lecturer at the London School of Hygiene and Tropical Medicine. In 1940 he joined the headquarters of the Australian Forces in Cairo as consulting physician and he was given the rank of colonel. He also acted as honorary consultant in tropical diseases at British Army headquarters as there was no consulting physician there at the time. When Japan came into the war, the Australian troops left for the Far East and Fairley went to Java. After the Japanese landed, Fairley escaped to Australia on one of the last ships to get away. He had arranged for the purchase of all available stocks of quinine in Java and shipment to Australia, but of the two ships carrying the consignment, one was sunk and the other was captured by the Japanese.

In Australia, Fairley became Director of Medicine in the Australian military forces. Later he was appointed chairman of the Combined Advisory Committee on Tropical Medicine, South Pacific Area, and was directly responsible to General MacArthur. In September 1942 Fairley was sent to Washington to obtain anti-malarial drugs for the Australian forces fighting in the South-West Pacific. He impressed military authorities both in London and in Washington of the seriousness of the malaria problem in the Far East, and as a result of his prodding ICI was encouraged to go ahead with research. With so many troops fighting in malaria-infested areas, the need for production of anti-malarial drugs was very urgent.

The development of mepacrine was a long, complicated process. 'Nevertheless progress was such that production of mepacrine grew from 22 lb. in 1939 to 12,500 lb. (equivalent to over 50 million tablets) in 1942, and by the end of 1943 production capacity had increased to a rate of over 100,000 lb. per annum. All this was achieved in the improvised experimental plant at Blackley, and it is not too much to claim that the manufacture of this drug in quantities adequate for the essential needs of Allied troops in the Middle and

---

* Nearly 40 per cent. of the British force went down with malaria and there were 693 fatal casualties.

Far East was a contribution to the war effort without which disaster might well have occurred.[2]

But how effective was mepacrine and what dosage was required to obtain that effect? The solution is an interesting example of the transmission of the fruits of scientific research. In 1937 experiments were made with atebrin by Dr. J. W. Field, then senior malaria research officer at the Institute for Medical Research at Kuala Lumpur (the drug had been obtained from a German pharmaceutical firm). Field wrote a monograph on the experiments which proved that prophylaxis was the best way to prevent malaria, and this was published by the Colonial Office. When the Japanese occupied Malaya, Field was taken prisoner. In November 1942, malaria among the Australian troops at Milne Bay, New Guinea, was so prevalent that on an average only 15 per cent of every fighting unit were capable of holding a rifle. Lt.-Col. E. V. Keogh, Director of Pathology in the Australian Army, remembered Field's work on the suppression of malaria and at once contacted Dr. R. Lewthwaite, who had been a colleague of Field's and who was then working in the Commonwealth Serum Laboratory at Melbourne. He asked Lewthwaite to obtain permission from the Colonial Office to reprint the monograph for use by medical officers in the Australian Expeditionary Force. This, in the confusion of the war at that stage, took some weeks, but permission was eventually given. Meanwhile Keogh had distributed the monograph in order to save the force in New Guinea. Later editions appeared with the sub-title 'With Permission of the Colonial Office' on the cover. Keogh discussed with Fairley Field's research and it was decided early in 1943 to set up the Experimental Malaria Centre at Cairns, in North-east Queensland, to test the effectiveness of mepa-suppressive treatment. Fairley, with his wide experience of tropical diseases, was made director. But the idea for these more detailed experiments sprang directly from Field's published work, and saved Fairley about six months' initial research.

At Cairns, about 800 soldiers, physically and mentally fit, volunteered to be 'the subjects of a variety of unpleasant experiments. The majority, having first been bitten by infected mosquitoes, were used in trials designed to determine the protective properties of different drugs. Others were used as controls, and for various related purposes. During the later trials of prophylaxis the volunteers were subjected to every kind of hardship which might be encountered on active service, such as long exhausting marches carrying full equipment, lack of sleep, extremes of heat and cold, and shortage of food and water. Without Fairley's fiery enthusiasm, which lit up everyone with whom he made contact, it is doubtful if a sufficient number of men would have offered themselves for these unpleasant ordeals. As it was, his appeals never failed, and at no time was there a shortage of willing victims.[3] The experiments proved that all types of malaria encountered in New Guinea could effectively be suppressed by administration of one tablet of mepacrine daily.*

With this fact established, military commanders were told that if the taking of mepacrine was strictly observed troops could fight in the jungle with the minimum of malaria casualties. Thenceforward commanding officers were made responsible for ensuring that anti-malarial discipline was carried out and were called to account if any cases of malaria occurred in their units.†

The malaria rate among the Australian troops was cut down from 740 per 1,000 to 26 per 1,000 in the period December 1943 to November 1944, and the mepacrine method of suppressing malaria was adopted by all commands in the south-west Pacific and south-east Asia. From 1942/43 in the latter area the sickness rate was of such proportions that almost every man was sick and admitted to hospital inside two months. The ratio of malaria admission to those from wounds in 1943 was 126 : 1 but by 1944, due to mepacrine, it had been reduced to 19 : 1. Malaria, to which the Japanese were equally susceptible, had hitherto caused an unacceptable number of casualties and might have been disastrous to the campaign but for mepacrine. In fact, it was now possible for the Fourteenth Army in Burma to operate in malarious areas where the Japanese, without mepacrine, were at a great disadvantage.

---

* There were two cases of malaria at Cairns. Fairley, who knew his Australian soldier, made a personal enquiry. One man hid his pill between his fingers and pretended to put it into his mouth; the other put chewing-gum in his mouth, pressed it onto his teeth and drove the pill into the chewing-gum for later extrusion.

† Similar disciplinary measures are taken by the US Army at present fighting in South Vietnam.

PART FIVE

AMPHIBIOUS WAR

Chapter 11

Maintenance of an Army: Transport of Supplies and Equipment

The experience gained in combined operations—landing on an enemy-held coast—in the First World War was not encouraging for future enterprises of this kind. Yet in the 1930s the Japanese made successful landings in China—admittedly against an inferior army—and they were the first to use specialised landing craft. The US Marine Corps, although tied to a restrictive budget, persisted in experimenting with amphibious techniques, using some of the paraphernalia that was to become familiar in the Second World War, such as mechanised landing craft to carry troops ashore and amphibious armoured vehicles. The first self-propelled barges to carry tanks were used in 1938, and by that time joint air, naval and army exercises had been held.

The British services were tied financially by the ruling of the Chiefs of Staff, who foresaw no need for amphibious operations in a future war. However, in 1938 the Inter-Services Training and Development Centre (ISTDC) was set up at Portsmouth. It recommended the construction of prototype mechanised landing craft and by the outbreak of war a small number of these were in use.

In October 1941, Headquarters, Combined Operations, under Captain (later Admiral) Lord Louis Mountbatten, became responsible for the working out of techniques, the development of ships, craft and gadgets. Hitherto known as a dashing destroyer commander, Mountbatten was also a signals expert and had an original and inventive mind. A new epoch in combined operations then began.

(i) Artificial Harbours

It is important to define the component parts of the artificial harbours used in the Normandy landings in the summer of 1944 before beginning to describe how the idea was born and how it developed.

There was an inner and an outer harbour. The inner one consisted of a number of blockships, individually known as 'Corncobs' and collectively as 'Gooseberries', which sailed across the Channel under their own power and were then sunk in line. They were required from the word 'Go' in order to provide shelter for light craft. The outer harbour was formed by concrete caissons known as 'Phœnixes' towed across the Channel and sunk in position. A floating breakwater of steel construction (the 'Bombardons') was anchored still further out to sea. Within the sheltered water the components of the 'Mulberry' harbour could now be constructed. They were a number of floating pierheads ('Whale') moored some distance off the beach and connected to it by a floating roadway of articulated steel construction. However, despite the publicity they have received on account of Churchill's minute which inspired their development, they were not of vital importance. The *sine qua non* was sheltered water. Within the Mulberry harbour, which covered an area as big as Dover harbour, large coasters, tank landing ships, smaller craft and amphibious vehicles were able to discharge their cargoes. In the shelter of the outer breakwater Liberty ships would be able to anchor and unload on to barges. The harbours were intended to be used for a period of ninety days after the assault. By then it was hoped that captured ports would be in operation.

The combined Army, Navy and Air Force commanders began to plan for a return to the Continent in the autumn of 1941. By the early summer of 1943 the Chief of Staff to an as yet unappointed Supreme Allied Commander (COSSAC)—General Sir Frederick Morgan—and his team of planners concluded that artificial harbours were essential to the operation. The painful experience of the Dieppe raid of August 1942 made it clear that a port of any size could not be captured in the early stages of an assault. Secondly, it was believed that the risks involved in maintaining an army across open beaches were too great. It was while trying to find a solution to this seemingly insoluble problem at a meeting at Norfolk House in London that the Naval Chief of Staff to General Morgan, Commodore (later Vice-Admiral) John Hughes-Hallett declared : 'If we can't capture a port we must take one with us.'[1] His remark was greeted with laughter.

In fact, work on pierheads for unloading stores on an open beach began soon after Dunkirk. A team of experienced civil engineers, all of them experts in harbour construction, had, on the Army's evacuation, put on uniform and joined the War Office Directorate of Transportation under a prominent civil engineer, Brigadier B. G. (later Sir Bruce) White. This group examined all ideas on the subject of returning to the Continent, and did not overlook the wildest-looking proposal which might nevertheless contain the germ of a useful idea.[2] In the early days of the project the War Office appreciated the complexity of the problem more than the Admiralty.

On 30 May 1942, when thoughts about the invasion of the Continent were beginning to crystallise, Churchill wrote his celebrated minute about pierheads to the Chiefs of Staff. 'They must', he said, 'float up and down with the tide. The anchor problem must be mastered. Let me have the best solution worked out. Don't argue the matter. The difficulties will argue themselves.'[3] Retained at the back of his mind was a problem then twenty-seven years old. At Gallipoli, the one major combined operation of the First World War (and one which owed its genesis to Churchill), he had proposed building a small harbour out of blockships and later he had pressed for some sort of portable equipment by which ships could remain floating while discharging cargo off an open beach.

The Prime Minister's minute seems to have 'drifted round' the Admiralty, who considered it impractical. With a lack of urgency, it was passed on to Headquarters, Combined Operations, and finally came to rest with Bruce White's team during a meeting at Montagu House. His chief assistant, J. A. S. Rolfe, an engineer with experience of harbour construction in India, and his colleagues, produced an answer in seven days.[4] Their proposal was based on a special dredger, built by Messrs. Löbnitz in 1923, able to anchor itself by pressing down spuds or legs into the seabed, thus providing itself with a rigid yet flexible anchorage. The dredger, which went out to the West Indies, withstood a sudden storm in which other ships were wrecked or driven ashore.

White's team was charged by Headquarters, Combined Operations, responsible for the study of all aspects of amphibious warfare, with devising a pierhead. Between September 1942 and February 1943 a prototype spud pontoon was built and tested off an exposed beach on the west coast of Scotland. The spuds enabled the pontoon to rise and fall with the tide, permitting ships to berth and discharge at any time. This ability to float up and down with the tide was very important, for the beaches in north-west France are flat with gentle slopes and there is a tidal range of up to 30 feet. (Planners of the landings and Sicily and Italy, where there is no tide, found it very difficult to appreciate this factor.) It must be remembered, however, that this scheme was devised without any thought of a protective breakwater.

Some means had to be devised for bridging the water gap between the pierheads and the shore, which might be as much as a mile on account of the low gradient of the beaches. Of three schemes considered by Headquarters, Combined Operations, the one evolved by one of Bruce White's team, W. T. Everall, was the best. This was an articulated steel bridge mounted on concrete pontoons (steel was not available) linked with the spud pontoon pierhead. Tested with the spud in Scotland, it was able to ride a rough sea without overstressing any of its components.

In February, DMWD had consulted White's engineers over the possible use of artificial breakwaters to be used in conjunction with the pierheads. Now, with a definite requirement, schemes were devised both by Admiralty scientists and War Office engineers—but with no central direction. The first scheme, the bubble breakwater, was one which had rested in the Admiralty archives for some years. A curtain of air bubbles was projected upwards from a pipe submerged below sea level; the constant upward flow or bubbles was supposed to have a neutralising effect on the waves. The idea had been patented by an American in 1907 and had also been described more recently in a Russian scientific journal. The second idea was evolved by R. A. Lochner, an electrical engineer, who had joined DMWD. It was called 'Lilo' and was to consist of vast rubberised canvas bags filled with air which were to be anchored partly above and partly under the water.

The port engineers in the War Office were opposed to a floating breakwater. Their answer was to build large caissons of reinforced concrete in docks in Britain, tow them across the Channel and sink them off the assault beaches. The idea was not new in harbour engineering. In 1940 an engineer, G. A. Maunsell, had designed concrete platforms to hold anti-aircraft guns which were prefabricated, towed into position and sunk in the Thames and Mersey estuaries. Maunsell passed his idea on to White. 'The problems which were new', states Rolfe, 'were those of towing and rapid placing. Neither of these presented any difficulty.'[5]

In the meantime Headquarters, Combined Operations, acted both as a catalyst for ideas on the harbour and as an intermediary between the Services and the Chiefs of Staff. For Mountbatten had been instructed to study tactical and technical developments as well as to direct and press forward research and development.

From the outset, Mountbatten insisted that he represented the three services, and, inevitably, he made enemies among the more orthodox-minded. His headquarters were well represented on the scientific side with Professors J. D. Bernal and Solly Zuckerman, both of whom had been working on problems arising out of enemy air attacks, and the erratic but fertile-minded Geoffrey Pyke. They advised the Director of Experiments and Operational Requirements, originally Capt. (later Rear-Admiral) L. E. H. Maund who was succeeded by Capt. T. A. Hussey. The scientific side not so much originated but stimulated and encouraged the principal devices in amphibious operations.

A fresh stage in the development of artificial harbours took place on 28 June 1943, when an important conference was held at Largs, on the Clyde, at which the lessons learned in previous combined operations were explained and decisions were made on essential requirements for the invasion. Hughes-Hallett stated that artificial harbours were essential to the enterprise. Mountbatten, meanwhile, intended to co-ordinate the diverse projects for the harbours. But already there was a strong naval bias, for the Royal Navy, as Rolfe points out, being the senior service was apt to bang the table. The result was that the Admiralty, having already produced a breakwater scheme, was told it was to be in charge of the layout of the artifiical harbours. The War Office protested in vain.

Meanwhile, the Vice-Chief of the Imperial General Staff, General Sir Archibald Nye, had come down strongly in favour of the caissons (Phœnix), and designs for this project were well advanced by the time the Combined Chiefs of Staff met at Quebec towards the middle of August 1943. This conference decided the timing, strength and location of the invasion. A decision had also to be made on the vexed problem of the artificial harbours.

Two important decisions were taken. In the first place the Americans accepted that the artificial harbours should be a British responsibility, although consultations between the Allies should continue and, in fact, much technical assistance was given by the Americans. Secondly, the Lilo and bubble-breakwater schemes were rejected as being impractical. The breakwaters were instead to consist of blockships, which hitherto had been ruled out on account of the shortage of shipping, and the War Office's caissons. On 6 September the Chiefs of Staff asked Bruce White's organisation to supervise the design and construction of the caissons and pierheads.

The Admiralty, undaunted, came forward with an alternative to Lilo—also largely the produce of Lochner's mind. This was another floating breakwater formed of Bombardons[6]—massive steel cruciform structures with rigid vertical sides and watertight buoyancy compartments, each weighing about 1,000 tons. A model of the Bombardon had already been made, and whereas the Lilo suppressed the waves through resilience, the Bombardons suppressed them by inertia; they rolled like a ship but the period of roll was never in phase with the period of waves they were likely to confront. They were always banging against the waves and knocking them back. It was decided that they should form the outermost breakwater of the harbour.

There were only eight months to go before D-Day. Yet from the end of the Quebec Conference, early in September, until 15 December 1943, a battle raged for control of the Mulberry project between Admiralty and War Office. It ended in a victory for the Admiralty, which was confirmed by COSSAC when he decided that the Admiralty should become responsible for the breakwaters and layout of the harbours while the War Office retained responsibility for the piers and floating roadways. But, says Rolfe, 'I think that the principle of handing over the whole requirement to one Branch (Transportation) was the correct one. Our difficulties arose when we had the Gooseberries and the Bombardons thrust on us.'[7]

In spite of all these difficulties, the construction of the Phœnixes had gone ahead. On return from Washington, Bruce White set up two committees, one of contractors under Sir Malcolm McAlpine, and the other of consultant engineers under Sir William Halcrow. (One engineer is said to have walked out of the first meeting, unwilling for his firm to be associated with so impractical an idea.) The caissons varied in size from 60 to 200 feet in length and 25 to

60 feet in height.* A special department was set up in the Ministry of Supply under J. W. (later Sir John) Gibson to deal with the problems of construction. The Ministry was also responsible for constructing twenty-three spud pierheads and ten miles of floating roadway.

But the work on the Bombardons, which was carried out by the Admiralty, drew away skilled labour and materials from the caisson project. When completed the caissons were to be sunk in 'parking places' off the south coast and at the appropriate time they were to be raised by naval salvage vessels in readiness to cross the Channel after D-Day. White's engineers, however, believed that they would be damaged in the process. Had it not been for the Bombardons, they could have been anchored on the surface, but the Admiralty kept these anchors for the Bombardons.

The work on the pierheads had been going slowly on account of the rival schemes already mentioned and despite constant prodding by the Prime Minister. By 4 May, Sir Walter Monckton reported to him that 80 per cent of Whale would be ready a week before D-Day.

In January, Mulberry became an operational command under Rear-Admiral Sir William Tennant with Capt. (later Vice-Admiral) H. Hickling as his Chief of Staff.

The first Bombardons were ready to be tested in January. They proved to be far from seaworthy and several of them broke up in a gale, thereby confirming the original doubts of the War Office port engineers. However, work on them went ahead and by mid-March ninety-three Bombardons were assembled at Portland, where they were held in position by the moorings that had originally been intended for the Phœnixes.

Great difficulty was experienced in getting the Admiralty to give up the merchantmen for use as blockships. Admiral Tennant, after one meeting, remarked to Hickling : 'We came here to get a gooseberry and all we seem to have got is a raspberry.' A ruling had to be obtained from the Chiefs of Staff, one of whom asked how the Admiralty would feel if the situation arose in which the invasion had failed for lack of fifty-three ships. At last four old battleships and fifty-three merchant vessels were released by the Admiralty. On the eve of D-Day they had all safely arrived at Poole harbour, having sailed down from the west coast of Scotland.

* Some of them were equivalent in size to a concrete building five storeys high.

Much depended on the skilful placing of the Mulberry components, especially the caissons. Every scrap of information about the state of the tides and the composition of the seabed was eagerly devoured by planners and engineers.

The story of the construction of the Mulberry units has often been told. It is sufficient to say that all the units were completed by the end of May—only just in time. The blockships had been sunk and the Bombardons moored a week after D-Day. By 19 June, 90 per cent of the Mulberry harbours had been completed and 2,000 tons of stores were being handled daily in the British harbour alone. But on that day the worst summer storm for forty years began to blow. The American Mulberry was wrecked and became unusable. The British Mulberry was severely damaged. A number of Bombardons broke loose in both harbours and barged into the caissons sinking several of them (although Lochner denied that the Phœnixes sank on account of the drifting Bombardons). Landing-craft were swept on to the floating roadways and several pierheads were driven onto the beaches. Most of the caissons in the American harbour sank into the sand, others partially turned over or broke their backs. According to Admiral Hickling they were badly sited with too wide a gap between each caisson.[8] The water poured through, scouring the sand from underneath the caissons. The American harbour was abandoned and unloading went on over the open beach.

How essential were the artificial harbours to 'Overlord'—the code name of the Normandy invasion? And how effective were they? Twenty-two years after the construction of Mulberry, feelings still run high over their value. There is no doubt that the 'improvised sheltered water' had averted disaster during the great storm which raged for a week. During that time hundreds of ships and small craft rode it out in safety and unloading went ahead. The value of the Bombardons will continue to be disputed. Looking back, it is difficult to see that they were essential to the harbour. The blockships, no novelty in naval warfare and only effective in shallow water up to 20 feet, in the event was probably the most useful of all the breakwaters. The most efficient breakwaters should have been the concrete caissons and, where sited properly, they performed the task required of them. On the other hand, the pierheads and articulated roadways were far less successful. The roadways were very difficult to tow across the Channel and 40 per cent was lost at sea. The first pier was not operating until 29 June—over two weeks after D-Day. The whole structure was too elaborate for the reason it had been designed for use on an exposed shore before the break-water was introduced.

The Mulberries cost £30 to £40 million in all. Were they worth it? In fact, some 35 per cent of the stores for the armies in Normandy was landed through the artificial harbour up to the end of August 1944; 50 per cent was unloaded over open beach sheltered by the blockships; 15 per cent was unloaded in the small harbour of Port en Bessin and Courseulles. On the other hand, it should be remembered that when the original design was considered, only three, not five, divisions were planned to take part in the assault, thus imposing additional strain on the capacity of the harbours. The Whale units were useful for offloading heavy machinery and other awkward equipment and also for embarking casualties and backloading damaged equipment; finally, the harbour provided shelter in the storm.

The artificial harbours were a very important, though in the end, not a vital part of the machinery for maintaining the armies. They were undoubtedly a fine achievement of British engineers and scientists, but the disputes that arose during their construction could have been disastrous to the landings. This factor underlined both the importance of effective central control and the failure of service officers to pay attention to expert advice—in the latter case the experienced port engineers. Inter-service squabbles would have been avoided had the engineers of different departments been welded into one team. Such criticism came from no less a person than the late General Eisenhower, who pointed out the dangers of dividing responsibility for Mulberry between the Admiralty, War Office, and Ministry of Supply.[9] It was fortunate for the enterprise that so much preliminary work was done by the War Office team before approval of the harbours was given only eight months before D-Day.

(ii) Naval Lighter Pontoons

The need to obtain sheltered water for the unloading of vessels was peculiar to the English Channel coast. A quick turn round for shipping lying off an assault beach where there were no port facilities was also necessary. Two solutions to the problem were the Naval Lighter Pontoon and the DUKW.

The Mediterranean is a tideless sea with gently shelving beaches. How were vehicles to be landed when the slope of the beaches was so little that the vessel would ground in a depth of water which exceeded the wading capacity of the vehicle? This difficulty had been foreseen by Capt. Maund at the ISTDC in 1939. He had designed a wedge-shaped landing-stage, but this never got beyond the embryo stage. The alternative was to fit the landing craft with a special ramp which would swing out on to the beach. Such a ramp was, in fact, built in 1940 but where there was a very shallow beach the ramp had to be constructed in three separate interlocking parts : it was too clumsy and had to be abandoned.

The necessity to bridge the water gap was first appreciated by Capt. Hussey who, as already mentioned, had become Director of Experiments and Operational Requirements at Headquarters, Combined Operations. The occasion was the planning of the assault on Sicily. On a visit to the United States at the end of 1941, the purpose of which was to persuade the Americans to build assault craft for Britain and which will be discussed later, Hussey had seen the Naval Lighter Pontoon which was a substitute for a pier, or landing-stage. It was a floating rectangular tank, 7 ft. by 5 ft., and any number of parts could be strung together to form whatever size or shape was needed. He also saw the US Army treadway bridging equipment.

Hussey remembered the pontoon and suggested it to Mountbatten, who was working out requirements for the landings. Mountbatten sent him out to Washington in March 1943 to make further enquiries. Representations made by the British Military Mission there had made no progress. 'I had', says Hussey, 'great difficulty in persuading the Americans that the Naval Lighter Pontoons were feasible and were necessary and should be made roughly as we suggested, at the greatest speed, and sent to the Mediterranean.[10]

Eventually the matter was taken up with the Combined Chiefs of Staff and two tank landing ships were put at Hussey's disposal. Trials, using the pontoons in conjunction with the treadway bridge, showed the practicability of the system. Motor vehicles were driven ashore within ten minutes of the landing ship beaching, and the equipment could be towed to another ship after all the vehicles had driven off. It was then decided that the pontoons should be made available for one in every six tank landing ships.

In the meantime, prototype pontoons were made in Britain, each

75 ft. long and with 15 ft. beam, specially shaped at bow and stern to facilitate towing. Ramps were devised like the treadway but were not ready for the Sicily landings. Instead, substitutes from Bailey bridge panels were improvised by the sappers.

Despite lack of experience in handling them, the pontoons were used successfully in the landings on Sicily. In the first place they were towed astern, and when the ship grounded, their momentum took them ahead of the ship where they were coaxed, one under the ramp of the ship and the other overlapping the first and reaching the shore in about two feet of water. Later, the Americans perfected a means of carrying them hoisted one on each side of the landing ship.

In Normandy, a new use was found for the pontoons. Sections were lashed together and fitted with outboard motors. In this guise they were called 'Rhino ferries', and brought ashore supplies from ship to land in the sheltered waters of the Mulberry harbour. The pontoon causeways, then, were important to all amphibious operations because, without them, no tanks or vehicles could have landed beyond their wading capacity on any beach.

(iii) The DUKW

Less complicated than the pontoons would be an amphibious vehicle which could take on cargo from a ship, navigate through the sea and drive ashore to dump its load. The DUKW,* or 'Duck', did just this. It also enabled ships to offload very quickly and this was an asset when there was a shortage of shipping.

The DUKW was an all-American idea and development, the idea for which came shortly after Pearl Harbour, when the U-boats were reaping a harvest off the east American coast. It then became necessary to exploit every ship's capabilities to the utmost. Vannevar Bush was the moving spirit behind the development of the DUKW, which was the responsibility not of the services but of the NDRC. In 1942, a small group of engineers and yachtsmen under Hartley Rowe, chief engineer of the United Fruit Company, began to design it. Rowe had acquired in South America before the war a good deal of experience in handling cargoes over beaches where long rollers came in. Col. (later Brig. Gen.) A. C. McAuliffe, who

---

* The initials stand for D—year 1942; U—Utility; K—Front wheel drive; W—Two rear-driving axles.

was on the staff of the Commanding General, Supply and Services, Lt.-Gen. Brehan B. Somervell, encouraged development of the DUKW but, in general, the Army opposed it.

The question was whether to convert a truck already in large-scale production into an amphibious vehicle or whether to develop an entirely new model. Bush chose the former. He got permission from General Somervell to produce a pilot model on condition that he cancelled three alternative designs. The vehicle chosen weighed $2\frac{1}{2}$ tons; it was available in numbers with spares, and all the teething problems had been solved. The idea was to fit a watertight hull round the truck and provide it with a propeller for use in the water.

General Motors took on the development work and a prototype was ready within thirty-eight days at the firm's proving ground at Milford, Michigan. On 3 June 1942, the first DUKW was water-borne. It carried fifty people, or an equivalent load of supplies at a speed of five miles an hour in the water. However, the Army was still disinclined to take the project seriously. Bush later wrote : 'There was probably more obtuse resistance to this device than to any other in the war.'[11] But when plans began to be made for the European landings and something was required for unloading shipping, more interest was taken in the DUKW. When asked by McAuliffe whether its wheels would stick in the mud, Rowe replied that the DUKW would be able to cross 90 per cent of the beaches in the world. Without leaving his seat the driver was able to inflate or deflate the tyres on all the wheels, according to whether the terrain underneath was soft sand, coral or hard road.

The Army was still not convinced, and was inclined to opt for more conventional models. At last a dramatic incident, in which an Army DUKW became a lifeboat, won over the prejudiced 'Brass'. One night when the DUKW was undergoing trials at Cape Cod, a coastguard boat with seven men aboard was driven ashore in a 40 mph gale. It was impossible either to launch a rescue boat through the heavy surf or to approach the vessel from the land side and use a breeches buoy. One of the original DUKWs went out into the gale and rescued the stranded crew, taking photographs as well. This was the first rescue of a naval vessel by an army truck. Bush showed the photographs to a Presidential meeting and, writes Bush, 'From that moment on we found less resistance to this new-fangled and strange contraption.'

The DUKW could drive ashore at full speed. As already shown, it could negotiate soft sand with deflated tyres; it could circle round a ship and take a 10-ton load off the booms; it was even able to land through surf. It could travel at 50 mph on a good road.

DUKWs were used to great advantage in Sicily, Italy, Normandy and the Pacific. The British took to them at once after seeing them in action in Morocco, but it is interesting to note that they did not appear in the Pacific until the end of 1943. They were particularly useful off the American beaches in Normandy after the US Mulberry had been destroyed. The DUKW had its drawbacks : it was small and difficult to unload; it was slow in travelling through water but it could stand up to rough handling; it could go through surf. Altogether it played a very important role in amphibious operations.

(iv) Landing Craft (Tank)

In July 1940, R. (now Sir Roland) Baker of the Royal Corps of Naval Constructors was asked to produce a design for a tank landing craft or LCT. It was to be a flat-bottomed craft able to carry five Valentine tanks, one behind the other, and land them in three feet of water on what was believed to be the average beach gradient of 1 in 30. The landing craft (tank) was to have a speed of nine knots.

Baker's design was ready within three days, and thirty of these craft were immediately ordered in spite of the urgent need for anti-submarine vessels. The first two were completed by Messrs. Hawthorne Leslie on the Tyne that November, and were sent out to the Middle East.

A second version of the LCT was designed so that it could be built by bridge builders in sections and assembled on improvised slipways on the mudbanks of rivers. They were also easier to load as deck cargo when built in sections. A total of seventy-three of these craft were built, each driven by Napier Lion aero engines, apparently designed in 1916. But this type of LCT had two defects; it drew too much water and the engine was not powerful enough. Hence the LCT (3), which was similar in design to its predecessors but had an additional section in the centre which carried a Paxman diesel engine. This craft was probably the best all-round type of its kind and was eminently suitable for landing on the shallow French beaches.

But the war was not only going to be fought on French beaches. The planners were closely studying the shores of Sardinia, Corsica, Sicily, the Dodecanese and, farther afield, the shallow inlets of Southern Burma. The LCT was not a decked vessel. With such cramped accommodation for its crew, it could not attempt a long sea voyage; it had poor sea-keeping qualities and too shallow draught. It could not carry more than three tanks. A large ocean-going vessel was required.

(v) Landing Ship (Tank)

The idea for such a vessel came from the Prime Minister, Winston Churchill.* On 7 July 1940, only a month after British troops had been evacuated from France, he minuted : 'Let there be built great ships which can cast up on a beach, in any weather, large numbers of the heaviest tanks.'[12] It is interesting to note that at the time this minute was written no craft existed in Britain capable of carrying even one tank, nor were any plans in existence for manufacturing such craft.

As a direct result of the Prime Minister's minute Roland Baker was asked to submit a design for a tank landing craft. 'There is no doubt', Baker has written, 'that it was the Prime Minister who first used the expression tank landing craft—later Landing Ship (Tank)'.[13]

Baker, we have seen, designed the LCT. But Churchill wanted ships capable of carrying sixty tanks and landing them on a beach-head anywhere in the world. This idea was given some point by the experience of the fiasco at Dakar in September 1940. Even if the assault from the sea had been successful its momentum could have failed for lack of tanks. Nevertheless, it gave birth to a war-winner —which sprang from the Prime Minister's brain. As Bernard Fergusson, the chronicler of Combined Operations, wrote : 'Most people are agreed that it (the tank landing ship) was the biggest of all material contributions to the successful landings in the Mediterranean and on the Normandy coast, as well as the spectacular performance of the Americans in the Pacific.'[14]

---

* Churchill was recalling a suggestion he made in 1917 for bullet-proof lighters and tank landing craft for a proposed landing on Borkum and Sylt.

Special ships would, of course, take time to build, whereas something was wanted quickly. A. T. Sheffer, a Lloyds surveyor who was on the staff of the Director of Naval Construction, remembered the special shallow-draught tankers used to load oil at Maracaibo, in Venezuela. Three of these vessels were requisitioned and converted. The first was ready for commissioning in June 1941 and went, as did the others, to the Middle East.

The naval constructors told the Prime Minister that it was too risky to put sixty tanks in one vessel. Instead they suggested a ship which carried twenty tanks each. The LSTs to be built on these lines were known as 'Winettes', and were given the aggressive names of *Boxer*, *Bruiser* and *Thruster*. They had a special ramp by which the tanks could descend on to the beach, over the bows of the ship. Loading took place over the stern with the aid of a 40-ton crane and the tanks or vehicles were carried on two decks connected by a lift. There is no doubt, says Baker, that the Prime Minister 'plucked the idea off his own ceiling' for the Winettes.

But there was a tug-of-war over the building of these special craft. The Admiralty wanted corvettes in a hurry to hunt U-boats. The Navy always believed that priority must be given to the defence of the trade routes which meant, in fact, the building of conventional warships. It also cast covetous eyes on the LCTs for purposes of its own.

For this reason it was necessary to look westwards to the United States. The need for mass-produced landing craft had, however, been foreseen by a number of British shipbuilders at a very early stage in the war. 'It was necessary', said one of them, 'to design a ship which could be constructed by the aid of a set square and a foot rule.' But this country lacked men, materials, and the space in which to build them. In the United States the technique of construction of specialised landing craft was already well advanced not only by the US Bureau of Ships but by private enterprise as well. One of the leading innovators was an energetic Irish-American—Andrew J. Higgins—from New Orleans, who had designed a number of craft originally intended to enable rum-runners to out-distance the revenue cutters. Now he worked on more lawful occasions with the US Marine Corps and designed the powerful 'Eureka' craft which could carry thirty-six men.

Goodwill for Britain in 1941 was abundant and there was a tremendous shipbuilding potential in the States, if only the Admiralty would state its requirements. This was confirmed by Edward Cochrane, US Bureau of Ships, and Francis Gibbs, the naval architect who had designed the liners *United States* and *America*. Rear-Admiral J. W. S. Dorling of the British Joint Staff Mission in Washington urged his colleagues in Britain to take action. Mountbatten, who had recently arrived in Headquarters, Combined Operations, was not slow in taking the hint. He sent out a mission to Washington under Hussey which included Baker, and Cdr. R. C. Todhunter, who had been recalled from ICI. They took with them plans for three types of assault craft which they were going to persuade the Americans to mass-produce. There was a design for a small LCT which could be shipped across the Atlantic as deck cargo; a Landing Ship (Dock) (LSD) which will be discussed later, and Baker's design for a simplified LST to be an alternative to the Winettes and which was eventually to see the light as the LST(2).

The time was November 1941. The United States was not yet in the war. Hussey and his colleagues described to American officers the need to land over open beaches in combined operations and how important tank landing craft were for a long haul, for instance, if an operation against North Africa were to be planned. The Americans were politely interested, asked to study the plans and kept them for a week. At the second meeting, only a week before Pearl Harbour, to the disappointment of the British party, the Americans advised them to concentrate on building warships. While the smaller landing craft presented no problem, construction of the larger one used up too much space for the building of merchant shipping. Naval officers further stated that they could see no requirement for specialised craft for amphibious operations. But General Marshall strongly opposed this view and afterwards urged the President to back the British request. Cochrane also spoke out on behalf of the British. He believed that there was plenty of space for shipbuilding, especially on some of the large American rivers.

Hussey felt despondent over the possibility of the mission foundering. Nothing could be lost, he felt, by approaching the President himself. He was rewarded by the offer of a meeting between the British mission and the President on 8 December—in the event, the eve of the Japanese attack on Pearl Harbour. This shattering blow put further discussion about making landing craft for Britain out of the question for the time being.

But Churchill and the Chiefs of Staff were soon conferring in

Page 221 (*above*) The British Mulberry Harbour on the Normandy beach-head showing sheltered water; (*below*) a 'Rhino' Ferry carrying three tanks.

Page 222: A Landing Ship (Dock).

Washington. Lord Beaverbrook was also in the party and eloquently advanced the requirements of Headquarters, Combined Operations. This time the President not only approved all the items in the list hopefully made up by Hussey six weeks earlier and which he never imagined would be obtained *in toto* but doubled the American requirement.

There were still obstacles in the way. This time they arose from the proclivity of the US Naval Chief of Staff, Admiral King, for operations in the Pacific. He was adamant in his belief that this theatre of operations should have top priority. Fortunately the President intervened once more and on 17 May 1943 issued a decree which placed landing ships and craft second in priority only to air-craft-carriers.

The Winette design was dropped and instead the LST(2), origi-nally known as the Atlantic tank landing craft, was designed for long ocean voyages. Hussey has written that 'the ultimate design as pro-duced in large numbers by the Americans bore little relation to the first shot made at the request of the Director of Naval Construc-tion . . . it was largely due to the badgering of Baker and, to a small extent, myself.'[15] Baker stayed in America for several months to help the Americans in the design which proved so successful. One of the difficulties was to construct a ship seaworthy enough to cross an ocean and yet of sufficiently shallow draft to be able to land on a beach. The Americans had the idea of welding the ships' hulls instead of riveting them and they put in eight diesel engines for motive power. Trials were completed by November 1942. Baker concludes : 'We realised that the Winettes were too large and com-plicated and it was our conception of the Atlantic tank landing craft, which became the LST(2), that more than anything else made winning the war possible.'

The LSTs were built in naval yards and cargo vessel slipways up and down the American coastline and large rivers. Altogether 115 of them were received by the British. It is the verdict of historians that the Allies would have been given greater flexibility with more of them and that their scarcity was a constant headache for the Chiefs of Staff. General Wilson, Supreme Allied Commander in the Mediter-ranean, wrote thus : 'Distribution and availability of craft became a permanently limiting factor in planning all amphibious operations, not only in the Mediterranean, but throughout all the Allied theatres of war.'[16] Against this must be balanced the pressing requirements for anti-submarine vessels. Yet when all is taken into account, one can only echo Churchill's conclusion that the major amphibious enterprises of the war would have been impossible without the LSTs.

(vi) Landing Ship (Dock)

This original ship was designed to carry several LCTs which were too heavy to be lifted by derricks or davits. It was a high-speed, self-propelled floating dock. The LCTs we have seen, could not make long sea voyages. On the other hand, they could beach their loads in shallower water than the LSTs and they could disgorge tanks onto the beach faster. They also presented a smaller target. The LSDs carried these craft into the battle area.

The LSD was a 'brain foster child' of Capt. Hussey. The proposal for such a vessel was made at an Admiralty meeting on 19 September, 1941. Before the sceptical eyes of his colleagues, Hussey produced photographs of a 'Popper' barge transporter (a paddle-steamer) used on the Danube. It could be flooded like a floating dock and two barges floated on, one on either side of the superstructure. The water was then pumped out and the barges were left high and dry resting on the part fore and aft of the paddle box. Hussey envisaged the LCTs being floated in through a gate at the stern of the vessel, and after landing their tank loads they could be used for other duties.

It was through making this proposal that Hussey earned his nickname of 'ITMA',* after Tommy Handley, the radio comedian. But the Director of Naval Construction, having overcome his surprise, agreed to make a design. The ship was to be able to steam 5,000 miles at fourteen knots and the two LCTs would carry twelve tanks or other vehicles and their crews or alternatively, a larger number of small assault craft.

During Hussey's visit to Washington, already mentioned, the Americans, although initially sceptical, agreed to build four LSDs for the British. They also built eighteen for themselves, most of which saw distinguished service in the Pacific. The British LSDs were used to good purpose in the Mediterranean and in the Normandy landings. They ferried various types of landing craft and amphibious vehicles to all parts of the world. Finally, they were used for the repair of small landing craft.

* 'It's That Man Again.'

Chapter 12

Landing on a Defended Coast

(i) Landing Craft Tank (Rocket)

The idea for the rocket craft arose out of the post-mortem on the Dieppe raid of August 1942. This costly attack has since been the subject of much controversial writing—a good deal of it ill-informed. A number of valuable lessons were learned which, however obvious they seem in retrospect, were less apparent at the time. Bernard Fergusson has written of the raid: 'It certainly showed up, in a brutal manner, the deficiencies of some of our thinking.'[1] The reports on the operation agreed that the chief lesson was the total inadequacy of the close support provided by the ships of the Royal Navy to cover the assault infantry and armour. It was necessary to drench the beaches and land overlooking the beaches with high-explosive immediately before the landing. Despite every precaution taken to identify enemy batteries and machine-gun nests for destruction by naval guns and aircraft, all the weapons could not be located. And these targets were difficult to engage after the attack had been launched because they were quickly obscured by the smoke and dust of battle.

The experience of Dieppe was assimilated by an assault warfare committee set up by Mountbatten in November 1942. At a higher level, the Chiefs of Staff formed a technical sub-committee the following month with representatives from all the services, Headquarters, Combined Operations, and the Ministry of Supply.

The Deputy Director, Experiments and Staff Requirements, Headquarters, Combined Operations, Col. F. H. C. Langley, was particularly struck by the inadequacy of fire support. He had seen service in both the Royal Navy and the Army, and in the latter had been a battery commander at the end of the First World War. He therefore had every qualification for being a member of a combined operations staff. He had been a civilian in the inter-war years, and was now enthusiastic about rockets. The solution was, he said, 'an extremely dense concentration of rocket fire from special craft, directed on the assault beaches in such a way as to make any form of enemy-aimed fire difficult, if not impossible, during the period just before the deployment of infantry and armour from the assault landing ships and craft.

'In order to produce as soon as possible a short-term answer to this requirement, it was suggested that LCTs should be made available in the required numbers, that the 5-in. chemical warfare rocket* armed with a high-explosive-filled head should be the weapon mounted in the craft and that, until the Admiralty were able to design and manufacture a projector capable of use at sea, the projectors designed for the chemical warfare rockets should be used. It was realised that if this form of weapon was to be tactically effective, it was essential that the best available fire-control system should be incorporated in the craft. This was the H₂S radar set mounted to scan horizontally instead of vertically downwards as in an aircraft.'[2]

Mountbatten at once approved the idea and made it an urgent operational requirement. The Director of the Gunnery Division of the Admiralty, who fortunately happened to be Langley's brother, after detailed examination of the project, gave it his blessing and the Admiralty made available a precious LCT. The War Office supplied the ammunition and, in the early stages, the projectors. The Air Ministry provided a small number of H₂S sets.

The experimental craft was assembled at Portsmouth and did its firing trials under the direction of the Controller of Projectile Development in the Ministry of Supply and later, under Admiralty gunnery experts. The first experiment was not encouraging for Langley and his fellow enthusiasts. An audience of distinguished officers, many of them sceptical about the ability of the projectors to fire accurately, was present. Langley asked the captain of the experimental rocket craft to fire six salvoes (sixty rockets in each) at intervals of five seconds. There was a short circuit and 360 rockets were fired simultaneously. Langley comments: 'The result was enough to remove my eyelashes and eyebrows and much of my hair!'

This mishap did not, however, obscure the possibilities of the new craft. On subsequent tests the projectors worked to plan, and approval was given to the project. Six LCT(R)s were ready to take

* Rockets will be discussed in greater detail in Part Six.

part in the Sicily landings. The tremendous power of these craft may be judged by the fact that one craft could discharge 840 rockets in twenty-six seconds. Later, this total was increased to 1,080 rockets which was approximately equal to a bombardment by eighty cruisers or 240 destroyers in the same amount of time. The maximum range was 3,500 yards.

One limitation was that at this time the rocket projectors were immovable and could only fire straight ahead. Thus the craft sailed at right angles to the beach and fired its rockets over the bows. The rockets could only be fired once, as reloading was a complicated process.

About thirty-six LCT(R)s were built and took part in Mediterranean amphibious operations and in north-west Europe. The Americans also used them to cover landings by their troops. The chief factor which gave impetus to the project was the drive of Admiral Mountbatten in his capacity as Chief of Combined Operations and also as a member of the Chiefs of Staff Committee when requirements for amphibious warfare were under discussion.

(ii) Radio Decoy

In a landing on an enemy-occupied coast the factor of surprise is vital. While preparing for the Normandy landings it was impossible to conceal the great assemblies of shipping on the English south coast. An invasion was on the way but at which point or points would the landings be made? One solution was to destroy completely the enemy's network of coastal radar stations, the principal means by which he could obtain early warning. A programme of attacks was laid on, but as the destruction of every radar station could not be guaranteed, it was also necessary to jam those stations which survived or which had intentionally not been attacked. For the planners had a scheme known as 'Fortitude', the purpose of which was to simulate an attack far distant from the actual invasion area. This plan provided fresh opportunities for the scientists engaged in radio countermeasures to exercise their ingenuity.

TRE had foreseen that radio countermeasures would be an important feature of the invasion plan but by the autumn of 1943 it had received only the most general indications of what might be required. Then, in mid-January 1944, Dr. Cockburn, in charge of radio countermeasures at TRE it will be recalled, was 'Bigoted' which meant that he was initiated into the highly secret planning then in progress at Norfolk House, in London. Here was a good example of direct contact between the planner and the scientist. Technical and tactical problems had to be solved in a very short time with the invasion due to begin in four months time.

Cockburn, having learned the nature of the deception plan, argued that jamming of radar stations was not enough. Simulated landings were to take place in the areas of Boulogne and Dieppe. Clearly, there were insufficient ships to spare for this purpose. But ships could be simulated by dropping Window—a new use for a device which previously had been thought of only in connection with jamming. The idea was received with scepticism because a very high degree of navigational skill would be required of the aircrews dropping Window to ensure its success. It had originally been decided that the jamming operations would be carried out by training squadrons.

However, some small-scale experiments, organised by TRE and conducted by the Royal Navy and tactical aircraft, proved that the simulation scheme was by no means impractical. Cockburn's proposals were accepted and from then onwards every assistance was given to the project.

The intention was to give the appearance of a mass of shipping covering a front of sixteen miles to a depth of sixteen miles. Only a few aircraft were needed. They were to fly very accurately on elliptical orbits about ten miles long, releasing Window over the straight runs of the orbit which were to be two miles apart. At each successive orbit they would approach nearer to the enemy coast according to the distance which a convoy would move during the orbit time. This was a speed of exactly seven miles an hour. In order to maintain the illusion of a surface force, the sizes of Window bundles were to be adjusted as the orbiting aircraft approached the coast. Thus the size of echoes produced would vary in accordance with the change in echoing power of surface targets with distance. Navigation was to be done with the aid of Gee and Gee-H.

As the flight plan was so complex and the accuracy of navigation required extremely high, it was decided to employ the famous No 617 Squadron, using Gee, to fly on the Boulogne diversion and No 218 Squadron, which was experienced in operating on Gee-H, to fly on the Dieppe diversion. Scientists from TRE helped No 617 Squadron with the navigational technique and the Operational Research Section of Bomber Command perfected the Window-dropping arrangements. There was also a small seaborne effort to deceive ASV and coastal radar sets.

At the same time, the airborne operations over Normandy were given cover and a diversion. Some aircraft from operational training units dropped Window over the coastal areas, while others dropped dummy parachutists in selected areas.

There was only a month in which to train the two principal squadrons for their task. Security was intensive. Imagine the surprise on the eve of D-Day when the selected squadrons were told that they would take no bombs and that each aircraft would carry thirteen men to help to throw out Window. Each aircraft of No 617 Squadron carried two Gee sets in case one should break down.

The decoy was an outstanding success. Looking back, it is probable that a smaller effort would have been just as successful. In operational planning the human element is sometimes apt to be forgotten—a nervous radar operator peering into his screen is an easy prey to alarm. There is no doubt that the whole deception plan contributed to the slowness of the enemy's reactions to the Allied landings and his failure to appreciate the situation on D-Day. From the scientific point of view, the operation was a model one. There was close collaboration between scientists, the planners of the operation, and the aircrew taking part. Once the idea had been accepted, every effort was made to make the decoy convincing.[3]

PART SIX

NEW WEAPONS

Chapter 13

Rockets

(i) British Development

Rockets in warfare went out of fashion in the nineteenth century with the improvement of artillery by rifled barrels, recoil mechanisms and colloidal propellants. Early in the twentieth century scientists turned to rockets for a new reason—the exploration of space. The three pioneers in this field were the Russian, Konstantin Ziolkovsky, the American, R. H. Goddard and the Roumanian, Herman Oberth. They all published papers or books on long-range rockets, but Goddard went further and was the first actually to build and fire rockets after the First World War. He designed a rocket gun which was the forerunner of the useful American 'bazooka' of the Second World War. The US Army neglected rockets until mid-1940 when they were stimulated by British development, and Goddard died in 1945 without receiving any acclaim for his pioneer work.

In 1929, the German Army began rocket research in conditions of great secrecy and persuaded a few civilian technicians to work for them. After several years, reports of this clandestine rocket development reached the War Office. The British Army had not used rockets since the Zulu War in 1879 and had abandoned all forms of rocket research at the end of the First World War. In December 1934, it decided, largely because of the interest of the then Master General of Ordnance, Sir Hugh Elles, and in view of the German activities, to form a small group consisting of Dr. Crow, a physicist and Director of Ballistics Research at Woolwich, a chemist, Harold Poole, and a ballistics expert, William (later Sir William) Cook, to investigate rocket propulsion. Needless to say the proposal at first met with opposition from senior artillery officers.

The group's first task was to find a suitable cordite propellant, one which burned steadily and controllably and which, at the end, left as little unburnt residue as possible. A special fuse was another

233

requirement. Research began at Woolwich in May 1935 and by the following year Crow, the leader of the team, reported that the stage had been reached where rockets could be considered for war purposes. The new propellant which was emerging was known as Cordite SC (Solventless Cordite).[1]

In July 1936, the Sub-Committee on Air Defence Research of the Committee of Imperial Defence took over direction of the rocket experiments. This committee was presided over by the Air Minister and was attended by service chiefs and technical experts. Winston Churchill was one of its members and was probably foremost in encouraging the development of rockets, influenced by Lindemann— a fervent believer in the rocket as a weapon of war. The committee decided that the study of rockets should continue in the following order of priority : (1) anti-aircraft defence; (2) long-range attack; (3) air weapon against hostile aircraft; (4) assisted take-off for heavy aircraft.

The pressure of rearmament in the late thirties caused rocket development to be put on a low priority, with the exception of the anti-aircraft rocket known as the 'Unrotated Projectile' or 'UP'. For the slow production of anti-aircraft guns in this country was causing great anxiety and the rockets, although very inaccurate, could serve as a useful substitute while more orthdox weapons were being manufactured. Another attraction was that the rockets required fewer men to fire them, compared with anti-aircraft guns, and they did not have to be highly trained.

Crow's first task was to produce a rocket which would parallel the performance of the 3-in. anti-aircraft gun. He decided to make a rocket of 2-in. calibre using cordite as propellant. Liquid fuel, used by the Germans for their long-range rockets, was rejected because of design problems and the likely unsuitability of liquids in small rockets.

Technical problems inevitably delayed development, and there is no need to do more than summarise them. It was thought that the highly combustible properties of cordite would melt the thin steel casing of the propellant container. Crow decided to fill with a plastic compound the gap between the cordite charge in the middle of the rocket and the inner side of the steel casing. Specially-thickened steel was necessary, involving a process which caused lengthy delays in production during the course of the war. Another serious setback was caused by the fact that the plastic material used inside the rocket was vulnerable to extremes of heat and cold. In February 1938 Crow decided to abandon the plastic surround and return to a loose charge. The metal casing would be specially insulated to protect it from the hot gases. These modifications led to a much lower performance of the rocket than originally anticipated. Nevertheless, as we shall see, the 2-in. rocket was the prototype for a number of original, if not always practical, weapons.

In October 1937, a year after work on the 2-in. rocket had begun, there was a demand for a rocket having the equivalent performance of the 3·7-in. heavy anti-aircraft gun. The Sub-Committee on Air Defence Research therefore decided that a 3-in. rocket was to take precedence over the 2-in. with the aim of obtaining 'an initial supply of a type which, though it might not be ideal, would serve as a weapon of war.' In fact, the rocket, until its development as an aircraft weapon for attacking targets on sea and land and its adoption as a novel form of naval bombardment, proved to be a stop-gap.

Crow used the loose type of cordite charge as in the 2-in. rocket. Although criticised at the time, he believed that this was a wise decision for when the need for the 3-in. rocket became acute early in the war there would otherwise have been no rockets of this kind available and ready for mass production. BSA and Vickers-Armstrong became responsible for the manufacture of rockets and projectors.

So far rocket development had not been invested with great urgency nor were the security arrangements particularly intensive. Sir William Cook recalls sitting with Colonel Kerrison over a sandwich lunch in a pub at Portland after a rocket trial when a fisherman inquired : 'How did them rockets go this morning?' The Munich crisis of September 1938, however, made it necessary to press forward with the experiments, but the General Staff eventually rejected the 3-in. rocket on the grounds that it was insufficiently accurate for medium and high level firing. Nevertheless, work continued on improving the rocket's accuracy up to the outbreak of war, when it was allowed to lapse in favour of more urgent priorities.

By that date, however, as a result of pressure from the sub-committee on Air Defence Research, Crow had become head of an independent department known as the Projectile Development Establishment located at Fort Halstead, in Kent—a fortification erected at the time of the Napoleonic wars. A proving ground had also been found at Aberporth in South Wales.

The use of the dive-bomber by the German Air Force against merchant shipping in the Channel and the North Sea early in the war revived interest in the 3-in. rocket. Rocket projectors were devised which were easy to manufacture and which could be handled by unskilled troops or seamen.

During the *Blitz* of the winter of 1940/41 the anti-aircraft defences were strained to the utmost, and the 3-in. rocket reverted to the function for which it had originally been intended—to supplement the overworked heavy anti-aircraft guns. But, although credited with a few aircraft kills, the general verdict was that rockets were too inaccurate and were no substitute for radar-directed anti-aircraft guns.

By contrast, the rocket fired from an aircraft proved exceedingly effective and was probably the most successful development. For instead of being used in an air-to-air role, rocket-carrying aircraft attacked tanks on land and ships and submarines at sea. To attack such targets effectively, much greater hitting power than that of any gun normally housed in an aircraft was required. And rockets had the great advantage of giving no recoil which, in the case of the gun, becomes more embarrassing as its size increases.

The idea was originally put forward by Crow's staff early in 1940, but it was not until 1942 that the proposal was taken up by the Air Ministry, largely on account of a report that the Russians were using rocket-firing aircraft against tanks and bomber formations. At the request of the Air Staff the possibility of using rockets in aircraft against ships and tanks was investigated, and the Ministry of Air-craft Production began experiments that November.

By August 1942 three Hurricane fighters fitted with projector rails had carried out tests with 3-in. rockets fitted with an armour-piercing head. Although they had primarily been considered as anti-tank weapons (Army support aircraft could have made good use of them in the Western Desert) early in 1943, the Air Ministry stated that the new weapon was 'capable of making very accurate and devastating attacks on U-boats.' Hitherto the use of rockets in anti-submarine warfare had not been taken seriously, although for long advocated by Nevil Shute Norway, who was attached to Goodeve's Miscellaneous Weapons Department. A complete change of attitude was brought about when the dynamic and technically-minded Admiral Sir Max Horton, Commander-in-Chief, Western Approaches, heard about the armour-piercing rocket and sent one of his staff to see the trials. As the officer's report was enthusiastic, Horton pressed hard for the introduction of the rocket in Fleet Air Arm and RAF coastal aircraft.[2]

Eight weeks later, aircrews had been equipped with the weapon and trained to use it. And the first U-boat kill came almost immediately when, on 23 May 1943, Swordfish aircraft from HMS *Archer* sank a U-boat in the North Atlantic. A few days later RAF Hudsons operating from Gibraltar despatched an Italian submarine. Next month RAF Coastal Command made its first extensive strike with rocket-carrying aircraft against shipping off the Norwegian coast. This is an interesting example of a case where the intended purpose for a device was expanded and introduced into another service.*

A special branch was now set up to deal with further development of the airborne rocket in the Ministry of Aircraft Production. For the anti-tank role, a rocket with a high-explosive head weighing 60 lb. was to be used. But the rocket for Army support did not develop with the same speed as the one intended for ships. There had been complaints that the RAE projector hindered the performance of the aircraft—the Hawker Typhoon, and the Establishment was instructed to make its equipment more streamlined. By November 1943 it became clear that the modified projector would not be ready for the operations connected with the Normandy landings the following spring. There was no time to waste and Hawkers were asked to produce their own design. Within two weeks this had been done and as soon as the design was approved an order was placed for 500 projectors.

Equipped only just in time, the Typhoons, carrying up to eight rockets, made devastating attacks against radar stations on the coast and bridges inland. When fully loaded they had the full firing power of a salvo from a medium cruiser and the diving speed of the Typhoon added materially to the striking velocity on impact.

During the battle in Normandy, Typhoons flew thousands of sorties against tanks and vehicles of all kinds. Their greatest success was probably at Mortain on the American front where, in August 1944, they succeeded in halting a German attempt to break through to the Atlantic, which would have cut the Americans' slender line of communication. Although the rockets could not penetrate tank

---

* It is perhaps surprising that no effective airborne anti-tank weapon was produced in the Second World War. The airborne rocket was essentially a multi-purpose weapon.

armour, the Typhoons were able to attack from any direction and direct the rockets against the most vulnerable parts of the tank. A direct hit usually caused fire or disablement and even a near miss was enough to make the crew abandon their tank.

The fourth of the original objectives of British rocket research was to investigate the possibilities of rocket-assisted take-off. When, in April 1941, the decision was taken to provide fifty merchant ships with fighter aircraft to intercept hostile bombers attacking convoys, rockets were used to assist take-off. Two systems were eventually evolved. In the first, the aircraft was catapulted into the air by a special trolley propelled by rockets, thereby avoiding any recoil effect on the ship's structure. In the second, the propulsion unit was carried on the aircraft itself and jettisoned when the aircraft became airborne. On 1 November 1941, catapulted fighters claimed their first victim—a Focke Wulf. The rocket catapult system was superseded with the advent of the escort carrier and aircraft were flown off the flight-deck by assisted take-off. Both systems were invaluable in that merchant convoys were able to send up fast fighter aircraft to intercept approaching bombers. It is interesting to note that research and development on liquid fuel rockets was initiated during this period in connection with the problem of rocket-assisted take-off. A liquid oxygen system was examined by a research team which included members of the research group of Shell. The work was eventually limited to the research phase.

Thus the free-flying or unguided rocket, though much less ambitious in scope than the German guided rocket with liquid fuel propellant, had a great influence on operations in the Second World War on account of its versatility and because, unlike the German rocket weapons, it came in time to influence events. It should be noted that the original specification was rarely adhered to and the rockets were hardly ever used in the role for which they were first intended. Outstanding instances were their employment against submarines and their use in naval bombardment.

(ii) German Development

In contrast to the British rockets, the original German prototypes served an offensive purpose and they represented an attempt to fulfil the dream of a number of artillery officers for a long-range bombardment weapon. Experiments began in 1929 under Karl Becker, head

Page 239 : (*above*) A V-1 flying-bomb in flight; (*below*) rockets being loaded on a Typhoon fighter-bomber.

Page 240 : A German V-2 Rocket motor and fin.

of the Ballistics and Munitions Section of the German Army. Like their British counterpart, the German team was small and at the outset consisted of four men. The only soldier in it was Walter Dornberger, a 35-year old artillery captain who had also been trained as an engineer. Several civilian rocket enthusiasts were recruited, including a young technician, Wernher von Braun. Work on rocket-propelled motor vehicles and rocket-assisted take-off apparatus for aircraft was currently in progress in Germany and had received widespread publicity.

Rockets, we have seen, had not so far been used in modern warfare. A Swedish officer named von Unge at the beginning of the century patented a rotating rocket which had a range of 4,000 yards.* More to the point was Oberth's and Goddard's work; like them, the Germans were convinced of the superiority of liquid fuel and oxygen to a solid propellant. Although the Germans had little information to hand, at least the time was propitious for rocket development. Light metals forming the casing of the rocket could be mass-produced inexpensively; efficient oxidisers were available; and contemporary electronic equipment was reasonably reliable.

The usual prejudices to be found in any conservative military establishment were encountered. From the earliest days, Dornberger, imaginative and at the same time practical and a good organiser, fought against the sceptical attitude towards the rocket experiments adopted by many officers. His immediate superior, for instance, refused to believe that a rocket propelled by liquid fuel would rise from the ground. At the same time as Dornberger tried to translate the vision of the scientists into a practical weapon for the Army, he had to curb the scientists' dreams of space travel and teach them to appreciate the fact that the government would only provide money for their research work if it was convinced that the final product would be of sound military value.

March 1936 marks the birth of the A (Aggregat) series, of which the A-4 rocket was to become famous as the V-2 when it was fired operationally eight years later. By this time Dornberger had become the leading rocket expert in the German Army and experiments with a liquid fuel propellant were under way. One day Dornberger, von Braun and Riedl, the chief designer, were discussing what should be the requirements of the rocket as they had no directive to work

* Von Unge's patents were bought by Krupps of Essen, but were never used, as the Germans could not make the rockets accurate.

P

on. Dornberger, thinking in terms of long-range bombardment, propounded the requirement that the rocket should have a range of about 200 miles and carry about one ton of high explosive, twice the range and weight of explosive of the shell fired by the Paris gun in the First World War. For several days following their discussion calculations were drawn up on this basis.

In May 1937 Dornberger's group, then numbering some 300 scientists and technicians, began to move from Kummersdorf to Peenemunde, on the Baltic, where it was to remain until the advance of the Red Army in January 1945 compelled it to retreat to southern Germany. Hitler, who had been told about the rocket experiments in 1933, visited Kummersdorf in March 1939, but, contrary to his usual keen interest in novel weapons, appeared to be unimpressed by the rockets. It seemed that there was no role for them in his plans for the future. It is possible he saw them at too early a stage and did not comprehend their potentialities. (In the British TRE it was arranged that, as far as possible, no distinguished visitor, apart from scientists, should ever see a poor demonstration.) This was a set-back for the rocket enthusiasts, and was followed by another shortly after the outbreak of war when von Brauchitsch, the Army Commander-in-Chief, was dismissed. Von Brauchitsch had given Dornberger permission to increase the establishment at Peenemunde to 4,000 engineers and technicians.

In spite of the general lack of interest, attempts to find a solution for a method of propulsion went on. A successful launching using a liquid propellant was made in October 1939. Much still remained to be done, especially in keeping the rocket as steady as a shell during its course of flight.

But still the greatest obstacle to success resided not so much in technical problems as in the failure of the scientists to impress the authorities. In the spring of 1940 the war was going so favourably for Hitler that rocket development with radar and jet propulsion was taken off the priority list. Then, in late 1941, the failure of the German bombing offensive against Britain gave the rocket protagonists the opportunity to argue that a missile would not only penetrate the air defences but would be a cheaper weapon than the manned bomber which experience had shown tended to be shot down after an average of five to six operational flights.

On 3 October 1942, there was a very successful launching of an A-4 rocket. The rocket had now almost reached the stage when it could be used operationally. It was 46 ft. long, 5 ft. 6 in. in diameter and weighed nearly fifteen tons at take-off. It carried nine tons of liquid oxygen and alcohol as fuel and one ton of high explosive. As the German bomber offensive against Britain had failed, the Peenemunde establishment was ordered to redouble its efforts. A high-powered, but unimaginative, business executive named Gerhard Degenkolb was to co-ordinate manufacture of the rocket.

Hitler was still unconvinced. In March 1942 Dornberger and his colleagues were told that the Fuhrer had dreamed that no A-4 would ever reach England. Shortly after this set back, a special commission was set up to adjudicate between the A-4 and the pilotless aircraft, or flying-bomb. The latter, which will be described later, had been developed as a rival weapon to the rocket by the Luftwaffe. Its advantages were that it was cheaper to produce; it had a lower fuel consumption and it was easy to transport to the launching site. Opposed to this was the necessity for a fixed launching site which, in turn, demanded that the aircraft followed a rigid line of flight, thus making it comparatively easy to shoot down. The flying bomb had a low rate of travel (about 350 mph) and its height of flight (600 to 6,000 ft.) also made it vulnerable to anti-aircraft weapons.

On the other hand, the A-4 rocket could operate from a mobile launcher and this made detection by reconnaissance aircraft extremely difficult. Its great speed made interception impossible. At the same time its cost was prohibitive, extensive establishments and installations were required for testing and supply of fuel, the complicated nature of its mechanism militated against rapid output.

The commission recommended that both weapons should be put into production. By this time (July 1943) Hitler had changed his mind about rockets. He had never seen a rocket in flight, but after a carefully staged demonstration organised by Dornberger, which included a film of a rocket launch, Hitler decided that the rocket should be mass-produced. He even went so far as to admit to Dornberger that, 'If we had had these rockets in 1939 we should never have had this war.'

But in spite of Hitler's volte-face it was too late to hope that rockets would save Germany. 'The military situation', wrote Dornberger later, 'had long ceased to be such that by launching 900 V-2s a month, each loaded with a ton of high explosive, over ranges of 160 miles, we could end the Second World War.'[3] Furthermore, the propaganda that now began to revolve around the A-4, renamed the V-2 or 'Vengeance' weapon, as to what it could achieve, did no good. The rocket was a weapon with severe limitations; it was no more than a long-range artillery weapon of uncertain accuracy.

The month following Hitler's decision came the massive attack by RAF Bomber Command on Peenemunde. As it turned out, the physical damage was relatively small. More significant was the loss of several valuable scientists among the 735 personnel of the establishment who were killed in the raid. The total effect of the raid was to delay, still further, development of the A-4.

In September 1943 an SS officer named Kammler was given the special powers for the development of the A-4 that Dornberger had been requesting for years. But political intrigue accompanied the intervention of the SS. Hitler's decision to boost the rocket as a war-winning weapon caused the Gestapo under Himmler to take a close interest in rocket research and, more particularly in some members of the rocket team. This reached the point where von Braun and other indispensable technicians were arrested on a charge of sabotage, based on the supposition that they were working in a military establishment merely in order to advance research on the rocket as a space vehicle. Dornberger, by then a major-general, had sufficient influence to obtain their release.

The V-2 attacks against Britain began on 8 September 1944. About 1,300 rockets were fired, of which 517 reached the London area. During the attacks, over 2,000 people were killed and over 6,000 seriously injured. Rockets were also fired on Antwerp and Brussels. But apart from the senseless destruction of life and property, the rockets did not affect the course of the war, and by that time the Allied armies were on the German frontier. Allied heavy bombers continued to attack production centres and the aircraft of the tactical air forces attacked communications leading to the launching sites and, when possible, the launching sites themselves.

The V-2 was only one of a brood of rockets to which the Germans turned in desperation as the war drew inexorably to its end. Several became operational, such as the HS 293 air-to-ship weapon used in the Mediterranean and the radio-controlled bomb FX 1400 which sank the Italian battleship *Roma*. Others, were either still in development or no more than ideas on paper.

Cheaper weapons than the V-2 would have been more effective. The V-2 was a remarkable scientific achievement but for the purpose of war it was too complicated. It suffered from being put into mass production before it was ready, it lacked a sufficiently sensitive fuse, and its possibilities were exaggerated. Pressure groups moved in, and soon it became the pawn of factions. 'Only one thing can be said with absolute certainty', wrote Dornberger after the war, 'the use of the V-2 may be aptly summed up in the two words "too late". Lack of foresight in high places and failure to understand the technical background were to blame.'[4] We may go further than this. Even if the rocket had come into operation earlier, it was too in-accurate to be a war-winner. On the other hand, the piloted bomber, on which the Allies relied, with radar aids, by attacking the research and development centres and sources of production of the V-weapons was decisive.

Chapter 14

Pilotless Aircraft

(i) British Development

In the twenties in Britain, attention was given to the defensive and offensive possibilities of pilotless aircraft. In the former case an aircraft, known as the 'Hornet', was intended to detect and home on to a hostile aircraft at any time of the day or night. Work on this scheme was initiated in 1924 by the Director of Scientific Research at the Admiralty. Methods of detection were to be either by acoustic means or by using the heat radiation from the target aircraft's engine. Research along the latter lines failed, rather obviously, because in daytime the pilotless aircraft would invariably head towards the sun—a far more powerful source of heat than any aircraft. Experiments were cancelled in 1927, but at least something had been learnt about thermal radiation from aircraft, although this became obsolete with the development of radar in 1935. As A. B. Wood wrote over thirty years later : 'What we needed in 1925 was a prophet.'[1]

Sir Hugh Trenchard, then Chief of the Air Staff, believed that a pilotless bomber aircraft would be valuable in the event of an enemy occupying the northern French coastline. He foresaw, over fifteen years before the event, the threat of a missile attack on London and southern England. Furthermore pilotless aircraft would be easy and economical to manufacture and in bad weather would replace the manned bomber.

An idea for a primitive flying-bomb was thus conceived in the Air Ministry and by 1927 it had reached the prototype stage. Known as the 'Larynx', it was similar in design to a conventional aircraft and was powered by a normal Armstrong-Siddeley Lynx engine of 180 hp. It had a range of 200 miles and, carrying half the explosive load of a contemporary bomber, was guided to the target area by an automatic pilot. In the first trials the Larynx was catapulted off a destroyer. As it flew, radio signals were emitted every ten miles which were then picked up by direction-finding stations along the south coast. On one occasion a French warship discovered the wreckage of one of these aircraft and the captain informed the Air Ministry with regret that the pilot had not been found. Trenchard then ordered the tests to be transferred to Iraq where such incidents would not occur.

By 1928 the accuracy of the aircraft was so improved that Trenchard applied for more money to continue the experiments. But the scheme was squashed mainly on financial grounds. Winston Churchill, then Chancellor of the Exchequer, tacitly approved this decision, even though less than £1 million was required to continue research.

(ii) German Development

Shortly before the outbreak of war, an idea for a pilotless aircraft submitted by the aero-engine firm of Argus was turned down by the German Air Ministry for three reasons.[2] In the first place, the so-called bomb would have been less accurate than one delivered by a piloted aircraft; secondly, the radio technique required for control was still in a comparatively primitive stage; finally, the German Air Force was confident of winning the coming war without resort to this device.

But by the spring of 1942, the Luftwaffe had not only failed to penetrate the air defences of Britain, it was also in danger of being unable to prevent the mounting British bomber offensive against Germany. The firm of Gerhard Fiesler, manufacturers of airframes, in the person of Robert Lusser, re-introduced the idea of a pilotless aircraft carrying high explosive. Now the German occupation of northern France made radio control unnecessary, and the aircraft's engine would only be required to work for half an hour to take the bomb from France to the London area. The flying-bomb would be launched from an inclined ramp by a propulsive charge employing hydrogen peroxide and a permanganate. An automatic pilot would control the flight to the target area. Having covered a predetermined distance, an electro-mechanical device cut off the engine thus bringing down the bomb, equivalent to the warhead of a V-2, to the ground.

Argus, then, had the idea; Fiesler's converted it into a practical weapon. At this stage it was known as the FZG (*Flakzielgerat*—anti-aircraft target apparatus). On 19 June 1942, just over two years before the flying-bomb became operational, Field Marshal Milch, Chief of the German Air Staff, ordered that top priority should be given to the production of the flying-bomb. His decision was made on the strength of a verbal description and a rough diagram. Development under the German Air Ministry now went forward as a joint venture by three firms, Argus, Fiesler and Askania, the latter firm being responsible for the control mechanism.

About six months after Milch's decision, the first flight was made by a German pilotless aircraft. It was anticipated that a year would elapse before the missile was ready for operational use. The V-1 was dogged by the same trouble that retarded the V-2; production was begun before the development stage was completed. Co-ordination became difficult on account of the number of agencies involved, including the manufacturers, the Luftwaffe experimental station at Peenemunde and the troops employed to launch the missile at Zinnovitz. In the summer of 1943 production was further set back when the Fiesler works at Kassel were bombed, and more delay was caused when changes to individual components made at Peenemunde had to be incorporated in the mass-produced design at Fallersleben. The factory did not start output until late September 1943, less than three months before the date originally fixed for the start of the campaign.

Meanwhile, an extensive programme of building launching sites along the northern coast of France had begun. This, too, was delayed by the heavy attacks of RAF Bomber Command and of the tactical air forces. Thus the flying-bomb attacks did not begin until 13 June 1944, a week after D-Day. They continued until the capture of the launching sites in the first week of September, although a few bombs continued to be launched on London by aircraft. The effectiveness of the defences against the flying-bombs has already been demonstrated, and these accounted for just under 3,500 of the 6,700 missiles observed. A total of 9,000 bombs were launched. They killed 6,184 people, mainly civilians, and injured 17,981 more.

The ordeal of attack by missiles had to be endured after Britain had been at war for four years. These weapons were frightening because they were an innovation in aerial warfare and their blast effect was worse than that of a conventional bomb. Nevertheless, they did not alter the course of the war, nor did they affect the battle in progress in France, though they did cause a serious diversion of the strategic bomber effort which might otherwise have been directed against German industry.

Just as the V-2 was rejected in the early stages of the war, so was the V-1 ignored; it was then taken up when the Germans had lost mastery of the air; but it was too late. Like the V-2, it also was bogged down in political intrigue and forced into production before the final problems of the design had been overcome.

PART SEVEN

THE FAILURES

Chapter 15

Failure in the Air

War and the threat of war have traditionally been an incentive to ingenuity. It has also encouraged the crackpot, the charlatan and the enthusiastic amateur. Sometimes the amateur submitted an idea which had already been translated into a device. On one occasion a Member of Parliament wrote to Rowe suggesting what, in fact, was radar. He had politely to be informed that his idea would receive consideration.

Yet there were failures on the Allied side that arose from untenable ideas which received support at a high level. On 24 February 1942, Professor A. V. Hill, Independent Member for Cambridge University, said in the House of Commons : 'The common objection to expert opinion, that it is sometimes wrong, is highly dangerous doctrine . . . there have been far too many ill-considered inventions, devices and ideas put across, by persons with influence in high places, against the best technical advice. One could tell a sorry story of them. They have cost the country vast sums of money, and a corresponding effort in development and production, to the detriment of profitable expenditure of labour and materials elsewhere.'[1]

Aerial Mines

Professor Lindemann, who had been a pilot in the Royal Aircraft Factory at Farnborough during the First World War, and afterwards had served on the Aeronautical Research Committee, became obsessed by two types of explosive aerial mine. First, the Short Aerial Mine, alternatively known as the parachute-wire-bomb assembly. These small mines would be carried in shells or rockets; on exploding, the shell would eject the mine which was attached to a strand of wire 100 ft. long with a parachute at the end to retard its fall.

253

The mines would be fired in a barrage round vulnerable points, such as airfields or factories. The second kind was the Long Aerial Mine which consisted of a 2,000 ft.-long spool of piano wire at the end of which was a small cylindrical mine about the size of a large cigar. The mines would be towed by slow-flying aircraft across the path of the incoming bombers. In both cases the mines would be sufficient to damage the wings of an aircraft and the wire might become entangled in the propellers.

By June 1935 Lindemann had joined the Tizard Committee, and he lost no time in pressing the case for small explosive mines.* He argued that with the speed of modern aircraft increasing rapidly and the ability of the pilot to take evasive action, the odds against shooting down bombers with anti-aircraft guns were very high. An ordinary shell, said Lindemann, must be made to explode in the right place and at the right time to within approximately one-tenth of a second. But with a shell distributing small mines, it was only necessary to make it explode in the right place with a period of tolerance of roughly ten seconds. (It is curious that he did not attach more importance to proximity fuses.)

Trials with dummy mines having proved inconclusive, the committee, with the exception of Lindemann, were sceptical of the value of the project. So were RAF officers, including Joubert, then Air Officer Commanding Fighting Area, who were called upon for advice. Moreover, the strewing of wires over the country would endanger vital communications and power supply. The aerial mines project stood still. Lindemann, annoyed at this, accused Tizard of moving too slowly. 'Your procedure', he wrote, 'would be excellent if we had ten to fifteen years' time.'[2] Lindemann then enrolled the support of his friend Winston Churchill, then a member of the Air Defence Research Sub-Committee of the Committee of Imperial Defence. This action angered Tizard, and in a letter written on 5 July 1936 he assured Lindemann that he wanted to co-operate with him. Lindemann's criticism was merely retarding progress. As for the aerial mines, Tizard continued, the other members of the Committee did not see eye to eye with Lindemann over their value. The two points of view were irreconcilable, and less than two months later the Tizard Committee was dissolved—only to be formed again without Lindemann.

* Lindemann's other predeliction was, it will be recalled, for infra-red detection as an alternative to radar.

Meanwhile, the Royal Navy had become interested in the Short Aerial Mine for the purpose of defending ships at sea and harbour installations. The trials, conducted at the request of the Ordnance Board, were unsatisfactory. It was calculated that 2,000 shells per minute were necessary to create a barrage one mile long with shells carrying wire and explosives, an altogether too extravagant an expenditure of ammunition. Equally pessimistic conclusions about the value of explosive mines had been drawn from tests at RAE. Undeterred, Lindemann from his position outside government circles, continued to agitate for further research and development, claiming that the Tizard Committee had deliberately tried to find fault with his proposals. However, on 6 May 1939, Lindemann was invited to Shoeburyness for further trials with the Short Aerial Mine. Results were again disappointing, but Lindemann complained that peacetime safety precautions did not give the device a fair trial.

When Churchill became First Lord of the Admiralty on the outbreak of war he at once invited Lindemann to become his scientific adviser. Lindemann had already addressed a memorandum to Churchill earlier that year warning him not to have too much confidence in radar; that 'the only thing in the present emergency is to revert to our original idea,'[3] ie, the strewing of aerial mines in the path of hostile bombers. At this time, it will be remembered, the War Office and the Admiralty, especially the latter, were taking a keen interest in rockets on account of the serious shortage of anti-aircraft guns.

In the early months of 1940, when German aircraft began to attack east coast convoys, the demand for anti-aircraft weapons became acute. The Admiralty had the year before, due largely to pressure from Lord Louis Mountbatten, then a staff officer in the Naval Air Division, ordered 1,500 Swiss 20-mm Oerlikon automatic anti-aircraft guns, but only a few had arrived. Substitutes had to be found. Hence the formation of the Anti-Aircraft Weapons and Devices Department already mentioned. Rockets and their projectors were easy to produce as we have seen. Now, through Lindemann's influence, there was a 'hideous spawn', in the words of Capt. Stephen Roskill,[4] of variations of the Short Aerial Mine. They included 'Pig Trough' which had a special mounting designed to keep the projector pointing vertical while the ship rolled. There was 'Pillar Box', a multi-barrelled rocket projector operated by one man. There was a compressed air gun called the Holman Projector*. Goodeve's team of young scientists and engineers enthusiastically developed these erratic weapons, but they were no more than a substitute for the far more accurate anti-aircraft gun.[5] 'The crews of the merchant ships and fishing vessels', Roskill has written, 'knew that an automatic gun like the Oerlikon, which fired an explosive shell, was the weapon they wanted and they felt it was a long time coming into their hands.'

The gap was filled, largely by the efforts of two men. One was Goodeve who convinced the Admiralty of the need to speed up production of the Oerlikon, and the other was S. (later Sir Steuart) Mitchell, who was on the staff of the Chief Inspector of Naval Ordnance and took on this task.

What had happened, meantime, to the Long Aerial Mine? The beginning of the night blitz on Britain led to a debate on whether or not to produce vast quantities of aerial mines. Beaverbrook, Minister of Aircraft Production, told Churchill that the Air Staff opposed aerial mines. They considered it would be impossible to lay mines with sufficient accuracy across the route of the bombers and were in no position to spare the precious aircraft which would have to be specially adapted for such a task. It was much more important to concentrate on the development of the Aircraft Interception set. In the autumn of 1940, 10,000 aerial mines had been delivered to the Admiralty and 2,100 of these had gone to the RAF. Beaverbrook himself was against further production until the mines had proved themselves in action.

Churchill—and this is an outstanding example of bad scientific advice—urged by Lindemann, decided not only to go ahead with production but actually increased the order to one million mines. Protests were made at the expense—estimated at between £7 and £10 million. Lindemann, undeterred, assured Churchill that a single mine cost approximately the same as one anti-aircraft shell and was more likely to destroy a bomber at night or in cloud.

Meanwhile trials with aircraft using the Long Aerial Mine, now known by the uninspiring code name 'Mutton', had been in progress since the summer. An experimental unit known as No 420 Flight was formed for the purpose at Christchurch under the direction of Joubert, then Assistant Chief of Air Staff, later moving to Middle Wallop on Salisbury Plain. After a number of mishaps with

---

* The work on these devices has been described in *The Secret War* by Gerald Pawle, Harrap, London, 1956.

aircraft damaged by premature explosion of the mines, the first operational flight took place under ground-controlled interception on 26 October. Incredibly, the pilot claimed a 'possible'. But it proved to be the only one.

Attempts to sow minefields over southern England continued throughout the winter of 1940-41. By December, twenty-four aircraft had been allotted to the task and No 420 Flight became No 93 Squadron. The laying of mines was extremely dangerous for the aircrew; apart from hang-ups and premature explosions, there was the danger of the wire becoming entangled in the towing aircraft. But the only casualties inflicted by Mutton were two horses. One was slightly injured by a wire trailing from an aircraft and the other, ridden by an officer during a demonstration of Mutton on Salisbury Plain, broke a leg after tripping over wire strewn on the ground. Not surprisingly, the morale of the squadron deteriorated in spite of visits from King George VI and Air Chief Marshal Sir Sholto Douglas, Commander-in-Chief, Fighter Command. The aim of the operation was never clearly defined and the squadron was harrassed by a stream of enquiries from the Prime Minister, Lindemann and the Air Staff. Attempts were made to lay the mines across the radio navigational beam used by the Germans in attacks on British towns—but with no success. The chances of a bomber fouling the wires were remote.

At last, on 19 November 1941, Mutton was cancelled—nearly six years after the first experiments made at the request of the Tizard Committee and a year after operational trials had begun. Sholto Douglas has written the final indictment of the Long Aerial Mine : 'The whole scheme was far too impractical and difficult to operate, if only because the defending aircraft had to be placed in exactly the right position to fly at right angles directly in front of the oncoming enemy bomber. This in itself was asking for more than could then be achieved by the controllers on the ground.

'We were compelled to go on with this ridiculous scheme long after it was proved to be a complete waste of time and effort, and even after a normal radar-equipped night-fighter squadron flying from the same airfield had proved that its simpler methods of operation were infinitely more effective.'[7]

Chapter 16

Failure on the Sea

(i) Habakkuk

Geoffrey Pyke, the son of a Jewish lawyer, was educated at Wellington College for two years, and then went to Pembroke College, Cambridge, to read law. On the outbreak of war in 1914, he was in
Germany reporting for the *Daily Chronicle*. He was interned in the
celebrated civilian internment camp at Ruhleben, from whence in
1915 he made a remarkable escape to Holland.

Pyke's mind was a breeding ground for original ideas. After the
war he tried his hand at business and as master at a progressive
school, but neither brought fame nor fortune. He became involved
in Left Wing activities in support of the Loyalist cause in the
Spanish Civil War, and in 1939 he decided to conduct an opinion
poll in Germany to discover whether the Germans wanted Hitler to
win if war broke out. Soon he attracted the attention of Leo Amery,
Secretary of State for India, with an idea for a small force to
operate in Norway mounted in special tracked vehicles, able to cross
the snow and destroy bridges, dams and power stations and other
strategic objectives. The Germans, argued Pyke, would be compelled
to maintain a very large force to protect these vulnerable points.[1]
Amery, impressed with Pyke's originality, sent him to Mountbatten
with a recommendation. Mountbatten accepted Pyke, despite his
strange manner and eccentric appearance, because he appreciated
that even if some of his ideas were impracticable he would at least
think along original lines. Pyke, like his raiding forces, would conduct pin-prick attacks on orthodox military thought.

Pyke's project became known as 'Plough' and he was sent to the
United States to advise on the vehicle, able to cross mud or snow,
that was to become known as the 'Weasel'. It was during this visit
that the idea of Habakkuk germinated in Pyke's mind. It was even
more ambitious than Plough and Pyke believed it to be a potential

war-winner. His idea was essentially based on a new material which was later named after him—pykrete. The elements were simply, wood, pulp and water. When frozen, this slush became as hard as concrete. Experiments made at Pyke's request at Brooklyn Polytechnic Cold Research Laboratory showed that pykrete was very much harder than ice. Even after the material's outer surface had thawed, the pulp insulated pykrete so effectively that it remained stable at high temperatures. Pykrete only required the expenditure of a small amount of energy to keep it frozen.

What would pykrete be used for? Pyke had the idea of constructing huge aircraft-carriers which would be unsinkable because the specific gravity of pykrete was lower than that of ice. He also contemplated the possibility of ice ships heading an assault on the ports of Naples and Genoa. It would have been better, instead of trying to discover a use for pykrete, to have circulated the information to all and sundry in case a requirement for its use should arise.

Pyke expounded his idea in a lengthy memorandum to Mountbatten. There was a separate page intended to catch the preoccupied commander's eye. On it was a quotation from one of Chesterton's 'Father Brown' stories which ran as follows : 'It isn't that they can't see the solution, it is that they can't see the problem.' Mountbatten read on, fascinated by Pyke's proposal. He instructed scientists to carry out tests on pykrete to prove Pyke's theory. Its properties were confirmed. Pykrete could not be crushed by a hammer, yet, it was easy as wood to turn on a lathe. A bullet fired from a rifle penetrated no more than six and a half inches whereas a similar bullet penetrated fourteen inches of pure ice.

Mountbatten hastened to the Prime Minister at Chequers and, finding him in his bath, made him watch a piece of pykrete float in the hot water without dissolving. Cherwell, hitherto unimpressed by Pyke's ideas, when he heard about pykrete, recommended that a committee be set up to study the possibilities of a project which was to be known as 'Habakkuk'.*

There was at that moment a critical shortage of long-range air-

* Pyke gave the project the name of Habakkuk (or Habbakuk as it was mis-spelled throughout its existence) because of a character in Voltaire's *Candide* who was able to do everything. The appropriate text from the Book of Habakkuk goes thus : 'Behold ye among the heathen, and regard, and wonder marvellously : for I will work a work in your days, which ye will not believe, though it be told you.'

craft able to cover what was known as the 'Black Pit'—the area of
the Atlantic beyond the range of coastal aircraft operating from west
and east. Habakkuk could be used as a base for aircraft hunting
U-boats. Alternatively, it could be used as an aircraft-carrier to
support an Allied landing on the west coast of France, a region out
of range of tactical aircraft operating from Britain. The idea of an
operation in the Bordeaux area was soon found to be impractical,
although it was to be considered later in the war as an alternative
to a landing in the south of France.

Churchill approved a plan to develop a prototype of Habakkuk,
but he insisted that only natural resources were used. He was impressed with the idea of a floating island for refuelling aircraft.

Hussey and Bernal from Headquarters, Combined Operations,
were sent to Canada to arrange for the construction of a prototype
Habakkuk. A 1,000-ton ice ship was then built on Lake Patricia in
Jaspar, Ontario. At least it was economical in materials. The re-
frigerating plant was operated by a 1-hp petrol engine and sheet
iron pipes carried cold air through the inner hull made of pykrete.

The actual ship, had it been built, would have been 2,000 feet
long and displaced 2,200,000 tons, twenty-six times the tonnage of
the *Queen Elizabeth*. Its great size would have precluded it from
operating in the shallow waters of the North Sea. Motive power was
to have been supplied by thirteen 1,000-hp electric motors housed in
nacelles on the sides of the ship. The iceberg ship was designed to
carry 200 fighters and 100 Mosquito bombers. The whole project
would have cost in the region of £17 million.

Mountbatten decided that the American Chiefs of Staff should
be given their first glimpse of pykrete when the Combined Chiefs of
Staff met in Ottawa in August 1943. But by that date Habakkuk
had already become redundant for two reasons. Firstly, its role in the
Battle of the Atlantic was finished, for Allied air and naval forces
had undoubtedly won victory over the U-boat by May 1943. The
causes were centimetric radar, the availability of larger numbers
of long-range aircraft, HF/DF, and the improved system of training for crews of ships operating in an anti-U-boat role. The critical
period of the U-boat war, when Habakkuk might conceivably have
been of some use, was during the winter of 1942 and the early part
of 1943. Secondly, the Normandy coast had been chosen for the
landings in North-west Europe—within range of the airfields of
southern England which had itself become a vast 'unsinkable' air-

craft-carrier. Nor was there any need for Habakkuk in the Mediterranean, for the Allies were in occupation of Sicily and had a foothold in the 'toe' of Italy. The crying need was not for Habakkuk but for more tank-landing ships.

Thus Mountbatten's celebrated demonstration of the toughness of pykrete before the Combined Chiefs of Staff when he fired at a block of pykrete, the bullet afterwards ricochetting round the room, had already lost its point. The incident caused even more alarm to staff officers outside who thought that a tense meeting which had preceded the demonstration was now developing into a shooting match. Mountbatten himself was shortly to take over south-east Asia Command where he was soon to experience how the shortage of tank landing ships could frustrate his plans for amphibious operations.

In spite of criticism from the Admiralty and the US Navy, a joint Anglo-US-Canadian Habakkuk committee was formed after the conference to decide on future development. Fortunately, the whole scheme petered out in December 1943. By that time the Allies had turned to the offensive in the Battle of the Atlantic and air bases in the Azores had been acquired from the Portuguese from which full air cover across the Atlantic could be obtained. Plans for 'Overlord' (the Normandy landings) were well matured and the war in the Pacific was proceeding far more rapidly than had been expected.

How much of the war effort had been wasted by Habakkuk? According to Pyke's biographer, no more steel had been used in building the prototype ice ship than would have been used for a destroyer, and the actual cost of development was in the region of thousands of pounds. No more than fifty men were engaged at any one time on the project. But a different view was expressed by Lord Alanbrooke, wartime Chief of Imperial General Staff, when he wrote : 'Heaven knows how much money went down the sink over this project!'[2]

Not surprisingly, a number of criticisms were levelled at the proposed scheme for Habakkuk. Bernal's estimates for steel, for instance, were considered to be too low. Some scientists thought that the propulsion units would have generated too much heat. To be fair, just as much ridicule was poured on the eventually successful Mulberry and Pluto. But more important, Habakkuk failed because there was a lack of co-ordination over the project. No one seemed to have asked himself when and where it would be used. This should have been done at the Quebec Conference. Habakkuk failed not because it was an imaginative idea, but because it was unrelated to current strategy. Would it, in fact, have worked? The answer is that in theory it would. But as with all prototypes, a very large number of snags would have been encountered and years would have elapsed before one Habakkuk could have put to sea. The cost in manpower and money would have been astronomical. All Pyke's ideas were equally impractical, with the exception of the Weasel. His last brainwave was that, in the final stages of the war in Burma, troops assaulting from the sea should be transported from their ships to the land by a pneumatic tube about three feet in diameter. The men were to be packed in shuttles and blown through at high speed. Pyke was furious when Hussey pointed out some of the more obvious drawbacks, and, in the event, the scheme never materialised.

PART EIGHT

CONCLUSIONS

Chapter 17

Conclusions

Now that we have completed the analysis of the forty-one items, chosen by some of the leading participants, that made the most important contribution towards the winning of the Second World War and for comparison have examined some outstanding enemy devices, and some failures, what sort of pattern emerges? What factors have been propitious, stimulating, or inhibiting for the development of novel scientific ideas?

(i) Pressure of Events

The old adage 'Necessity is the Mother of Invention' is undoubtedly true in the case of most warlike inventions. Radar was developed in response to the need for Britain to look to its air defences. Again, it was the need to find a means of detecting the small shape of a submarine in the vastness of the ocean and the bomber in the space of the night sky that stimulated the development of the magnetron valve and short-wave radar. Radio and radar aides for navigation and bombing were developed in response to the failure of RAF Bomber Commander to reach and locate its targets.

In the sphere of amphibious operations, only after the British Army was evacuated from the Continent in June 1940 did the construction of all kinds of landing craft begin. Artificial harbours for the return to the Continent were built because the capture of a port was too costly an operation. The development of a rocket craft sprang from the painful experience of Dieppe.

The intensification of the U-boat campaign stimulated, on the one hand scientific application to the problems of attacking U-boat transit areas and, on the other, planned flying and maintenance.

In the medical field the Japanese victories in the Far East compelled the development of synthesised anti-malarial drugs—a process which the Germans had already begun in the inter-war years.

Pressure of events again revived German interest in rockets and pilotless aircraft when orthodox aircraft had failed to achieve success and air superiority had gone to the Allies. Although the Germans had a strong lead in this field, early successes in the war reduced the urgency for development and these revolutionary weapons came too late to turn the tide for them.

(ii) Development in Response to Enemy Technical Innovations

The war at sea was notable for providing a number of examples of technical measures and countermeasures. Within a few weeks of the outbreak of war counters to the German magnetic mines were devised. As it was appreciated that the Germans would continue to use influence mines, a sweeping organisation was set up to deal with every type of mine likely to be used, with the result that the Royal Navy was never again taken by surprise.

In the war against the U-boat, the development of ahead-throwing weapons—originally proposed in the First World War—became feasible with the employment of asdic and the requirement to follow up detection with rapid attack before the U-boat escaped. The sonobuoy came into its own when the schnorkel-equipped U-boat was able to remain submerged longer than the conventional submarine.

The German dive-bomber which had become invincible on the Continent stimulated the initial development of the proximity fuse, and the British development of rockets was in direct response to German developments in this sphere. Although the idea for the Kerrison predictor had long matured in the mind of the inventor, the opportunity to apply it only arose with the choice of a new light anti-aircraft gun—the Bofors.

The growth of the combined British and American bomber offensive against Germany caused the strengthening of the German air defences, and this in turn led to the introduction of radio countermeasures by the British in order to reduce casualties and mislead the enemy.

In the war on land, the great tactical opportunities opened up by the tank provoked a concentration on defensive measures—

especially minefields. Therefore mine detectors and mine destroyers (flails) became very important items of equipment in mobile warfare.

Three other factors which are related to technical considerations should be mentioned. Firstly, a device must be easy to mass-produce. For instance, one of the advantages of the cavity magnetron over the klystron valve was that it was easier to manufacture in large quantities. Secondly, it was better to have an equipment in operation although it might not give an ideal performance. Examples may be found in the radio telephony system for fighter control in the Battle of Britain and the early gunlaying radar sets. Nevertheless, mass production was not always essential to achieve an operational result. A dozen pathfinding H_2S sets could influence the bombing offensive just as a dozen ASV sets might turn the tide in the Battle of the Atlantic.

(iii) Foresight

Necessity was the spur. But given this there were notable examples of foresight. The most important was surely the decision to build the radar Home Chain which was in operation a year before the outbreak of war. Again, the idea for the Kerrison predictor had been thought out well in advance of the requirement, while Donald Bailey combined the advantages of the Martel box girder and Inglis bridges, incorporating them into a design capable of carrying the heaviest tanks. In the radio field there were a number of examples of foresight. The system of radio communication between tanks on the move, largely sponsored by Hobart, was evolved by 1935—only to be copied by the German Army. The importance of radio telephony for linking fighter aircraft with ground control was foreseen, but the equipment was only ready at the last moment. Tizard foresaw the need to work out a technique for daylight interception before the introduction of radar. High-frequency direction finders for the assistance of air and naval forces were operating successfully before the war and undertook a new role of intercepting radio orders to U-boats and thereby locating their position—after the outbreak of war.

As for radar, its possibilities as an airborne detector, a navigational and bombing aid and as a means of discriminating between hostile and friendly aircraft were foreseen by some at Bawdsey at an early stage, but these ideas had to be put 'on ice' and prior attention given to the completion of the Home Chain. The ISTDC belatedly set up, anticipated by the time of the outbreak of war some of the requirements for specialised landing craft. The Americans appreciated the need for a quick turn-round in craft or vehicles when landing supplies on a beachhead; the answer to this problem was the DUKW.

There were certain inventions or innovations which were evolved before the war the full significance of which was not perceived until a critical moment arose. Thought had been given to the most economical use of aircraft in Flying Training Command, but it was the lack or inability of aircraft to maintain constant maritime patrols that made the RAF aware of the necessity for planned flying and planned maintenance. Some devices were tried out in the inter-war years but were then neglected for one reason or another. The pilot-less aircraft was sponsored by the Air Ministry only to fall a victim to cuts in defence expenditure. It was left to the Germans to perfect this weapon and to use it in war for the first time.

(iv) Organisation, Propinquity and the Human Factor

In matters of the organisation of science the British, and later the Americans, were far superior to the Germans. Close liaison was established between the scientists and the services. Which of our items were assisted by this factor? First and foremost, the Tizard Committee had the most profound effect on all types of radar. The cavity magnetron owed its rapid emergence to co-operation between the services, groups of academic scientists and industrial laboratories of firms. TRE, in particular, evolved a high degree of co-operation between scientists, service officers and civil servants in its 'Sunday Soviets'.

Two important factors should be noted here. One was the decision to recruit outstanding young physicists of the country a year before the war began, to work in the revolutionary field of radar. The second was that scientists trained in one discipline turned with great effect to something entirely outside their province. Sir Thomas Merton, the distinguished spectroscopist, and himself closely associated with wartime science, has written : 'During the war, when once a requirement had been clearly stated, someone, somewhere or other, nearly always turned up with the right answer; and the answer was often provided, not by an expert in the seemingly obvious field, but by some man whose pre-war activities were associated with some completely different discipline. It is usually more difficult to ask the right questions than to get the right answers.'[1]

The final point to be made in regard to organisation is that the ideas for the most important contributions came from individuals within the service scientific establishments and not from small back rooms. Lord Hankey, who had long and close experience of science and war, wrote: 'The fact is that useful inventions come almost entirely from technical people who are immersed in the business of war. For the most part it is found that the "bright ideas" of the outside inventor are not new and that the new ideas are not bright. It is only very rarely that a really valuable new idea comes from outside. The tank is a good example, but even in that instance those concerned were all to some extent inside the official circle.'[2]

To what extent did propinquity contribute towards the fruition of an idea? Radio and radar navigational and bombing aids and aircraft interception equipment all owed much to propinquity because views on ideas for air warfare were exchanged at the 'Sunday Soviets' at TRE. The personality of the scientist working in conjunction with the services was another important factor. Tizard was outstanding in many aspects as adviser. Dee, Reeves, and Bowen had energy and determination in pushing through radar equipment. Ratcliffe was admirable at initiating scientists into the novelties of radar. Goodeve's knowledge of naval habits and his ability for organisation were of great help in the degaussing operation. Kerrison, apart from possessing a fine scientific mind, was a good team leader. Blackett and E. J. Williams, in the role of operational research scientists, won the respect of service officers. They worked as civilians and held that their neutral garb made them accessible to all ranks. On the other hand, there were a few, and Goodeve was one of them, who believed that the scientist was equally effective in uniform. Certainly it was useful in the degaussing operation and in circumstances where the scientists had to go to sea. Even the supporters of civilian status for scientists agreed that there were times, for one obviously on operations, when uniforms must be donned.

Finally, the scientists' task was made easier by the presence of senior officers who were receptive to new ideas.

(v) Factors Impeding the Development of the Idea

(a) Lack of Requirement

The failure to ask the right questions was indeed serious and it was the inability to see the need for requirement that so often delayed the adoption of a scientific device. Thus the Admiralty in 1928, or the Admiralty and the War Office in 1931, given more imagination and foresight, should have been in possession of radar. With this inability to see the requirement there were usually obstructions put up against scientists. The Anti-Non-Contact Committee did not listen to Wood's advice on demagnetisation, and there was, on the part of the RAF, a failure to see the need for developing navigational and bombing aids.

(b) Inter-Service Rivalry

Perhaps the outstanding example of this disruptive factor in the items under discussion was the construction of the artificial harbours, responsibility for which was disputed by the Admiralty and the War Office, and which might have severely delayed the whole project. In the United States, the DUKW was the victim of disputes between the Army and the Navy, neither service believing it to be practicable. For the Germans, this factor was disastrous and politics further impeded development of scientific projects, in particular, the 'V' weapons.

(c) Excessive Secrecy or Caution

A feature of scientific and technological progress which was unappreciated during the Second World War was that ideas are slow in coming to fruition but, once they reach the development stage, the idea occurs in different countries at about the same time and despite stringent security precautions. Radar had reached about the same stage in Britain and Germany by the outbreak of war, each country believing that it was ahead of the other. No important scientific discovery has remained hidden from other nations for long. Yet the exploitation of the idea must be kept secret. It would have been disastrous if the efficacy of radar had been revealed in time for Germany to defeat it by jamming and other measures.

Secrecy, however, often limited the value of a device because information was restricted to too few, and there were several wartime examples of excessive secrecy. The proximity fuse might have been exploited more widely if more senior officers had known of its existence. The Hedgehog would have been more effective if more information had reached those who were to operate it. The revised setting for the depth charge was kept so secret that orders for its employment still included the outmoded figures of 50 to 500 feet.

There were occasions when the decision had to be made whether the weapon, device or idea would be more useful to the enemy than to the originator. Both Britain and Germany were reluctant to start using Window, and it was only when the British bomber losses became almost unsupportable that it was used. Similar lengthy discussions preceded the use of H_2S which involved the certainty of making a present of the priceless magnetron to Germany.

(d) The Pace of Development

In the analysis of the forty-one items we have noted the time taken from the birth of the idea until it reaches the hands of the user as device or weapon. The following comparative table shows the pace of development. (In a number of cases such as Gee, or the Bailey bridge, to take two at random, the idea lay dormant until it could flourish in the right environment.)

TIME TAKEN FROM START OF DEVELOPMENT
TO OPERATIONAL USE

Device/Weapon	Days	Weeks	Months	Years	Remarks
Degaussing		3			
Double-L Sweep		6			
Acoustic Mine Sweep		3–4			
Pressure Mine Sweep				3	Approximate
Acoustic Torpedo Decoy			18		Approximate
ASV Metre				1	
ASV Centimetre				2	
Naval Early Warning Radar (7m)				2	Air warning
Naval 271 Radar (cm)			9		Anti U-boat

Device/Weapon	Days	Weeks	Months	Years	Remarks
Naval 281 Radar (3m)				1	Control of short-range AA fire
Naval 284 Radar			8		Control of surface gunnery
High-Frequency Direction Finder				2	Seaborne set
Sonobuoy			5		
Hedgehog				1	Approximate
Planned Flying and Maintenance			4		Approximate
Coastal Radar Chain				4	Chain of 20 stations
Chain Home Low			4		
High-Frequency Direction Finder				3	RAF
VHF/RT				4	RAF, approximate
Aircraft Interception Radar (metre)				4	
Aircraft Interception Radar (centimetre)			10		
Plan Position Indicator				1	
Ground Control Interception			6		Approximate
Identification, Friend or Foe				1	Approximate
Cavity Magnetron			1+4 mths		
Gee			4		Not used for seven months
Oboe			7		Eighteen months before German targets bombed
H$_2$S				1+1 mnth	

Device/Weapon	Days	Weeks	Months	Years	Remarks
Window				2+7 mths	
Kerrison Predictor				1	Approximate
GL (metre) for AA				3	Approximate
GL (centimetre)				3	Approximate
Proximity Fuse				1+2 mths	US development
Tank R/T				3	Approximate
Microwave Communications				1	Approximate
Bailey Bridge			10		
Polish Mine Detector			6		
Flail Tank				1	
Artificial Harbours			8		
Naval Lighter Pontoon			5		
DUKW			9		Approximate
Landing Craft (Tank)			6		
Landing Ship (Tank)				1	
Landing Ship (Dock)				2	
Landing Craft Tank (Rocket)			10		
Radio Decoy			5		For 6 June 1944
Rockets (AA)				4	Approximate
Rockets (Aircraft Take-Off)			8		
Rockets (Anti-ship)			2		
German V-2				6	
German V-1				2	

R

That certain items took longer than others did not necessarily mean slow progress. The coastal radar chain, for instance, required extensive construction work; the important point was that it was operationally ready by the outbreak of war. Other items, as we know, evolved rapidly because of the pressure of events, such as the naval 271 radar set, aircraft interception equipment, or Oboe. Others, such as Window and H_2S, were held up for non-technical reasons. It will be seen that the V-2 rocket was the longest in coming to fruition. But for Hitler's confident belief that there would be no need for such weapons, any more than there would be for sophisticated radar, this might indeed have become a war-winning weapon for the Germans.

The crucial factor behind all the items was that technical ingenuity counted less than integration of military and scientific disciplines. The Germans and their allies failed to achieve such collaboration. In war, it is vital to reduce as far as possible the interval of time between the birth of the idea and the arrival of the equipment in the hands of the user.

ACKNOWLEDGMENTS

While I was seeking information for a less ambitious book, also on science and war, Dr. A. P. Rowe drew my attention to the lack of any analysis of the growth and development of scientific contributions to the Second World War. He has watched with a critical, but kindly, eye the growth of the book that subsequently was written.

I am also greatly indebted to Mr. J. E. N. Hooper, a member of the Telecommunications Research Establishment, and more recently of the Royal Radar Establishment, who prepared the draft chapters on radio and radar navigational devices.

The detailed research that was necessary for the study required the interest and co-operation of many people, all of whom it would be impossible, in the limited space available, to thank. I must, however, acknowledge with gratitude those who gave up their valuable time to read and comment on parts of the text, or who provided extensive material. They are: Dr. W. A. S. Butement, Sir Robert Cockburn, Sir William Cook, Sir Charles Goodeve, Dr. C. J. Hackett, Mr. C. E. Horton, Capt. T. A. Hussey, RN, Dr. R. Lewthwaite, Major-Gen. H. M. Paterson, Mr. A. H. Reeves and Mr. N. H. A. Warren.

My thanks are also due to Mr. L. A. Jackets and his staff in the Air Historical Branch of the Ministry of Defence and Mr. H. L. R. Hinkley, Secretary and Editor of the *Journal of the Royal Naval Scientific Service,* for their unfailing and invaluable help; also to Sir Basil Liddell Hart for allowing me to draw on the extensive historical material in his possession, and to the Librarian of Nuffield College, Oxford, for the use of the late Lord Cherwell's papers.

I am also indebted to Miss Margaret Joy and Mrs. Audrey Tester who typed the successive drafts, and to the latter for a number of helpful suggestions on presentation. Last, but not least, I owe much to my wife who enabled me to concentrate on the writing of the book.

GUY HARTCUP

275

BIBLIOGRAPHY

PUBLISHED SOURCES

Air Ministry, Air Publication 3368, *The Origins and Development of Operational Research in the Royal Air Force,* (HMSO, 1963)

Baxter, James Phinney, *Scientists Against Time,* (Boston, 1946)

Bernal, J. D., *Freedom of Necessity,* (Routledge & Kegan Paul, 1949)

Birkenhead, The Earl of, *The Prof in Two Worlds,* (Collins, 1961)

Blackett, P. M. S., *Studies of War,* (Oliver & Boyd, 1962)

Boyce, J., *New Weapons for Air Warfare,* (Boston, 1947)

Bryant, Arthur (Ed.), *The Turn of the Tide,* (Collins, 1957)

Burchard, J., *M I T in World War 2,* (John Wiley & Sons, New York, and Chapman & Hall, London, 1948)

Bush, Vannevar, *Modern Arms and Free Men,* (Heinemann, 1950)

Chalmers, Rear-Adm., W. S. *Max Horton and the Western Approaches,* (Hodder & Stoughton, 1954)

Churchill, W. S., *The Second World War,* Vols. I-IV, (Cassell, 1948-54)

Clark, Ronald, *Battle for Britain,* (Harrap, 1965); *The Rise of the Boffins,* (Phoenix House, 1963); *Tizard,* (Methuen, 1965)

Clarke, Maj-Gen. Sir Edward, *Royal Artillery Commemoration Book,* (Bell, 1949)

Collier, Basil, *The Defence of the United Kingdom* (HMSO, 1957)

Cowie, J. S., *Mines, Minelayers and Minelaying,* (OUP, 1949)

Crowther, J. G., *British Scientists of the Twentieth Century,* (Routledge & Kegan Paul, 1952)

Crowther, J. G., and Whiddington, R., *Science at War,* (HMSO 1947)

Davies, J., *Prime Minister's Secretariat 1916-20,* (R. H. Johns, 1951)

Dornberger, Walter, R., *V-2* (Hurst & Blackett, 1954)

Douglas of Kirtleside, Lord, *Years of Command,* (Collins, 1966)

Ellis, L. F., Capt. G. R. G. Allen, RN, Air Chief Marshal Sir James Robb, Lt.-Col. A. E. Warhurst, *Victory in the West,* Vol I, (HMSO 1962)

Fergusson, Bernard, *The Watery Maze,* (Collins, 1961)

Galland, Adolf, *The First and the Last,* (Transatlantic Books, 1957)

Goudsmitt, S. A., *ALSOS—The Failure of German Science,* (Sigma Books, 1947)

Green, F. H. K., and Covell, Maj-Gen. Sir Gordon, *Medical Research,* (HMSO, 1953)

Gretton, Vice-Adm. Sir Peter, *Maritime Strategy,* (Cassell, 1965)

Hankey, Lord, *The Supreme Command, 1914-18,* (George Allen & Unwin, 1961)

Harris, Sir Arthur, *Bomber Offensive,* (Collins, 1947)

Hickling, Vice-Adm. Harold, *Sailor at Sea,* (Kimber, 1965)

Hill, A. V., *The Ethical Dilemma of Science,* (OUP, 1960)

Jewkes, J., Sawers, David, and Stillerman, Richard, *The Sources of Invention,* (Macmillan, 1958)

Lampe, David, *Pyke: The Unknown Genius,* (Evans, 1960)

Liddell Hart, B. H., *The Tanks 1914-1945,* (Cassell, 1959); *Thoughts on War,* (Faber & Faber, 1944); *Memoirs,* Vol I, (Cassell, 1965)

Martel, Lt.-Gen. Sir Giffard, *An Outspoken Soldier,* (Sifton Praed, 1949)

Maund, Capt. L. E. H., RN, *Assault from the Sea,* (Methuen, 1949)

Morgan, Gen. Sir Frederick, *Overture to Overlord,* (Hodder & Stoughton, 1950)

Morison, S. E., *The Two-ocean War,* (Little Brown & Co., 1963)

Pawle, Gerald, *The Secret War,* (Harrap, 1956)

Pile, Gen. Sir F. A., *Ack-Ack*, (Harrap, 1949)

Postan, M. M., Hay, D., and Scott, J. D., *Design and Development of Weapons*, (HMSO, 1963)

Richards, Denis, and Saunders, Hilary St. G., *The Royal Air Force 1939-45*, (HMSO, 1953-4)

Roskill, S. W., *The Strategy of Sea Power*, (Collins, 1962); *The War at Sea*, Vol I, (HMSO, 1954)

Rowe, A. P., *One Story of Radar*, (CUP, 1948)

Scott, J. D., and Hughes, Richard, *The Administration of War Production*, (HMSO, and Longmans, Green, 1955)

Watson-Watt, Sir Robert, *Three Steps to Victory* (Odhams Press, 1957)

Webster, Sir Charles, and Frankland, Noble, *The Strategic Air Offensive Against Germany 1939-45*, Vols I-IV (HMSO, 1961)

Weeks, Sir Ronald, *Organisation and Equipment for War*, (CUP, 1950)

Wood, Derek, and Dempster, Derek, *The Narrow Margin*, (Hutchinson, 1961)

Zuckerman, Sir Solly, *Scientists and War*, (Hamish Hamilton, 1966)

REFERENCES

PART I

INTRODUCTORY

CHAPTER 1

1   Jewkes, J. *et al.*, The Sources of Invention, *passim*

2   Rowe, A. P. 'From Scientific Idea to Practical Use', *Minerva* Spring (1964), pp 303-4

CHAPTER 2

1   Tizard, Sir Henry, 'Science and the Services', *Jnl. Roy. Unit. Serv. Instn.* Vol XLI, No 563 (Aug. 1946) p 338

2   Crowther, J. G. *British Scientists of the Twentieth Century*, p 78

3   Postan, M. M. *et al. Design and Development of Weapons*, Chap XVI

4   Goodeve, Sir Charles, Conversation with the author

5   Hankey, Lord, Technical and Scientific Manpower, Lecture 29 Aug. 1951

6   Barfield, R. H., Letter to the author, 23 Nov. 1965

7   Burchard, J., *M.I.T. in World War* 2, Pt 2 *passim*

8   Rowe, A. P., *From Scientific Idea to Practical Use, op. cit* p 309

9   Terman, F. E., Letter to A. P. Rowe, 23 July 1962

10   Clark, Ronald, *Tizard*, p 268

11   Hill, A. V., *The Ethical Dilemma of Science*, p 277

12   Clark, Ronald, *Tizard, op. cit*, p 253

13   Goudsmitt, S. A., *ALSOS*, p 156

14   Baxter, J. P., *Scientists Against Time*, p 10

PART II

THE WAR AT SEA

CHAPTER 3

1   A. B. Wood Memorial Number, *Jnl. Roy. Nav. Sci. Serv.*, Vol 20, No 4 (July 1965), p 84

2   Harris, Sir Arthur, *Bomber Offensive*, pp 38-9

3   Wright, Sir Charles, Letter to the author, 6 April 1965

4   Kelly, H. W. K., 'Historical Introduction to Degaussing', *Jnl. Inst. Brit. Elec. Eng.* (4 April 1946)

5   A. B. Wood Memorial Number, *Jnl. Roy. Nav. Sci. Serv., op cit*, p 82

6   Wood, A. B., 'Stephen Butterworth, OBE—An appreciation', *Jnl. Roy. Nav. Sci. Serv.* 1 (1945-6), pp 96-8

7   Goodeve, C. F., 'The Defeat of the Magnetic Mine', *Jnl. Roy. Soc. Arts.*, Vol XCIV, No 4708 (4 January 1946), p 81

8   *Ibid*, p 87

9   Bullard, E. C., 'The Protection of Ships from Magnetic Mines', *Roy. Instn. Gt. Brit.* (15 Feb. 1946), p 17

10   *Ibid*, p 19

11   Goodeve, C. F., *op cit*, p 81

12   Pawle, Gerald, *The Secret War*, p 24

13   Phillips, Vice-Adm. H. C. in discussion with Goodeve, *op cit*, p 89

14   A. B. Wood Memorial Number, *Jnl. Roy. Nav. Sci. Serv., op cit*, p 275

15   Pickles, A. T., 'Sweeping Division', *Jnl. Roy. Nav. Sci. Serv.*, Vol I (1945-6), p 144

16   Pickles, A. T., Letter to the author, 10 March 1965

17   Roskill, S. W., *The Strategy of Sea Power*, p 149

18   Gretton, Sir Peter, *Maritime Strategy*, p 120

CHAPTER 4

1   'Radar—A Summary', *Office of Scientific Research and Development Report*, Technical Report of Div 14, NDRC, Vol I

2   Crowther, J. G. and Whiddington, R., *op cit*, p 71

3   Horton, C. E., 'The Royal Naval Scientific Service and the Seaman', *Jnl. Roy. Nav. Sci. Serv.*, Vol II (1947), p 192

4   A. B. Wood Memorial Number, *Jnl. Roy. Nav. Sci. Serv.*, *op cit*, p 76

5   Roskill, S. W., Letter to A. P. Rowe, 1 Dec. 1961

6   Landale, S. E. A., Letter to the author, 23 March 1966

7   Brundrett, Sir Frederick, Letter to A. P. Rowe, 21 Sept. 1962

8   Horton, C. E., Letter to the author, 2 Sept. 1965

9   Morison, S. E., *The Two-ocean War*, p 127

10 Herrick, John, 'Subsurface Warfare', *Office of Scientific Research and Development Report*, NDRC, (1 Jan. 1951)

11 Davies, J., *Prime Minister's Secretariat*, 1916-20, p 75

12 Cherwell Papers

13 Snow, Lord, House of Lords, *Hansard*, 2 Dec. 1964

14 Blackett, P. M. S., Evan James Williams, 1903-45, Obituary notice, *Fellows of the Royal Society*, Vol V, March 1947

15 Bernal, J. D., *Freedom of Necessity*, p 276

16 Air Ministry, Air Publication, 3368, Ch 5

17 Cuckney, Air Vice-Mshl E. J., Letter to the author, 8 March 1965

18 Obituary Notice, Dr. Cecil Gordon, *The Times*, 8 April 1960

PART III

THE WAR IN THE AIR

CHAPTER 5

1   Randall, J. T., The Cavity Magnetron, *Proc. Phys. Soc.*, Vol LVIII, 1946

CHAPTER 6

1   Wood, Derek, and Dempster, Derek, *The Narrow Margin*, p 129

2   Rowe, A. P., *One Story of Radar*, pp 4, 5

3 Rowe, A. P., *op cit*, p 18

4 Wood, Derek, and Dempster, Derek, *op cit*, p 128

5 Crowther, J. G., and Whiddington, R., *op cit*, p 4

6 Wood, Derek, and Dempster, Derek, *op cit*, p 17

7 Butement, W. A. S., Letter to author, 17 Jan. 1967

8 Cockcroft, Sir John, 'Sir Winston Churchill', *Nature* (30 Jan. 1965), p 425

9 Butement, W. A. S., Letter to author, 17 Jan. 1967

10 Wood, Derek, and Dempster, Derek, *op cit*, p 168

11 Rowe, A. P., *op cit*, p 59

12 Collier, Basil, *The Defence of the United Kingdom*, Appendix XXXIV

13 Rowe, A. P., *op cit*, p 70

14 Richards, Denis, and Saunders, Hilary St. G., *The Royal Air Force, 1939-45*, Vol I, p 214

15 Postan, M. M., *et al, op cit*, p 414

16 Bowden, Lord, Letter to author, 3 Oct. 1967

CHAPTER 7

1 Rowe, A. P., *From Scientific Idea to Practical Use, op cit*, p 307

2 Dippy, R. J., Information supplied to author

3 Watson-Watt, Sir Robert, *Three Steps to Victory*, p 173

4 Rowe, A. P., *One Story of Radar, op cit*, p 108

5 Saward, D., *The Bomber's Eye*, p 53

6 Reeves, A. H., and Jones, F. E., Information throughout this section supplied to author

7 Watson-Watt, Sir Robert, 'The Evolution of Radiolocation', *Jnl. Inst. Elect. Eng.*, Vol XCIII, Pt IIIA, 1936

8 Watson-Watt, Sir Robert, *Three Steps to Victory*, p 403

9 Rowe, A. P., *One Story of Radar, op cit*, p 117

10 Watson Watt, Sir Robert, 'The Evolution of Radiolocation', *op cit*

11 Brandt, L., German Centimetre Wave Technology, *Radar Conference*, Frankfurt, 1953

12 Jones, R. V., Letter to A. P. Rowe, 15 May 1962; 'Infra-red Detection in British Air Defence, 1935-38', *Infra-red Physics,* Vol I, pp 153-162, 1961

13 Webster, Sir Charles and Frankland, Noble, *The Strategic Air Offensive Against Germany,* Vol II, p 144

14 Galland, Adolf, *The First and the Last,* p 218

PART IV

THE WAR ON LAND

CHAPTER 8

1 Kerrison, Col. A. V., Conversation with author

2 Green, Constance McLaughlin, Thompson, Harry C., Roots, Peter C., *The Ordnance Department, Planning Munitions for War,* OCMH, Washington, (1955)

3 Pile, Gen. Sir F. A., *Ack-Ack,* p 243

4 Warren, N. H. A., Letter to author, 10 May 1965

5 Pile, Gen. Sir F. A., *op cit,* pp 65, 66

6 Butement, W. A. S., Letter to author, 17 Jan. 1967

7 Watson-Watt, Sir Robert, *op cit,* p 381

8 Clarke, Maj.-Gen. Sir Edward, *Royal Artillery Commemoration Book*

9 Butement, W. A. S., Letter to author, 17 Jan. 1967

10 Johns Hopkins University Applied Physics Laboratory, 'The "VT" or Radio Proximity Fuse', Silver Spring, Md. (1945)

11 Morison, S. E., *op cit,* p 579

12 Boyce, J., *New Weapons for Air Warfare,* p 155

13 Pile, Gen. Sir F. A., Letter to *The Times,* 5 April 1946

CHAPTER 9

1 Liddell Hart, B. H., *Thoughts on War,* p 70

2 Liddell Hart, B. H., *Memoirs,* Vol I, p 248

3 Cole, Maj.-Gen. E. S., 'Military Telecommunications of the Past, Present and Future', *Radio Soc. of Gt. Brit. Bull,* March 1961

4 Butement, W. A. S., Letter to author, 17 Jan. 1967

5 *History of Pye Radio* (privately produced)

6 Butement, W. A. S., Thesis for Doctorate of Science

7 Bailey, Sir Donald, Conversation with author, 5 April 1965

8 Baker, J. S., Inglis, Sir Charles, Obituary notice, *Fellows of the Royal Society*, Vol VIII, (1952-3)

9 Information supplied by The General Sikorski Historical Institute; *Canadian Army Journal*, Vol I (1947-8)

10 Hobart, Maj.-Gen. P. C. S., Papers in Liddell Hart Collection

CHAPTER 10

1 Slim, Field Marshal the Viscount, Letter to A. P. Rowe, 23 Aug. 1961

2 ICI Ltd, Pharmaceuticals Division, *Pharmaceutical Research in ICI*, (1936-57)

3 Boyd, Sir John, Sir Neil Hamilton Fairley, Obituary notice, *Fellows of the Royal Society*

PART V

AMPHIBIOUS WAR

CHAPTER 11

1 Morgan, Gen. Sir Frederick, *Overture to Overlord*, pp 261-2

2 White, Sir George B., 'The Mulberry Harbour', *The Central*, Vol XLI, No 93 (June 1946)

3 Churchill, W. S., *The Second World War*, Vol V, p 66

4 Rolfe, J. A. S., Letter to author, 2 June 1965

5 *Ibid*

6 Inst. Civ. Engrs., *The Civil Engineer in War*, Vol II

7 Rolfe, J. A. S., Letter to author, 2 June 1965

8 Hickling, Vice-Adm. Harold, *Sailor at Sea*, p 204

9 *Report by the Supreme Commander to the Combined Chiefs of Staff on the Operations in Europe of the Allied Expeditionary Force, 8 June 1944 to 8 May 1945*, HMSO, p 67

10 Hussey, Capt. T. A., RN, Information supplied to author

11 Bush, Vannevar, *op cit*, p 39

12 Churchill, W. S., quoted in Grindle, Commodore J. A., RN, 'Development of Combined Operations Materials and Techniques', *Jnl. Roy. United. Serv. Inst.*, Vol XCIII, (No 572), Nov. 1948

13 Baker, Roland, Letter to Captain Hussey, RN, 29 Nov. 1961

14 Fergusson, Bernard, *The Watery Maze*, p 68

15 Hussey, Capt. T. A., RN, Information supplied to author

16 Wilson, General Maitland, *Report to the Combined Chiefs of Staff on the Italian campaign, 6 Jan. 1944-10 May 1944*, HMSO (1946)

CHAPTER 12

1 Fergusson, Bernard, *op cit*, p 168

2 Langley, Col. F. H. G., Letter to author, 30 July 1965

3 Cockburn, Sir Robert, Information supplied to author

PART VI

NEW WEAPONS

CHAPTER 13

1 Crow, Sir Alwyn, 'The Rocket as a Weapon of War in the British Forces', *Jnl. Instn. Mech. Eng.*, Vol CLVIII, No 1 (1948), pp 15-21

2 Chalmers, Rear-Adm. W. S., *Max Horton and the Western Approaches*, p 193

3 Dornberger, Walter, R., *V2*, p 108

4 Dornberger, Walter R., 'The German V2', *History of Rocket Technology* (ed. Eugene M. Emme) Detroit Wayne State Univ., 1963

CHAPTER 14

1 A. B. Wood Memorial Number, *Jnl. Roy. Nav. Sci. Serv.*, *op cit*, p 68

2 Collier, Basil, *op cit*, pp 353 *et seq*

PART VII

THE FAILURES

CHAPTER 15

1 Hill, A. V., *op cit*, p 293
2 Cherwell Papers
3 *Ibid*
4 Roskill, S. W., Correspondence with author
5 Pawle, Gerald, *op cit*, Chap 10
6 Roskill, S. W., *The War At Sea*, Vol I, p 140
7 Douglas of Kirtleside, Lord, *Years of Command*, p 107

CHAPTER 16

1 Lampe, David, *Pyke: The Unknown Genius*, Chap 7
2 Alanbrooke, Lord, 'Notes on My Life' IX, from *The Turn of the Tide*, ed. Arthur Bryant

PART VIII

CONCLUSIONS

CHAPTER 18

1 Merton, Sir Thomas, 'Science and Invention', *New Scientist*, 11 Feb. 1965
2 Hankey, Lord, *The Supreme Command, 1914-18*, Vol I, p 231

INDEX

Illustrations are indicated by page references in italic type.